May 12, 2017

Dear Sharrone,

Sincerely,

Dr. Melvin R Hall

To God be the glory!

THE SKY'S THE LIMIT

Go For the Gold!

Dr. Melvin R. Hall

authorHOUSE®

AuthorHouse™
1663 Liberty Drive
Bloomington, IN 47403
www.authorhouse.com
Phone: 1-800-839-8640

First published by AuthorHouse 8/21/2009

ISBN: 978-1-4389-8776-7 (e)
ISBN: 978-1-4389-8775-0 (sc)
ISBN: 978-1-4389-8774-3 (hc)

Library of Congress Control Number: 2009905004

Printed in the United States of America
Bloomington, Indiana

This book is printed on acid-free paper.

ACKNOWLEDGMENTS

First, I must give all honor and glory to God, who not only gave me the words to write, but empowered me to have this book published. To Him all honor and glory is extended.

Thanks to the Publisher and Editor (Tony Johnson) of *Our Times* who actually planted the seed in my thinking about publishing my essays. He not only started my thinking process on the possibility of compiling all I had written into book form, he often e-mailed me about how much he enjoyed them. He furthered encouraged me by sharing compliments from the readership.

Words cannot amply express my gratitude to my goddaughter, Dr. G. Faye Wilson who painstakingly perused most of my manuscript, making (deleted and, inserted a comma) a number of grammatical corrections. She has encouraged me in many ways, but her statement about my being ever young as I approached the beginning of my octogenarian year added much to my thinking **that age is just a number**.

My dear sister in Christ, Dorothy Gantt, has shown herself to be a true friend for more than forty years. She has come to my aid or assistance voluntarily on many occasions. She too shared time and interest reviewing the manuscript and encouraging me by writing little notes of approval and making corrections.

To many others who have telephoned, emailed and personally spoken to me about publishing my essays, I say, "Thanks for your encouragement. The book is now in your possession; please enjoy it as you did the essays in *our Times.*"

The author

OPEN YOUR HEART

Twenty-six years ago God allowed my path to cross with that of a blessed man of God, Melvin Raymond Hall. There he was – already in his mid-fifties-working and serving diligently at Grace United Methodist Church St. Albans, New York.

Dr. Hall, known fondly as "Mel", "Melvin" or "Raymond" was a one-man wunderkind. An excellent writer, his essays in our church newsletter, Grace Notes, were resplendent with details that could make you believe that you were at whatever event that he was discussing. He served on various committees, his organizational skills enabled any program to be developed and implemented creatively.

What was most intriguing was how deeply he connected with the youth in the church. They loved him because he listened and that he cared. The youth knew that he would laugh with them and cry with them as well as correct and encourage them.

It was during those times of working with youth, that he extended an invitation to me to continue to be a blessing to me today. He volunteered to be my godfather and that came with a gift a woman could ever need in her life. There was no topic that was taboo, no subject too trivial. Whether I needed a shoulder to lean on, an ear attuned to hear, or someone to rejoice with me, I found that person in my godfather.

In this book, you too will find that you have found a friend. His essays are designed to teach the power of positive thinking, the reward of making quality decisions, and the strength of staying focused on God in every area of your life. As you read them, you will think that he has listened to your internal thoughts and eavesdropped on your conversations with your best friend. Don't worry – every secret is safe with him.

I ask only one thing; as you read this book, let the wisdom of the ages-revealed to us by God through the anointed writings of my godfather, Dr. Melvin R. Hall- speak to your heart and guide your steps.

Faye Wilson, Ed.D.

DEDICATION

This book is dedicated to my cousin, Florence Delorez Griffith Joyner (1959-1991), THE DAZZLING Olympian who was awarded two gold and one silver medal in the 1988 Olympics in Seoul, Korea.

"Dee Dee," as she was fondly known by family and close acquaintances, was not only a superb athlete, but a very inspirational and motivational speaker and a role model to all aspiring young persons who desired to realize their dream for greatness.

For her, the sky was indeed the limit as she went for the gold in the Olympics.

The author

CONTENTS

FRONT COVER

BRIEF DESCRIPTION OF THE BOOK

This book of essays is especially designed and written for the sole purpose of encouraging, inspiring and motivating you so that you can claim and enjoy the greatness that you were created to have.

Some famous people we read and hear about have been able to discover and determine very early in life what they wanted to be or accomplish and they have pursued their dream to fruition. You may be one among others who have not been that fortunate, but it is not too late. Know that the sky is your only limit. Your opportunity and potential for successful and greatness is limited only by your own action.

It is hoped that as you read each essay you will find and dwell upon the ones that speak to your own personal situation and you will be encouraged, inspired and motivated to take whatever action necessary to achieve your dream and goals.

It is up to you. There is nothing standing in your way but your own shadow of doubt and fears. Former President of these great United States Franklin Delano Roosevelt who suffered from Polio most of his life said,"Man has nothing to fear but fear itself."

After reading this book of essays any fear that you might have will vanish and be replaced by enthusiasm, confidence and a new sense of self that you never dreamed possible!

You can be a winner. You will be a winner. **Go for it!**

The author

FOREWORD

How I met Dr. Melvin Hall was quite unusual. But it does explain why I think the man is so special. It was a bright beautiful Sunday morning, and I was riding my daughter's purple truck-bike to the park to play basketball. Mel was dressed for church in his shirt, tie and jacket, also walking on the other side of the block. So I don't know why I decided to make a u-turn and approach him.

Maybe it was his afro-centric Kofi he wore and the Bible in his hand, which gave Mel a scholarly look that embolden me to ask, "Are you a writer?" A light that seemed to illuminate from his very soul filled his face before he answered, as though I was the answer to a silent prayer.

It has been over four years since we first met and discussed the idea of Mel writing for *Our Times*. And he hasn't missed an issue. His contribution to the paper has been immense. Through his essays, he has touched lots of lives. I know this for many have told me so personally.

It's a privilege to be in the position to publish Dr. Melvin Hall's column. Using the ancient form of storytelling, Mel the griot weaves situations that we can all relate to. With his education in psychology, and wisdom derived from a loving heart, Mel writes essays that inspire.

I enjoy reading Mel's articles. His non-judgmental style of writing most would describe as simply folksy, grabs the reader's attention. In the search for self, a life-long journey, Mel gives ample food for thought. He saw beyond my ruffled self on that faithful Sunday morning, and believed in a perfect stranger. How many of us have been shown opportunity, yet had doubt?

During times of tribulations, Mel's articles have encouraged me to preserve through the hardships. The challenges of being a Black publisher and editor of a Black community newspaper have been trying for me, and I'm fortunate that I have a motivator as Mel on our team.

I believe in the power of the word. There's an undeniable spirituality to Mel's writing that affects you whether you are religious or not. It comes from a sincere heart. We are blessed to have talent as Mel who is dedicated to understanding the human element. What role God plays in all this, through His wisdom, Mel boldly tackles.

I admire Mel. There is purpose behind his writing. I know it takes courage to freely express yourself. Mel has the confidence to tell the story, having faith that it will be well received by the audience. I wish him continual success as he uses his God-given craft for all our benefit.

Tony Johnson Publisher & Editor of *Our Times*

ASPIRING TO INSPIRE
BEFORE EXPIRING

"...I have prayed for you, that your faith will not fail;
and when you are converted, strengthen your brothers."
Luke 22:32

A dear friend either begins or closes her e-mail with saying something cheerful. And I notice that the advice she gives, she honestly feels. Can you imagine what our world would be like if each of us did this on a daily basis to everyone we meet?

Every day we find ourselves in the land of the living, we can find someone needing to be inspired. I am sure you know what the word means, but for my own sake and to encourage you, I am going to share what Mr. Webster has to say about the word "inspire."

But first we have to aspire to inspire so let us be sure we know what the word aspire as well. *Aspire is to have an ambition to do something or to want to do something.* Some meanings for the word inspire are *influence, bring about, and stir into action.*

When we see a person looking sad, perhaps we can say something kind and uplifting. By lifting the person's spirit, we inspire him or her. When we lift a person's spirit, ours automatically is lifted. Saying something kind to someone often causes the person to smile, and we all know what a smile does.

We won't bother with the term "expire" because when that happens all conversation about anybody who has experienced it, evokes the use of the verb "was." We need to stay in the "now."

Children are so impressionable and the best gift you can give them is to tell them how well they did something, even how nice their mud pies are if they still make them today. Of course, they have more expensive toys these days. Some would not be caught playing with mud! But whatever they are doing, inspire them.

1

We expend too much energy telling people what's wrong with them rather what is right.

We need to hear that what we do is appreciated and be encouraged to do better.

When we bring something to a person's attention that needs correcting, why not mention first their good qualities and what you like about them? Then when you do mention possible corrections, why not soften it a bit? The world is not going to fall apart because of mistakes or a person's inappropriate handling of a matter or an incident.

Let's say that you as an administrator overheard one of your supervisors speaking harshly to another worker and you aspire to inspire the supervisor to be kinder. How do you think you should handle it so that the person begins to aspire to inspire rather than condemn or ridicule?

Your first impulse may be to give the person a "taste of his or her own medicine" but that would prove nothing and not help anyone. But to show the supervisor how to correct a worker will enable the supervisor to function better and enable the worker to feel inspired. Here's an example:

An administrator says to the supervisor, "I can understand your frustration in having to correct your supervisees as often as it is required, and you are a good supervisor. Do you think it would be better if you spoke in a softer tone? Do you think that the person you are correcting will be more acceptable to your instructions? Suppose you speak to her as I am speaking to you? Our jobs require that we enable people to correct their mistakes. How do you feel by my approach to you? I hope that you will extend the same courtesy to your worker as I am extending to you. Okay?"

The way we treat others ought to show the way we want to be treated. So since we all like to be inspired, inspiring others sends a message for others to inspire us. And, do it now – everyday – because it is too late once we have expired. You get my drift?

The way we treat others ought to show the way we want to be treated.

A STATE OF BLISS

"..the joy of the Lord is your strength."
Nehemiah 8:10 (NIV)

We may not verbalize it, but each of us would like to experience a state of bliss. Some may ask, "What is meant by a state of bliss?" It is a feeling of peace, joy and happiness. It is a feeling of being wanted, being loved, being accepted as people worthy of recognition and respect. We crave these feelings whether we are able to verbalize them or not.

We were created to enjoy life in abundance. A multiplicity of problems exists because of the lack of sense of wholeness. Each person unconsciously seeks to find what he or she was created to enjoy. To be able to laugh and enjoy life is one of the many blessings of humankind. To be able to enjoy the company of others is a predisposed blessing that is given to us from our birth. It is a desire to feel high.

However, it is most unfortunate that too many people find artificial and nefarious ways of trying to reach a state of euphoria that makes them think they are "feeling good." In doing so they find themselves breaking the law and doing great damage to their minds and bodies. Their "sense" of high causes them to experience false grandiose and unrealistic mild-altering negative thoughts placing them in a strange world without connection to the real world. Their grossly damaging "high" destroys them and their relationship with their loved ones who love them unconditionally, but feel so helpless in their quest to get them to realize the damage they are doing to themselves and their relationships. Do you find yourself in this situation? If not, do you have loved ones who are?

I don't want to remain with this thought. Being a positive person, I am going to move on with my thoughts and speak on the "real high",

3

"True High" and "blessed" high we were created to experience and enjoy.

We were created in this vast universe with the wherewithal to not only obtain greatness for ourselves, but to encourage all persons we meet to be the best that they can be. We should be able to invoke laughter and lightheartedness. We should be able to smile and to bring good cheer to the stranger we encounter in our day to day living. We should be able to offer hope to those who seem to wallow in a sense of hopelessness. We should be able to introduce others to the One who created us in this wonderful place we live in.

Our Creator expressed great loving care and smiled at the completion of each creation saying, "That is good!" After creating the best for us, He crated us to enjoy it all. (I refer to the book of Genesis in the Bible.) The book also warns us in a most interesting way of the deterrents in life which would keep us from enjoying the best that life has to offer. This portion refers to the "tree of knowledge." I strongly suggest that if you have read about the "tree" you read again slowly and prayerfully. If you have not read it, I suggest you do because it will whet your desire to read more and reading more will show you how to take full advantage of what has been created for you and me by the One who loves us unconditionally.

What can possibly exceed being loved unconditionally? Absolutely nothing! Just think. Even persons who are doing great harm to themselves and their bodies and minds in trying to obtain their "high" by artificial / nefarious means are loved by the One Who created them. They are still precious to Him and always will be.

There is a song with the words, "There is nothing like the real thing baby!" I submit to you that this is a true statement. The real thing is what the Creator offers. So you have tried your way. Where has it gotten you? Why not try the real thing and see what happens? You cannot possibly make it on your own. There is help. All you have to do is go to someone whom God has created and simply say, "Please help me. I am caught up in a wicked vice, using stuff that is hurting me and I want to rid myself of this demon. I am looking for happiness, peace, and contentment." If you find yourself not able to go to someone, just sit, stand, or fall on your knees and just plead to the One who will give you the strength and direct you to willing arms, ready to take you to the Source that will provide the help you need. There are many who have done just that and have found the real thing.

> **We were created in this vast universe with the wherewithal to not only obtain greatness for ourselves, but to encourage all persons we meet to be the best they can be.**

AVOIDING BITTERNESS

"Wherefore is light given to him that is in misery, and
life unto the bitter is sod."
Job 3:20 (KJV)

Bitterness rears its ugly head in many forms. It has many companions and they aren't lovely. Some of its many bosom pals are resentment, anger, jealousy, and hatred. If we want to dwell on bitterness, we could think of many more. However, the purpose of this essay is to talk about avoiding it, not perpetuating it.

Oh, how we endanger ourselves by courting any one of bitterness's companions! Each one alone can do great damage to the body and the human spirit. Each is an attacker. Each can make sure that life is tough and rough and perhaps lead to an early grave. Can you imagine it if we allowed them to work together? It is a strong possibility that we would find ourselves spaced out in a mental institution. But we don't want to go there. So what can we do?

The good news is – it can be avoided. We are blessed with the ability to make choices. You may ask, "How?" The answer is we can be the master of our own destiny. We can trust the inherent power within ourselves.

We have the ability to think positively or negatively. Positive thinking leads to positive emotions and those emotions lead to like behavior. So positive thinking frees us from those monsters. While some persons are entertaining bitterness and its companions, others are giving them the boot by refusing to get caught up in their mess. We don't have to follow others' bad choices. Because others are disrespectful toward us, we don't have to respond in kind. Let us look at each companion of bitterness separately and not only discover what each is, but how to avoid it.

Resentment does not like someone to accomplish more, give more, or be more successful than it. What resentful people fail to realize is that if they spent the same amount of time praising and rejoicing with the successful ones, they too, would be successful in their endeavors. People who love seeing others achieving cannot help but achieve their dreams, aspirations and goals.

Anger can cause resentment and it comes with no small amount of acidity. Acid burns and destroys and causes one to be consumed with bitterness. It does great damage to the person who holds it. It may encourage one to plot against another to do harm. It keeps a person from being productive. Getting rid of the feeling can enable and empower the person to be a winner or be successful in the fruition of their dreams, aspirations and goals. And they will be able to sleep well.

Jealousy and hatred act as if they are conjoined twins. Whenever such persons are in the presence of the object of their jealousy, they are so consumed by it that they lose all sense of reasoning. They cannot concentrate on what they should be about. If they would only realize that they are just as capable and can accomplish whatever they set their mind to, they would be free to put forth whatever efforts are required to succeed. They would also realize their inherent gifts, talents and abilities, and in realizing, will see there is absolutely no reason to be jealous.

Hatred becomes an illness. The mere mention of the name of the one being hated makes the hater ill. The illness may manifest itself as an emotional or mental breakdown. It is a disastrous feeling sometimes becoming dangerous and perhaps deadly. Some persons who are experiencing this bitterness may not remember why they harbor such feeling or when it began. Their cloudy mind (thinking) gathers more negative ideas overtime. Those persons need some kind of help. Depending upon the depth of their hatred, they may need professional help. Once the help is sought and heeded, the persons would be free to go about their business and become winners.

All of these "conditions" keep persons from being free. Once the chain is broken, they can become very successful. Most of the time their new freedom causes them to work extremely hard because they want to make up for wasted time. One can never make up time. As long as the past remains the past, whatever one does that is positive today will pay big dividends either today or tomorrow.

We are blessed with the ability to make choices.
We can be the master of our own destiny.

"Back in the Day...."

Love is patient, love is kind. It does not envy, it does not boast, it is not proud."
I Corinthians 13:4 (NIV)

"Back in the day...." sentences are very frequently heard coming from younger and older adults alike these days.

This reminds me of a very important rule of respect which I was taught over three quarters of a century ago, and it is as important to me now as then. Embodied in respect is the rule of good manners.

A part of good manners is the use of such words as "please, " "thank you," "excuse me" - all accompanied by a smile. It would be nice if people who refer to "back in the day" would make sure that we recall and exercise such courtesies.

I am sorry to say that today one sees too much discourteous behavior which seems to indicate most people seem quite angry. A smile ought to induce a smile, but I have heard it asked, "What are you smiling at?" That was a mild question. That question also has been punctuated with some choice words and instead of a smile - a frown - letting you know that the person did not appreciate an unknown smiling person (stranger) at him or her.

When we think about respect and disrespect, "back in the day" it was linked to age.

Now age does not matter anymore. A child at any age may consider himself or herself equal in status to any older adult. I still believe that in order to get respect one has to give it; but I have seen respectful adults being disrespected just on general principle by children of all ages but especially teens.

The use of foul language is not only distasteful but disrespectful, and is often used with great ease and at great volume. Some people young and old seem to want to be heard by persons who haven't the slightest interest in their conversation. Now that cell phones are widely used, persons talking on them must be speaking to someone on the other end who suffers from partial deafness.

When we talk about "back in the day," certainly someone must ask"What has happened to "Do unto others as we would want done unto us?" (Matthew 7:12)

Similarly, we can also ask what has happened to" Teach (train) a child in the way he/she should go so that when he/she is older will not depart from it?" The book of Proverbs in the Bible is rich in instructions to parents and to children. There was a time in most

households the Bible was read daily; the family would gather and the head of the household would read. Depending upon their age, children were encouraged to participate in the discussions. I wonder how many households take the time to read together today.

I strongly believe that whatever profession people eventually embrace, their best skills are grounded in how they perform in terms of interacting with others. An example is a doctor who exerts patience and listening skills, perhaps this was learned in his or her home as a youngster. Teachers, lawyers, bus drivers, taxi drivers, and clerks: in fact, all persons employed or unemployed should treat those with whom they come in contact with the same measure of decency and respect they want to receive. This is true "back in the day behavior." Interacting lovingly with others is a must-have skill whether one was taught (or not taught) this in their home.

Being a one parent provider is no excuse for not bringing up a child in the way he or she should grow. Whether one is poor or rich should not matter. There is no price tag on respect. Home is the foundation; that is where we learn how to function in our world.

Unfortunately, our world is heavily populated with young mothers and fathers who have not completed the "growing up" process. There is no way in which young parents who lack being fully maturated are going to be able to teach their children in the way they have not been taught. Observing immature parents sometimes makes me want to intercede, but I know that I am going to hear their response in a language their children should not hear. I have to restrain myself from telling them what they should not do in the presence of their children with an explanation why.

I don't think some parents even give thought to what they say and how they say it and that their children are very impressionable and will repeat what they hear.

Sometimes I am somewhat amused by the fact that very young children seem to know that what they are saying, in repeating their parents, should not be said. I am amused because they know they will get some kind of reaction from adults who feel strongly about proper behavior and conduct. And children quickly learn how to get over. They will quickly take the upper hand and use this "skill" better than their parents.

Some parents (single or as a couple) choose to laugh at something the child does that is wrong but considered by the parents as "cute," The child plays on that and will repeat it being aware of his or her parents' approval.

Parents who holler, scream or yell and curse their children will eventually cause major problems for themselves and their children. Moreover, children who are put down by verbal abuse grow to have low self-esteem and self-worth. There is no way they will feel good about themselves unless they get professional help. Their life's blueprint is going to set them up for failure and a life never intended by God. .

I don't necessarily want to see everything from "back in the day" repeating itself, but most certainly the values and attitudes taught to us in those days regarding respect need to return. We can most certainly enjoy with great thanksgiving the boundaries and discipline we were raised with even though at times we felt our parents were too strict, old fashioned, and not wanting us to have fun. Personally, I do have to admit; those thoughts never crossed my mind. Why? Because I was so caught up in thinking my mother could "read my mind," I was too afraid to entertain many private thoughts about her as a mother and me as her child. Children who have heard these words, "I brought you into this world and I will take you out" thought twice before provoking our parents.

We didn't want to know if they could or would "take us out."

Yes, "back in the day…" there seemed to have been greater security, respect and love. I wish that would come back. What do you want?

I don't necessarily want to see everything from "back in the day" repeating itself, but most certainly the values and attitudes taught to us in those days regarding respect need to return.

BEAUTY IN SIMPLICITY

"Teach me your way, O Lord; lead me in
a straight path...."
Psalm 27:11 (NIV)

Blessed are people who find happiness, joy, and contentment in simple things. They have the gift of receiving peace and joy from little things that others are not able to see.

An example of this is a simple "Hello" with a smile helps some people to see the good in a brand new day bringing many wonderful possibilities. And adding a sincere and genuine compliment to the greeting will boost their spirit and increase their sense of well-being.

I remember being around my young cousin as a child. If a person gave me a nickel, I was much appreciative; but one particular cousin would say that my nickel was nothing because he was given a quarter. That did not steal my joy. I have always found beauty in simplicity.

Small acts of kindness meant a great deal to me as a child and it still does as a senior person. I think it may mean even more now that I am much older and have had so many years of experience of having little, and sometimes, much. Having had to make myself content with whatever came my way has prepared me in my old age to appreciate even more whatever good falls onto my path.

When I express enthusiasm for small favors (blessings), it is not a put on. It is a genuine appreciation for all blessings big or small. Realizing that people operate from the goodness of their heart gives me that wonderfully warm feeling of heart to heart. I guess this gives me away as being a sentimentalist. I have to admit I am.

Even small expressions of kindness mean a lot to sentimental people. We look for the good in all situations and find excuses for those who unkindly represent themselves.

We see beauty when others see plainness or smallness. Why is this? It is because we see the spirit of love in every thing. We look for and feel the love that is a part of the giving.

We are grateful receivers. Sometimes a simple wink at a moment when we are feeling a little low in spirit boosts or lifts our spirit. It doesn't take much because there is beauty in simplicity.

When it comes to material things such as furniture and furnishing, for example, we believe the plainer the better. We pride ourselves in keeping these items polished and well arranged to suit our taste. Our plainness does not negate our desire to be neat and orderly.

The beauty we feel extends itself in other areas of our life which makes us feel good about ourselves, our environment, our jobs, our ministries, our place of worship, our spiritual leaders, our neighbors, and our various interpersonal interactions. We are not jealous or envious because we are pleased and satisfied with whatever comes our way. We do not compare ourselves to the "Jones." We just hope they are as happy with their blessings as we are with ours. Why? The answer is simply because there is beauty in simplicity.

We find so many good things happening each day that enables us to cope with anything that may give us grief. We are not immune to pain and grief, but we do not allow ourselves to mentally add more than what truly exists. We realize a bad situation could be worse. So we are thankful that it isn't and, therefore, able to move on to do what we have to do by the power of our ever-loving God.

When we think of and truly feel God's unconditional love, we are able to overlook minor infractions, behavior, unkind remarks, unkind deeds, and the thoughtlessness of others. Why? Because we realize that people show their hurt and pain in a variety of ways, and to expect kind words from a hurting person is not being realistic. So we pray for them and ask God to bless them mightily by removing their pain.

If only all of us could find beauty in living our lives even when our world is sometimes topsy-turvy, we would find that sense of peace that passes all understanding. Many times when we hear people saying, "How can you remain so cool and calm with all that is going on?" They do not understand how we can stay focused on the beauty of life and the simple, and sometimes grand, things it brings.

For those of us who find beauty in simplicity, we keep on "keeping it simple" and enjoying life as it unfolds and keep wishing, hoping and praying that **all of us** find the peace that passes all understanding.

If only all of us could find beauty in living our lives when even our world is sometimes topsy-turvy, we would find that sense of peace that passes all understandings.

Being Better Than We Are

"Love does delight in evil but rejoices with the truth."
I. Corinthians 13:6 (NIV)

Even though as humans we will never obtain perfection, nothing should keep us from trying to be better each day. Before we can accomplish anything-great or small- we have to recognize that each of us has shortcomings. There is always something about us that needs correcting or changing.

If we would spend a few minutes thinking about what happened between us and others during the day just before drifting off to sleep, we will find something that needs changing. If we did this on a daily basis, we would not have to concern ourselves with making and breaking New Year's resolutions, we would practice self-correction on a daily basis.

We do not always intentionally do something to hurt or offend another; they just happen. And there are many reasons why they happen. One is a lack of control of our emotions. The lame excuse of just being "ourselves" is a rationalization that just doesn't work. Actually, we are not being ourselves.

We can greatly benefit by focusing on small things which we should take notice of and do something about them. An example is when we are about to speak beyond a certain point, some of us get a feeling that we should not say anymore. Unfortunately, we take the "bull by the horn" and "speak our piece." That piece opens the door to more angry words until it seems we are trying to out do one another. No one comes out a winner.

When we are hurt by some angry words, we just want to get back at the person and our emotions go into overdrive. After a time (shorter for some), the anger manifests itself in a physical form and we are out to physically hurt someone. Again, no one wins.

Does this sound like you? Are you hurting so badly that you just want to "get back" at someone, and you find yourself scheming how to do more to the person than what was done to you? Does it keep you awake at night? You know what? The bitterness you are harboring is doing you more physical, mental, and emotional harm than the person to whom you are directing the anger. Physically, you are causing an internal imbalance which keeps the body from fighting germs or ward off internal agents that interfere with your health. Mentally, we are a wreck and can't think with any good reasoning when we are emotionally out of control. We then blame others for making us upset and out of control.

In reality, no one can make us do anything. Yet, when we let people "play" on our emotions, we choose behaviors based on our emotional response to someone else's wrong behavior. How many times have you said so and so "made me mad?" Again, you just got mad. No one can make you angry. No one can do anything to you that you don't allow. You may be manipulated and provoked when you respond with angry words and fist; you are letting it happen whether you want it to happen or not.

How can you avoid this? First, think about an incident where you became so angry that you wanted to strike back in words or with some object that can cause harm. Think about what contributed to your feeling of rage. Ask how could this have been avoided? All of us have some weak areas and some of us have exposed "buttons" that others can push with little effort and we"fly off the handle." Some people get a secret joy in pushing other people's buttons. Those persons have their own insecurities that they are not trying to correct. If they can get you to show your insecurities, they can "prove" to themselves that you are worse than they are.

What happens then is that you both are so negatively emotionally tied to each other with your love/hate relationship that the only way to communicate is to keep something going until you reach the point of hurting each other severely. Come on! Do you really want that? Deep inside of you, you don't, but both of you are too prideful to admit the truth and call a truce, asking for forgiveness and admitting you are wrong. Rarely are people happy with the relationship being in turmoil.

Since you are a reader who can identify with this problem, it falls upon you to take the necessary steps to straighten things out so that your body becomes more conducive to helping you stay healthy, mentally and physically.

Thinking about this several nights before drifting off to dreamland, you will find yourself gaining the strength, fortitude and desire to release the anger, you will be moved to right the wrong between you and the person you actually love, or refuse to keep the feud going. Ultimately, you will and let hate (with all its ugliness) drift off into the sunset.

The ultimate reward is not only being better than we are for now, but for the rest of our lives.

When we are hurt by some angry words, we just want to get back at the person and our emotions go into overdrive.

Being Inclusive

"The lips of the righteous know what is acceptable;
but the mouth of the wicked speaketh forwardness."
Proverbs 10:32 (KJV)

I was invited to a marriage reception recently which inspired me to write this essay. Normally, I don't give thought to why I'm invited, but for some reason the invitation as well as another 50th Anniversary invitation has prompted me as a senior citizen to take note of being wanted as a part of friend's celebrations.

Everyone from the crib to the grave likes to be included in whatever is going on and particularly if it recognizes the person. If you would like to test this statement, just ignore an infant in his or her crib or a senior citizen who does not get around anymore and see what happens.

Another reason, more even than procreation, is why Adam got his mate Eve. God made us sociable creatures. We like to be in the company of people similar to us. People who share our ideas, yet are different, interest us.

Depending upon how well we like ourselves, we don't always want anyone too much like us. Often, we see ourselves in others and if they have the same qualities, we can't "stand" them. It is ironic that we become quite annoyed when we are around "such people." The problem is we don't stop to think that perhaps we may have the same annoying habits. There seems to be dark spots in ourselves which keep us from even thinking we could be anything "like them."

I learned very early in life to examine the possibility that what I find distasteful in another may be the same as another finds equally upsetting in me. Since my mother was a strict disciplinarian, I had to check myself to see if I were truly deserving of her strictness. To be quite honest, I actually thought that I did not deserve the punishment in some instances. Consequently, when I am criticized, I carefully review in my mind the incident to see if I am at fault or if it is just another's opinion. This has enabled me to be more considerate of others and not to be too hasty in wrongly judging them or myself.

What about you? Do you find yourself letting other people's opinions be the last word in your life? Do you give others more credit than you give yourself just because they are "supposed" to know? You must have observed that some people are overly forthright in expressing their opinions. Sometimes that serves (for them) a cover-up for what they don't really know, and that is their façade. It is a type of face-saving coping mechanism that will eventually be exposed in a matter of time.

I find life extremely interesting because of the people I have the good fortune to meet, observe, and I often wonder who they think they are fooling. God has blessed me with years of studying, training and experiencing human behavior. It is amazing how some of us with "one foot in the grave" are still so persistent in our behavior which does nothing for the enjoyment of others or ourselves. I wonder when we are going to wake up. How long will it be before the other foot follows the one that is already in the grave? Time is something we do not know when it will come to an end. That is why procrastination can be a disservice to us.

I think that all of us would want to be inclusively happy to the end of life as we know it. It would be nice to be able to laugh and talk with babies as we laugh and talk with people of all ages. Too many much older persons are neglected. We need to include them in our conversations and when possible, one on one conversation with lots of laughing and lightheartedness.

There is a little girl not quite two years old whom I see every Sunday in church. She is a delight! She has a smile for everyone. She claps her hands (not singing yet) and dancing in her seat to the music. Whenever the Praise and Worship Dancers are expressing their praise, she is right with them in her seat, and you can see her face lighted up.

If you happen to be a person who feels caught in your little box when outside there is joy, happiness, laughter, good times, and people enjoying life, why not ease out of the box and take a chance for your own happiness? "What chance?" you may ask. The chance of helping someone else may just help you to reap some of the rewards of life that you wish for yourself.

There is nothing wrong with saying to a stranger, "What a beautiful day! How are you?" If the stranger is still in his or her box and not ready to come out, don't let it bother you. Say it to someone else, and you will find yourself facing a wide smile because you have reached a person who wants to be included in your social circle even for a moment. To be included is to offer inclusiveness to others.

If you happen to be a person who feels caught in your little box when outside there is joy, happiness, laughter, good times, and people enjoying life, why not ease out of the box and take a chance for your own happiness?

BEING INTELLIGENTLY IGNORANT

During my childhood one of my mother's favorite expressions to me was to be "intelligently ignorant." I knew what each word meant separately, but it didn't make sense used together. As I grew older I was still puzzled and it made even less sense. But when maturity caught up with me and I became able to analyze what I heard and read, I became a critical thinker. It was then what she said made good sense.

Mother's formal education was completing the 5th grade plus enrollment in an adult education program with her aunt in Harlem. There they improved their reading, writing and arithmetic. She developed such hunger for learning proper English and to be able to speak well. To me, she was the greatest! I loved to hear my mother talk.

Thanks to my mother's insisting that I become intelligently ignorant, I have learned a great deal just listening to people talk and saying as little as possible. Why? When people think that you don't know as much as they do, they feel safe in telling you things about themselves, well garnished and wrapped in lies. Well, being intelligently ignorant, you know how to respond and how to elicit more information. It also reduces the amount of words needed from you to learn as much as you can if you are interested in the games they play.

Do not be mistaken that being intelligently ignorant means playing dumb. It does not. It just allows one to not say every thing he thinks or knows at the wrong time. There may come a time when you have to speak on what you know, otherwise you may lose out on a job, a promotion, or other benefits.

Have you ever heard of a joke being told differently from what you have heard? Well, the intelligently ignorant person keeps his or her mouth shut as if he or she were hearing it for the first time. Perhaps this will help him or her to learn something.

Has someone tried to show you something that you knew well? Did you tell him or her that you already know it or did you thank the person for showing you? In some instances I have to admit that I let the person know I knew, simply because he was telling me the wrong thing and I didn't want him to waste anymore of his and my time. Had the person been my supervisor or a person with authority, I would have listened without saying a word except acknowledging I understand what is being said. On some occasions, I had to let the person know that I had done it before and it turned out well.

Being intelligently ignorant has kept me from many arguments. How is that? When I clearly know the facts and I am told the contrary, I don't challenge the person I just do what I have to do the correct way. You see, sometimes people have a hidden agenda and they purposely give you the wrong information. I do not divulge that I know differently because I am checking to see how far this person will go and what his motive is, and why he is playing a game with me. Keeping my mouth shut enables me to learn how far he will attempt to push his dishonest behavior. My being intelligently ignorant does not alert persons that I am on to them. Rather, they think I am not so smart. Being intelligently ignorant does not mean I am actually ignorant, but the persons may err in thinking that I am not one of the smartest person on the block. People who think that will expose themselves with false confidence while I am busy checking to see just how far they will go in their game playing.

One big eye opener for me when I finally learned what the phrase meant and how to apply it was remembering how my mother interacted with people. I mentioned earlier I loved to hear my mother converse with people and listen to the poignant questions she would ask. Their answers revealed much more than they may have known they were telling. Because I enjoyed her technique of asking questions, I have developed a style similar to hers. When people are less than honest, they inadvertently slip up and, because of my being intelligently ignorant, they never knew that I caught them lying.

This worked quite well when I had to interview applicants for employment when I worked for a private firm and later for New York

City Social Services. This was quite an effective technique because people, when they are trying to be impressive, don't always remember their words. So when I asked well placed questions perhaps fifteen minutes later I had to say to myself, "Oh!" A number of persons weren't hired because of the lies they told, and I don't think they knew they did it to themselves.

A technique many interviewers use is complimenting applicants. This is a technique used to help the interviewee relax. But it backfires for the interviewee when he relaxes too much and begins to say too much, and he talks himself out of a job.

This same technique can be used in other circumstances such as when a person who ranks higher than you in your employment but pretends to be smarter than he or she is. What a person thanks of him or herself is okay with me. But when the person attempts to block my progress, my use of the being intelligently ignorant techniques work very well for me, thanks to Martha Banks-Hall.

Being intelligently ignorant has another role other than those mentioned. It is also a strategy for keeping our emotions hidden. Others do not need to know how deeply we are hurting at times. While we are not exposing ourselves, we can deal with our hurt by saying to ourselves, "this too shall pass."

Being intelligently ignorant allows one to not let people know how their callous remarks hurt whether intentional or unintentional. Being intelligently ignorant allows the user to know that jealousy is actually a misplaced compliment. One must be doing something right and well if persons are jealous of their performance. Being intelligently ignorant allows the user to silently say, "Thank you for the recognition!" Jealous persons especially in employment do not realize how their behavior is observed by those in position to elevate the person who is the object of the jealousy. Those in position to elevate the status or promote a worker take notice of what is causing the jealousy and begin to carefully observe the worker who is the object of the jealousy. It is possible that the worker may be elevated or promoted over the one who is jealous. Have I seen this happen? Yes I have, as a city government employee who was the object of jealousy many times.

Being intelligently ignorant is a positive mode of behavior, and it causes good things to happen to persons who use this method of dealing and interacting with others. In a sensible quiet way, the user remains calm, cool, and collective under trying circumstances and no one knows what is going on in the mind and heart of the user. No wonder I found my mother so cool and so did others that she worked for and interacted with. It is definitely a way to earn people's respect, and they don't know why they respect you so much.

Being intelligently ignorant keeps me from many arguments.

BEING TOO CRITICAL OF SELF

"Therefore, as God's chosen people, holy and dearly loved,
clothe yourselves with compassion, kindness, humility,
gentleness and patience."
Colossians 3:12

While there are populations of people who have inflated egos, there are others who are too critical of themselves.

If you think you are one of the persons who is too critical, here is your opportunity to closely examine yourself to determine whether you are moderately critical (as we should be) or super critical (which, of course, we shouldn't be).

Let me give you a little definition about inflated egos, and then we will move on to help persons who are too critical. People with inflated egos always talk about themselves (me, myself and I). They have a tendency to put others down or make light of their accomplishments while promoting themselves.

If you cannot be counted among them, this essay is for you. Certainly, we all should be critical of ourselves as we are far from perfect persons. However, we sometimes find ourselves being more critical than we deserve. And, there are reasons for that.

Let us explore some, you may find yourself in some of the scenarios. Some people as far back as they can remember have been mistreated by words or action. They have been yelled at, cursed and slapped for no apparent reason by their caregiver or older family members. Some have been harshly scolded in the company of others. Some have been told that they were dumb, stupid, and never amount to anything. Does any of this sound familiar to you? If any or all of this does, you have been a victim early on in your young life.

At that time, you had no control because you were too young to know how to handle the tirade put upon you. But now, if you are old enough to read this, you are old enough to begin to see that the people who victimized you were acting out of their own fears and insecurities. This is absolutely not your fault. In all probability you were acting as the child you were, and as children, we do senseless things because our minds are not always on what we are doing. Someone lost patience and addressed the situation in negative ways.

What has happened is that you, as a victim, have internalized their inappropriate scolding, have begun to feel that you are less worthy then others and consequently, became very critical of yourself. Most unfortunately, you believed that you are less than what you really are; therefore, you began to be critical of yourself. As you continued to receive such scoldings, put downs, and physical attacks, you confirmed to yourself that you are less than worthy of good treatment. Actually, contrary to your feelings, you are worthy of the best treatment any caregiver can possibly give. You were not created (born) to be mistreated, but to be loved and to express love.

Since everyone wants to be loved and express love, you began to do things to attract attention to yourself; but unfortunately, they were negative things, and they placed you in position to be scolded again. After awhile you realized that the only way that you are going to get any recognition (love) is by doing what the caregivers apparently find displeasing to them in their lack of patience and compassion.

If you are a child reading this, please go soon to a loved and highly respected adult in your life and let that person know of your hurt. We know that absolute trust is a must, so be sure to go to someone whom you know you can trust to deal and treat your situation as a matter of strictest confidence.

That person will be able to help you to remove (hopefully erase) all of your hurting experiences so that you can be the happy child that you were born to be.

If you are an adult, you have probably lived with your hurt since childhood, so it is more ingrained. You, too, ought to speak to someone you love and respect who will treat whatever you are feelings with confidentially. If that person is unable to help you to your satisfaction, you may need to see a counselor who specializes in situations that you are experiencing. Being too critical of yourself is crippling you from even recognizing what your potentials are and that you are a "candidate" for greatness in something.

Once you are free from past treatments and hurt, you will be able to not only realize that you have special talents, you will be able to do what is necessary so that you can develop your talents and bring them to fruition.

As a result, it is hoped that you will look for others who are experiencing what you have experienced and overcome so that they, too, will be able to realize their great potentials as you have done.

**You were not created (born) to be mistreated,
but to be loved and to express love.**

Blessed: Neither Boasting Nor Complaining

*"...seek first the kingdom of God and His righteouness
and all these things will be given to you."*
Matthew 6:33 (NIV)

When we are blessed we cannot boast because it is not our doing that we are blessed. We cannot complain because we are receiving grace and mercy from our Most High God. Blessings aren't earned; they are given. Every accomplishment that we have made is a blessing (gift) from God. It is not we who have accomplished anything.

We were born to be blessed. You may ask, "So where is our blessing?" The answer is simply this, you are blessed. The mere fact that you woke up this morning is your first blessing for the morning, and many have fallen upon you from the moment you got out of bed.

Blessed are those who are aware of most of their blessings. Being cognizant of the blessings you can see, feel and enjoy makes you grateful and happy. There are many persons who are unhappy simply because they don't see their blessings; therefore, they are not aware. Since they are not aware, they are not grateful. Because they are not grateful, some of the blessings God would like them to have are withheld.

Folks who complain a lot miss out on the blessings all around them, within them, about them and for them. Unfortunately, they apparently take every thing for granted so they see nothing special in anything, even life itself.

There is nothing we can do for them to see the Light, but to point them to the Light. Who is the Light? God is the Light. Looking for the light somewhat reminds me of a person driving and seeking directions from another person whether in a car or from a person at gas station. The other person gives the directions but he or she cannot get in your car and take you there. In this case the light to where you want to go is given to you. Now you have to follow directions in order to reach your destination. If you choose not to follow them, you remain lost.

As you are looking for the Light, that process is going to make a difference in you, resulting in a transformation. You will find yourself reading the Bible along with praying (talking to the Light).

Talking to the Light will briug you directly where you want to go, in terms of your life becoming more meaningful, fuller, richer, happier, peaceful, joyful, and more loving. That is not to say that you are not going to have any bad days, but you will have help to bring you through the rough times and you will be able to say with conviction, "This too, shall pass!" When you are lost and can't seem to find your directions, simply say, "I am lost now but I know I will be happy and at peace again soon."

Stop the negative thinking. Remember it is just common sense to ask for help when we are lost. Driving around and around seeing the same scenery and living the same scenario is foolish when help is only an asking away. The asking is simply saying, "I am lost. Please help me find my way."

Admitting being lost is the first step, asking for help is the second step and by those two steps, other steps will be taken by the Light who will send someone to help you.

There are those who are in the dark who don't believe in angels. But each person who comes to your assistance is an angel sent by God. However, if you are in the dark you may not want to believe what I'm about to say, but hold on, keep reading and prepare yourself for something hard to swallow and believe.

Now, God sometimes chooses the most unlikely person (perhaps in your estimation) to help you find what you are seeking. Just like when you are physically lost, you often ask the very first person you can find for directions. You don't pick and choose the "right looking person." Anyone will do as long as you get where you want to go.

The one who gives you the correct information is an angel sent by God, and you thought you were finding someone on your own. You may think anyone will do as along as you get where you want to go.

And do you realize that you have been an angel without realizing it? Each of us who has helped someone at any time has played the role of an angel. Your helping was not your doing. Your doing was to follow with what you thought was your idea, but God guided you and you willingly responded even though you may be in the dark about many things, especially finding the light.

God has tapped you on your shoulder more times than you can account even if you were not aware. I have more strange things to say, but I think this is enough for you to think about and digest. You will find out for yourself as you read the Bible, talk to God and open your heart and mind to what He is going to feed you.

The time will come again when you, as His angel, will realize that you are, and willingly, joyously, happily, and gratefully so. At that time you will also find your blessings beyond measure, neither boasting not complaining, because you will have found the light.

Blessed are those who are aware of most of their blessings.

Blessings Ever Overflowing!

"Praise be the Lord God, the God of Israel, who does
marvelous deeds.
Psalms 72:18 (NIV)

Blessings tangible and intangible are ever overflowing! God planned this even at the time He created the universe. It was His good pleasure for us to be blessed beyond measures (Genesis 1). He was thinking about us even while creating the universe and humankind. Just take a few minutes to very slowly read the first chapter of Genesis relax and meditate on it. Then continue reading this essay. Something is going to happen which you might not have ever experienced. You are going to receive a blessing so strange and wonderful you will not be able to restrain the indescribable feeling that is going to consume you for a fleeting moment. If you previously had had the experience, you will get a larger dose this time.

What a wonderful God we serve. You do serve Him, don't you? Can you imagine being love unconditionally?

Have you ever tried to count your blessing? Impossible isn't it? That's because there are intangible and tangible blessings. Intangible blessings cannot be seen by the naked eye. It takes the spiritual eye to "see" and recognize them. Those blessings are felt in the heart. What a feeling! Now, tangible blessings can be seen, touched and handled but seem often lost in our memory and replaced by the next tangible blessing. Remember how excited you felt when you were blessed with a new car? A few weeks later the joy seemed to have subsided.

Just think, God loves us so much that He sent His Son to die on a cruel cross suffering excruciating pain so that the joy of heaven would be ours to claim. And just think some people do not believe in Him. Nevertheless, God's unconditional love is just as much theirs as ours who believe He came, died and went to prepare a place for us, free from pain, suffering, malice evilness, and much more, too vast to name. What magnificent love He has for us! (John 14:2-3).

How wonderful it is to have a love that we can depend on. His love never wavers, remains steady, constant and dependable. It is ever present regardless of our behavior. He promises "when the praises go up, blessings come down." The more we give Him the honor and glory, the more we are blessed (I Corinthians 2:5). It costs only our time and energy. Actually, it's not our time, but His time. So we are really giving Him that which belongs to Him. All of what we think we own belongs to Him. All we think and claim that we have is borrowed. When our time is up on earth, He claims it back and gives it to someone else. This is expressed in a will written by the borrower. The borrower thinks he or she is passing whatever on to loved ones of his or her choosing, but he or she is only following what God has placed in his or her heart.

You see, God has prepared for our earthly life through His creations and prepares for our heavenly life having died on the cross and ascended into Heaven where he prepares a place for us after our time on earth is up.

While we are journeying on planet earth, it is so wonderful to be able to enjoy the things seen and unseen that God has prepared for us. Oh yes! Blessings are ever overflowing!

The tremendous appreciation and enjoyment are for those who believe. Those who do not believe are blessed as well, but the believers are blessed indeed in greater abundance because their blessings continue into another glorious dimension.

All that we think we own belongs to Him.

BUSY ENOUGH!

"Many are the plans in a man's heart, but it is the Lord's
purpose that prevails."
Proverbs 19:21 (NIV)

Whether you are retired or still employed, this essay will speak to you and to your heart.

Some of us have too much on our plate and others do not have enough. The art of living dictates the extent of being busy enough.

Just what does that mean? If your busyness gives you personal satisfaction and a sense of accomplishment without feeling pressured, then that's the answer to the question, "are you busy enough?"

There are myriad reasons why we commit ourselves to too much. Check the following list to see if you are "guilty" of one or more of these: (1) Are you trying to avoid boredom? (2) You just can't say "No?" (3) You have a lot of energy? (4) You like to be asked to do something? (5) Is this your way of being accepted by your peers or colleague? (6) You love/like the limelight? (7) You just love helping others and being a part of a team? (8) You enjoy working with people? (9) Keeping busy keeps you from thinking about yourself too much? (10) It gives you a sense of accomplishment?

After you recognize and take ownership of your reason (s), you may want to cut back and place yourself in your own "comfort zone" that fits with a sense of satisfaction and accomplishment. Sometimes the heart is willing but the body is not able to withstand the pressure that we put on it.

Let's address some of the reasons why we may or may not over extend ourselves and how we can address them:

Avoiding boredom is the first on the list. Our busyness should include doing something personal for ourselves and that could be reading, writing letters (for those who don't have the privilege of e-mailing), telephoning the sick and shut-in (especially if we are also a shut-in).

Just can't say "No." Trust me, if you cannot do what is requested, someone will agree to do it, we are not indispensable by any means. There is no reason to feel guilt unless you are doing nothing and are just plain lazy.

You have a lot of energy: You are probably the most popular person because others know about your energy and you are the very first one they call. And if you are known to do a good job, you are a sure hit with those looking for someone to do something or other. You are blessed by your having a lot of energy.

You like to be asked to do something. You are probably not a volunteer but people know if they call you, you will jump at the chance to be helpful. That's just fine!

Being accepted by your peers: Whether we admit it or not, everyone wants to be accepted and there is nothing wrong with that. However, depending how much you want to be accepted determines if this is a positive or a negative. Self-acceptance is more important and speaks of your self-confidence.

Liking the limelight: All of us do, but terribly shy persons shun it, but still like some recognition. It is similar to people liking sunshine but not too much. On the extreme, there are those who, for some reason, just can't seem to get enough attention. They become a nuisance "hogging" attention and they place themselves in the middle of any discussion even if they know very little on the subject. And there are those who arrive late to any event, and if the place is crowded, they like to be ushered to their seat.

Like helping others and teamwork: This type of person must enjoy accomplishing things with others. It gives him or her the opportunity to work with others on a common goal.

Enjoy working with people. For the most part, such a person enjoys being in the company of people and is much like the person who likes helping others.

Keeping busy so as not to think of self too much: One may find himself or herself busier than he or she should be. One needs to look into why it is so necessary to think too much about oneself. Getting help addressing the self-acceptance issue would be interesting.

Having a sense of accomplishment: Most successful and professional persons are motivated by having a sense of accomplishment. This is a good thing. It is healthy and personally rewarding. Such persons probably take pride in time management and organization for it affords them the ability to accomplish a number of things without too much pressure (if any).

Listen to your body. It will tell you when you are being too busy. Continue to enjoy whatever you are doing without pushing too much. Believe it or not, as good as we think we are, we can be replaced in a heartbeat. For proof of this, how many people have moved away or passed away who were in your circle, organization or place of worship? The work continued to get done with little or no problem.

**There are myriad reasons why we commit ourselves
to too much.**

BRILLIANT PEOPLE

"…what else will distinguish me and your people
from all the other people on the face of the earth?"
Exodus 33:16 (NIV)

Brilliant people are humble enough to let God's light shine through them. And by their brilliance, we see God's light!

If the above is true, and I truly believe it is, education, special talents, honed skills, and experiences, being affluent, personal possessions and elaborate homes have absolutely nothing to do with brilliance. However, being so blessed allows brilliant persons to share their gifts.

People tend to have greater respect for persons who seem to be financially endowed, but such persons are not necessarily happy. There is absolutely no doubt in my mind that people who are humble are happier and people who share what they have are continually blessed.

Humble people do not have to prove anything to anyone. They are loving, relaxed (cool), calm and magnetic. People are drawn to them. The light that shines through them has a very powerful drawing effect. Humble people are easy to define because of their personal relationship with God. Persons who do not have a relationship with God are difficult to define.

One feels good being in the company of brilliant people. They have a way of reducing or dispelling tension. Those who are wise enough to follow God's directions and instructions have been able to be blessed spiritually and materially. They realize that they have been entrusted with abundance that is supposed to be shared with those less fortunate, even those who do not heed God's directions and instructions.

When we accept the fact that God created this magnificent universe with all its vastness, and order of things, we can see greater possibilities to use what He has already provided. We can invent other things for our use and share with those who do not see any possibilities to make a difference for the use and enjoyment of all.

Brilliant people realize that they own nothing; what God allows them to use and share is only by His grace. They know that when this life as we now know it is over, we leave all of our material "loans" behind. Now, the persons who inherit what's left will continue to either share or become selfish. Sharing is the only way that they will reap happiness, joy, peace, contentment and, of course, remain brilliant.

People who give continue to receive. They give not to receive, but from their heart because the light that shines through them directs and instructs them to do no less. That which is given is replaced by the same amount, and often, by much more. The word is love. The light of love fills ones heart and the heart has to share. This is why the Bible says, *"It is more blessed to give than to receive."* But the more we give the more we receive.

Two factors so necessary to heeding God's instructions are trust and faith. But they have to be consistent and unwavering. Without that it is impossible to acquire anything. By trust and faith, it is easy to follow what God says in His book and when He "speaks" to us. God speaks to us in dreams, our thoughts, and our strong feelings and from our loved ones and others. We wisely should listen and do just what he says. We need to trust and obey.

People sometimes miss out on their blessings because they become so rigidly "religious" that they miss God entirely. Messages are not heard. Some mistakenly think that God is telling them something when He hasn't spoken. Some are confused by what they want to do and find "justification" for doing it, but it profits them nothing.

And there are those who believe that God wants them to be poor and humble (as if the two were synonymous). They don't know what true humbleness is. They confuse the word with having nothing (being poor). When they stop to read the Bible telling us how God created the universe with means and ways of increasing so we all can enjoy His ever providing bounty, how can they possibly think that humbleness means poverty or being poor?

Unfortunately, some religions preach that kind of humbleness. Well, my friend, if that is what you believe, don't you think something is wrong with your thinking? And are you going to allow someone to draw you into that kind of thinking while he or she prospers? If that is the case, you need to read the Bible for yourself.

The Bible teaches empowerment, prosperity, sharing, loving unconditionally, helping one another, and treating others as each of us wants to be treated (Matthew 7:12).

I don't know about you, but I strongly believe that a good relationship with God does not mean that I have to go without anything. God fills our needs. What do you believe? Your understanding of being humble (humility) makes all the difference in your spiritual world and adds to empowerment beyond measure. Be brilliantly humble.

> **Humble people do not have to prove anything to anyone. They are loving, relaxed (cool), calm and magnetic. People are drawn to them.**

CHANGES AND CHALLENGES

*"Consider it pure joy, my brothers, whenever you face
trials by many kinds, because you know that testing of
your faith develops perseverance."*
James 1:2-3 (NIV)

Any change calling for action on our part is a challenge.

Some people are more inclined to accept changes so they are able to roll with the punches. Others have a difficult time for many reasons. One of the reasons is some people are complacent or satisfied with things as they are. They say, "As far as we can remember, things have been just fine and we see no reason to change. They worked for our grandparents and they seem to be working quite all right for us."

Whether we like it or not, change is inevitable because nothing remains the same forever. The more difficult we find accepting change, the harder life is going to be. As far back as you can remember what do you see that has not changed? Some changes are so subtle that you do not actually see the process. Then one day you suddenly notice change has taken place.

What I have so far talked about are physical changes which we are more prone to accept, but the changes I am going to refer to now are the ones we encounter in our place of worship. People are used to things being a certain way and "suddenly" someone or a group decides things ought to be done differently to keep up with the changing time.

Changes in the House of Worship

For some reason this becomes a great concern for some members. The thought of changes as presented to them sometimes causes or produces negative feelings and they feel the changes are going to "mess everything up" They ask, "Why don't they leave well enough alone? Why do they have to come here and change things? If they don't like the way we do things, why don't they go back where they came from?"

Every time there is a transition in a church those comments are voiced. The complaining members have been in the same house of worship for a great number of years and are used to singing and praising their way and they consider themselves the "pillar and post" of their church. They become resentful of any changes taking place. They do not realize that a newly arrived member is just as much a members as a member of 50 years or more. The fact that the church is God's house and not theirs has not occurred to them.

The old timers complain about the activities of the children and that the children should have their own worship services. One of the complaints is the younger children have to go to the bathroom during worship service, but there is no problem when the older folk have to go as well.

Even though the Bible tells us to make a joyful noise unto the Lord, ((Psalm 66) the complainers find the drum makes too much noise, the organ music is too loud, the pastor is preaching too long. "We used to have one hour service now we are in church for two or more hours." You hear this mumbling, but the Bible tells us the Sabbath day is the Lord's Day to worship and praise Him. Some don't like praise service shortly before the regular Sunday worship service. Some of them voiced concerns that they don't want dancing, and have all kinds of musical instruments making loud noise. The Sunday service is getting too long. The preacher used to give us 20 minutes of good quiet preaching; now he is longwinded and he takes from one half hour to three quarters an hour just preaching. And he has the nerve to tell us to 'wake up.' They know Sunday school starts at 10 AM, but the service is too long and we are cheating the children of their time. The air-condition is too cold and bad for our arthritis." When the air condition is not on, they say," It's too hot in here. Why don't they turn the air condition on?"

Ready for the Changes and Challenges

For those who have a sense of humor welcome change, they take the above diatribe with a grain of salt and hope that the persons complaining will begin to see the value of changes and enjoy the introduction and implementation of something new in their place of worship.

Changes and Challenges for You and Me

Whatever the changes, we must muster the challenge to embrace them. We will find that life would be better than we can possibly imagine it to be. We should be able to step up to the plate and meet present and future challenges squarely, without excessive fear, doubt and resistance. We will find it worth every ounce of sweat we put into it. This has been proven over and over.

Whether we like it or not, change is inevitable because nothing remains the same forever.

CHILDREN IN CRISIS

"Wait for the Lord; be strong, and take heart ... "
Psalm 27:14 (NIV)

Unfortunately, it is not often that children who excel are reported in the news media. We can always read about the children who "fall between the cracks." That gives the impression that all children are lost. But we know better. Don't we?

What we need too do is become cognizant of why we have children in crisis. Too often I have heard parents saying, "I can't do anything with my child." This statement was made even before the child was five years old. As soon as children hear that, they have "won" the "freedom" to do just as they please. But the freedom is costly to the child and the family. Believe it or not, children understand such talk as early as their toddler years starting at the period of their "potty-training."

It's sad (and bad) for just one parent to say that, but it's even worse when both parents throw up their hands in desperation. That is a sure sign that the family is dysfunctional. Dysfunctional families lack unity. Children pick up on this and they play one parent against the other. They soon become experts in being manipulative.

When parents work together with one set of rules and boundaries are firmly set with "no" mean no, children respect and adhere to the rules. They may temporarily complain, but deep down inside of themselves they feel safe, secure and protected. We would have fewer children in crisis if we would seek help early in life as partners in parenting.

In dysfunctional families the parents compete for the affection of their children. Since they are not favored in each other's eyes, they get whatever they can from the children and the children take full advantage of it to the family's and each child's detriment.

Children in crisis become adults in crisis unless help is sought and efforts are made to resolve issues in the family. Families are sometimes in denial. Denial is one of the ego defense mechanisms which make people think and say,"that's not our family. Surely, we have our share of problems as other families, but we are not that bad."

There is, of course, no perfect family, but a family in crisis needs to realize that something is very wrong when most days are spent in anger and family members are not able to be civil, kind, understanding and patient with each other. This shows that the members are unhappy and not only displeased with others, but themselves as well. Whether they want to admit to it or not, they need help!

One of the reasons families are in denial is because too much has to be shared with a counselor (an outsider) and families would rather have their business kept private. But as long as we have children in crisis, the family's business will be known to the general public because the news media take delight in negativity. If people didn't enjoy hearing, reading and seeing how poorly people are getting along, the media would have to change to reporting the positive things that are happening. Wouldn't it be wonderful if there were such a thing as "The Family of the Month" and family would be shown on television, written up in newspapers and talked about on radio?

I envision so many families wanting to be recognized in positive ways that they would seek the help needed in order to qualify for this distinction. Count me in believing that people can and will change if given the support of other loving and caring believers, especially those who have the power and the means of giving assistance to feeling the stress of dysfunctioning.

Amazing changes can take place when people first get rid of the awful deceiver called denial and replace it with a desire to bring harmony, peace, caring, patience and unity (homeostasis) into the family. It we would take firm stance in our belief that everything we as humans make can be changed with great effort and determination, we would become enablers to families who need our help. Belief in their ability to change in partnership with a strong desire will make all of the difference in the world.

For us who are sick of the news media putting our families down by drawing attention to the dark side of our existence, let us push forward by writing empowered newspersons our discontent in reading, hearing and seeing defeating news about our citizens and leaders of tomorrow. Let us encourage them to recognize and publicize our children and young people's accomplishments. Can you imagine what that would do for our young people who will eventually become our leaders of tomorrow? At least, no harm could come of it. The possibility of great potential in motivating our young population seems large in the mind of people who always look on the bright side of life.

**We would have fewer children in crisis
if we would seek help early in life as partners in
parenting.**

CHRONIC COMPLAINERS

"Peace I leave with you; my peace I give to you. I do not give to you as the world gives. Do not let your hearts be troubled, and do not let them be afraid."
John 14:27 (NIV)

Everyone complains from time to time because it is natural to not like everything and everyone all the time. Those persons who say they do are not being truthful with themselves and anyone else.

Chronic complainers find fault with everything. Nothing is completely right. They are hard to please, and consequently, hard to get along with. Our saving grace is not trying to please them because you cannot win. They will use that as a means of controlling. They have a right to be as they are, and we have a right to learn how to ignore them and let them be.

No one was born this way. It is an acquired habit that needs to be broken. But you and I cannot break the habit for anyone. Each of us has a full time job working on our own idiosyncrasies. As much as we want to think we have it pretty much together, we don't. Have you ever heard the expression "the pot calling the kettle black?" That's us. We see ourselves in others. So if we don't want to become a chronic complainer we have to check ourselves to see if we do indeed have the same traits that we do not like in our relatives and loved ones.

We see ourselves in others (especially persons we like the most). As much as we love our parents, there are traits they have which we do not like and to the extent at times they get on our nerve! But do you know what? Even though we consciously say that we will not be like them, we unconsciously emulate them more than we think. Just think about that for a moment.

If we are truly honest we would admit this as a fact. So what do we do? We can deliberately make the effort to rid ourselves of those habits or traits we find annoying in our loved ones (especially our parents), I wouldn't advise saying anything to them because we can't win. I have to admit that as a child the one trait my mother had which I found quite embarrassing was "speaking her mind." I decided quite young that I would be a bit more diplomatic and watch my tone of voice as much as possible. I felt sorry for persons who were getting "told off" by my mother. Consequently, I have learned to keep some opinions to myself.

As we change ourselves we will find that we like others better. Why is that? We are able to become more tolerant, and we also realize that no one is perfect, including ourselves. This enables us to stop looking for perfection in others but closely examine ourselves with the intent of making necessary or appropriate changes we need to make.

The question is now is how do we live in peace with someone who is always complaining? Do we purposely avoid them? Do we ignore their telephone calls? Do we confront them directly? Do we let them know how much they annoy us? Each of us has to find his or her own answer. You have to find what works for you.

If you don't mind, I would like to share what works for me. I find peace in the ability to ignore chronic complainers to the point that I don't "hear" them anymore. They have come to realize that I am ignoring them. Their complaint to others is that I don't really care about them. That is not true and they know it is not, but it is their way of trying to "draw me" into their pity party again.

The thing is that we do not have to prove ourselves to anyone. When we feel we do, this gives them the license and opportunity to control us. We should be our own person, but just make sure that we are happy being the person we are.

I cannot say and I will not say that I don't complain, but I will pay close attention to how I register complaints. Using diplomacy, I will let my displeasure be known and insist on appropriate treatment.

The thing is to get to know yourself well enough to be honestly critical and put forth the required effort to make whatever changes you deem necessary. This is not what others think. It would not hurt, however, to give some thought to the possibility that they may be right. If they are, it will be time to do some self-correcting. If they aren't, just drop it in "file 13."

If you truthfully find yourself as a chronic complainer, for your own sake and the sake of your loved ones, put forth your best effort to change. You deserve to be happy. You deserve to find joy, peace, harmony and contentment while on your earthly journey. Apparently, you have been missing out, and you have set out and done a good job in making everyone you love as miserable as you are. The buck stops with you.

Do yourself a favor and start counting your blessings. You will find more to praise God about than to complain about. Try it. You just might like it, if not love it!

Chronic complainers complain about everything.
Nothing is completely right.
They are hard to please, and consequently, hard to
get along with.

COMMUNICATION

"That their hearts might be comforted, being knit
together in love..."
Colossians 2:2 (KJV)

You probably know that verbalization isn't the only way that we humans communicate. And you must know that body language sometimes "speaks" louder than words.

In silence we can communicate. This is especially true with people who are very close emotionally. It is almost like close identical twins. Couples who have been married for many years and know each other quite well enjoy communicating in silence. In fact, there is a multiplicity of ways to communicate.

When some people are emotionally close, deep thoughts concerning the other can be "picked up." An example of this is sometimes when an identical twin feels something is physically or emotionally wrong with the other twin; he or she knows that something is not right with his or her twin. If you are a twin (identical or fraternal) have you had this experience?

As I attempt to jar your memory, you will probably give some thought to some experiences you have had in communicating with a loved one very close to you emotionally.

I begin, however, with the more common way of communicating and that is using the spoken word. Then we will move into strange ways of communicating that people don't normally talk about to a large extent. I will not give any hints here. You will recognize it when I get to it. (Don't peep by reading ahead.)

Before infants learn to speak, they are able to communicate most effectively with whoever the loving caregiver is. As soon as they are able to control their focus they attempt to make eye to eye contact with the person they are most familiar with. We know, of course, how crying and cooing lets us know how the baby is feeling. Then they try to learn to talk by repeating as best they can what they hear. And, finally, they learn to talk and they may repeat something they heard the caregiver say about a person to that person. How embarrassing! Well, your "old- enough- to- talk- baby" is exercising his or her right and new skill by talking, and that is the beginning of their life-long chattering.

At some point in nearly any relationship, people tend to speak hurting words rather than loving and soothing words. We tend to use hurting words when disagreeing instead of trying to encourage another to understand what we feel as we express the opposite point of view. Or we become too emotional and let the emotion rule in a disagreement, rather than trying to communicate in a manner that will either persuade another to our way of thinking, or let the person know that we can disagree in a kind and friendly manner. When a small child has learned to talk, he or she will pick up not only our words but the attitude and the emotions displayed. An example of this is when little girls play with their doll; the conversation and the behavior they heard and observed are played out with the doll.

If a male figure was the dominant one, your male child would emulate the male figure and you may overhear him acting in like manner with his friends his age or younger. Why? Because the adult male unconsciously demonstrated how males are suppose to act. This is that male child's frame of reference in the treatment of others. And we wonder where he got his behavior from...hmm.

So you see, verbal communication is learned early in life and the ones talking are the teachers. People who work directly with children may not always be fully cognizant of what influence they have on children, especially in communication. So Communication "101" is the very first course, beginning when the child arrives from the birth canal.

Our insecurity comes out in the spoken word. Even when we love each other and are engaged in conversation, our words and attitude reflect our feeling of insecurity and inferiority. This is especially true when one love partner feels he or she does not measure up intellectually to the other. The same applies when one feels he or she is not as smart as the other. Do you see yourself in this scenario? Do you see your partner? If you do, it is time to give some deliberate thought to how you handle situations in communicating with loved ones and significant others.

What we sometimes miss is the opportunity to examine another's point of view and learn from it.

The next manner of communication is the nonverbal (body language). Young people in your household are known to speak "volumes" with their bodies and that seems to drive mothers absolutely wild. The feeling that the one in authority gets cannot be explained. The body language in addition to young people verbalizing their point of view seems to make communication so difficult these days. And some young people threaten to call 911 or the abuse hot-line after they have worked their parents into frenzy. This happens more often in a single parent family, it seems. In a single family the one parent has all of the responsibility of rearing the child and because of feeling so overwhelmed at times, the parent overlooks some behavior that should be addressed. The child soon learns how to manipulate his or her parent with threats.

The verbal and the nonverbal together as a pair can make any mother's blood pressure go up today. Back in the day children wouldn't dare express their point of view, but body language was at least tried once. For the most part, it was only once because parents did not tolerate what was considered disrespectful by a child regardless of the age. But this is a different age and time and unless the child was taught very early on, we will find old habits are hard to break. This reminds me of planting a tree and working with that tree while it is pliable. When that tree gets old enough (and set in it way) there is no way the tree is going to straighten up if it was allowed to bend in any direction when malleable.

Non-verbal communication between two adults is a different matter. Any negative communication, regardless in what form is hard on any relationship. The best way to handle it, as with a child (and a newly planted tree) is in the very beginning the parties let each other know what the other is not going to tolerate in disrespectful communication.

Let's move to other forms of communication I alluded to earlier that we actually have no control over for they seem to come from a different place than us. That is why I referred to them as strange.

Dreams: Are you a nocturnal dreamer? Do you dream in color? Do you remember any of your dreams? Have you dreamt of a recipe, how to make something or created something in your dream? Have you had disturbing dreams? What about erotic dreams? Have you ever dreamt of a person you can't recall ever meeting and then you subsequently met the person? Have you ever had a question and discovered the answer in a dream?

Inner small voice: Have you felt as if a message was given to you but not by a regular voice, but you "heard" the message? Have you heard your name called and there was no one around but you?

Other inexplicable means of communication: Have you ever felt someone staring at you and you looked up and directly in the person's eye? Have you felt something tingling on your the back of your neck and you turned and saw someone staring at you. Have you ever felt something was terribly wrong with a loved one and surely there was an accident at or close to the time you received the thought? Have you felt that you were given a message for someone and you gave the person that message?

Have you had a strong feeling to call a friend or family member? Have you had an urge to go somewhere (a store, a friend's house, a walk)?

As strange as all of the above may appear to you, they do happen to some folk. Without going into detail, some of these I have experienced and I didn't find it frightening at all. I think it was because of the book from which the scripture was taken (quoted) after the title of this essay).

Whether you believe in inexplicable communication or not, it will not hurt to check when you get the feeling that a loved one is in need of help. Following a creative dream may change your life for the better. When suddenly finding yourself looking into eye of a person, why not give a nod with a smile (unless you do not feel comfortable doing it)?

The more attention we give to communication the better we will be as individuals in relationship to others. We have such a short time on earth and we never know when that day will come and our time on earth ends. Let us spend as much time as possible perfecting our means of communication. Let us expend quality time verbalizing with appropriate body language the three most important words in any language *I love you* to loved ones far and near as often as we can.

What we sometimes miss is the opportunity to examine another's point of view.

Comparing Ourselves to Others

"There are diversities of gifts, but the same Spirit."
I Corinthians 12:4 (KJV)

We do ourselves a disservice when we compare ourselves to others. Why? This is because we are all uniquely different. That is the way life was planned by or Creator.

Can you imagine how disinteresting and boring we would be if we were all the same?

When we compare ourselves to others, we find we are less than some or more than others in terms of intellect, abilities, talents, looks, and achievements. So we assume either an inferior or a superior internalization of our own self-worth. This affects our self-esteem as well.

Our ability to have a sense of accomplishment is endangered when we see ourselves "superior" to others. We are not able to truly enjoy what they have to offer which would broaden our scope and knowledge of our world and ourselves.

Conversely, when we see ourselves as "inferior," we falsely believe that we are not worthy or that we are less worthy than others. And we tell ourselves that we should not attempt to grow spiritually, intellectually, and economically.

Let us examine both superior and inferiority in depth. Superiority invites a closed mind. When we refuse to receive, we limit our knowledge; therefore, we have less to give or to share with others. Worse still, we are unable to receive from others. The exchange of ideas builds and enhances relationships.

With a closed mind, we think we know everything. Because of our limited knowledge, we become boring and turn others off and it takes but a few minutes to achieve that. All communications begin and end with the first pronoun "I" and all conversations are about "me," mine" and "myself." Since we are limited in our knowledge, we soon run out of interesting things to talk about that includes others.

Inferiority has us thinking that we are not capable of being as good as others. We think we cannot learn, not able to accomplish even some of the smallest tasks, so why should we try? Consequently, we do not grow spiritually, intellectually, and we adopt a "woe is me" existence. We feel sorry for ourselves and view others as "looking down on us." We become dependent on significant others or anyone whom we can influence to give us an emotional hand out.

Feeling neither superior nor inferior enables us to realize our own uniqueness and, we can appreciate being different. We come to grip with the fact that we are not perfect human beings, and although we strive to do our best in our endeavors, we inevitably make mistakes and from those mistakes we grow. We accept the act that we are no less human because of them. In this realization we see ourselves as good and honorable persons who want to be the very best that we can be. So we are eager to learn, to explore, to grow intellectually, spiritually, emotionally and economically.

In wondering how we came to feel superior, inferior, or "normal," we have to first do a little self-assessment which includes thinking about past experiences as far back as our memory would allow us. What were those experiences? Were they uplifting with praises? Of those feeling superior, were you compared to a sibling or siblings as smarter? Were you told that you were the smartest in the family? Could you do no wrong? If so, everything that you were told was internalized and you grew up thinking "you were the greatest and no one could ever measure up to you!"

For you who find yourself in an inferior mode, were you screamed at? Were you put down and told to "shut up" by your parents or other adults in authority? Were you abused by any form? Were you teased negatively? Did people shun or ignore you? Were you asked why can't you be like someone else?

For you who consider yourself "normal," did you grow up in a loving household where you were respected, listened to and encouraged to express your point of view? Were you allowed to respectfully disagree without being ridiculed?

If you did not have the blessing of growing up in a household last described, do not be dismayed. As long as you have a desire to come into your own as a very capable individual who desires to find your uniqueness, there is hope. One of the best avenues is a very positive person who is non-judgmental and is a very good listener. This is especially true of a person who has been where you are and has conquered his or her inferior feelings. That person, you can say, has "done that," and "been there," That is the person who can help you to overcome your feelings and help you out of your darkness into the light.

Moreover, you should find that person easy to talk to and with. You will get very little from someone who has a bad case of superiority or inferiority as yourself. Both will probably cement your current feelings about yourself, life, and the world.

Why don't you check out someone whom you feel can help you by observing the behavior of those around you? Or you can ask a respected leader to help you or steer you to someone. If you are not used to being hugged, watch out, here it comes. The person who once walked in your shoes now knows what a hug can do. The person who can help you is probably someone you know and like. Let's waste no more time because life is too precious to waste!

When we compare ourselves to others, we find we are less than some or more than others in terms of intellect, abilities, talents, looks and achievements.

"Coincidence"

*"In all thy ways acknowledge Him, and
He shall direct thy paths."*
Proverbs 3:6 (KJV)

Mr. Webster defines the word *coincidence* as "an accidental and remarkable occurrence of events, idea, etc. at the same time in a way that sometimes suggests a casual relationship." Actually, there is no human explanation beyond saying that a coincidence is a Divine Intervention, miraculous interaction from God to humankind.

Humankind is not, and will never be, wise enough to know how God does anything. All we can recognize and know is by what we see. The inner workings of anything are beyond human ability to actually see.

If people were more obedient by following through when a subtle "voice" tell us to do a certain thing, go to a certain place, or move from a particular spot, we would experience more surprises and blessings.

Think about this for a moment. Have you ever gone somewhere just because you "felt" you should go? Did you find yourself surprised by something good? Was the surprise something you had said you wanted but never put forth any effort to get it?

Now, have you ever had a thought to go somewhere or do something and your reasoning kicked in and told you there was no reason for your going there or doing it? I don't know about you but this has happened too many times for me not to be obedient. But I have not always been obedient and I have regretted not following through. One prime example is being "told" to take my wallet when I was going to a cookout. I reasoned with myself and decided that I didn't need my wallet, because I was only going to a cookout and someone was picking me up and bringing me back home. Don't you know on the way to the cookout, we passed a store with a big for sale sign, and the driver decided to check it out? There were some items at such a bargain but I had no money or credit card with me.

Have you ever had a sudden feeling to give someone some money and you questioned and didn't? At another time did you have a stronger feeling you should give some money to a person (stranger or known) and you did? How did you feel?

Divine intervention is God instructing you to do certain things because He has a purpose for you. You see, physical happenings are made possible by physical means and God uses His people to do certain things He wants done. The messages come in a multiplicity of ways. It may be a dream, a thought, a feeling or a "voice." Let us examine each of these means.

Have you ever heard or read of a person inventing something with which they were given the formula in a dream? Madame Walker, a woman of color and a cosmetologist, dreamed of creating a product to be used on the hair of people of color. Following through, she became a very wealthy entrepreneur. I would imagine many other inventors were also given instructions in a dream.

Many ideas come in a thought that suddenly popped into someone's head. And when the person followed through, a new product or idea was made possible and the person reached financial rewards by working on or with the thought.

Persons who have learned to follow through with their strong feelings have saved lives, discovered something of value hidden, or have come into a wonderful surprise.

People have claimed to hear a voice urging them to go some place or do something. In following through they have been amazed by what they found.

Since some of us don't know how or why we are chosen or called to receive messages in various strange ways, the only answer we can understand is a coincidence, understanding Webster's definition of as an accidental and remarkable occurrence of events, ideas, etc.

Others of us who have learned to recognize and believe in Divine Intervention and are most eager to do what is "told" to us, we find much joy, peace and happiness in following through with the message regardless of how it is manifested.

Those persons who simply want to continue believing that things happened by chance and that they just ran into a bit of luck from time to time, all through life, will miss much of what life itself has to offer and what is promised to those of us who believe in Divine Intervention.

Divine intervention is God instructing you to do certain things because He has a purpose for you.

Confusing Miracles and Magic

"Ye shall know the truth and the truth shall set ye free."
John 8:32 (KJV)

Unfortunately, the saying, *"Truth is stranger than fiction"* is true. Some people confuse miracles and magic. Magic is sleight of hand; the hand is quicker than the eye. Magic is fiction. What you think you are seeing is not really happening.

Admittedly, magical tricks are very entertaining, fun and mesmerizing, and will keep you spellbound for hours. There may have been some arguments about what was seen or not seen; done or not done. Children are not the only ones who are caught up in the entertaining experience of the moment. Adults are often children at heart. Children and adults get "carried away" under the spell of magic.

Magic tricks are performed by gifted persons who have practiced long and hard to perfect their craft of fooling their audience. Strangely enough, we enjoy being fooled and it puts us in a happy frame of mind. We laugh and wonder how this or that was done. Then the show comes to an end and we have to face reality. Humankind can perform magical tricks, but only God can perform miracles.

Miracles come from power greater than humankind. Conception is a miracle. Because of modern science we can view different stages of human development, but we can't begin it. Miracles are happening all around us. In fact, everything related to life is a miracle and man has absolutely no control of the miracles happening in us and all around us.

It seems strange to me that we believe what we think we are seeing by magical tricks, but cannot believe in things we can actually see such as the growth and development up until the birth of the child of an embryo which takes place in the early stage after the male sperm fertilizes the egg of a female. We can see the different progressive stages of development up until the time of birth of the child.

Right in front of our eyes we see the results of a child's growth. What we don't and cannot see is the actual movements of the increasing in height and weight gaining. We, of course, see the results of the activities. In all manners of growth of plants and flowers, we see the results, but not the actual movements as the plants and flowers change in their stages of fruition. Similarly, we see and feel the results of the wind in motion, but we don't see the motion. And humankind has very little control if at all, any.

Just as we have no control over the creation of life, we have no control over death. Both life and death come from power greater than ourselves. Sometimes, when parents get frustrated with their children, they may say,"I brought you into this world and I will take you out." They, of course, have no power to do so. Only God determines when the last breathe leaves anyone. He is the One who breathes into us the breath of life.

I enjoy observing what is happening as I sit in the audience of a magician performing his skill; I also enjoy reading a good fictional novel. The enjoyment is so great because it allows me to get into the mind of the characters. Excellent writers can evoke various emotions: anger, joy, peace, happiness and so forth. In some stories, I find myself wanting to "choke" the life out of some evil and demeaning character or characters. Some characters I hate with a passion and some I love dearly. But it is all fiction. While deeply engrossed in the novel, I may lose all sense of reality, but once I close the book, I realize it was only fiction and my emotions return to normalcy.

When reading such books, the author's skill as a story teller is much like that of a magician. Each knows how to grab your attention and play with your mind and your heart. You lend your full attention for a time, and when it is over you return to reality. I would be remiss if I didn't mention the same happens when viewing a good story on television, movie or play. The only difference is my emotions may lead me to tearing. To be honest I have found myself crying at times. But again, what I was seeing was not real.

We can cause multiplicities of problems by not being able to distinguish magic (fiction) from miracles (divine reality). Would you believe there are people who claim what they "see" (magic) is real? Then we wonder why we have so many confused people in our world.

If you, perchance, find you are also confused, there is hope. There are ways to search for the truth. First and foremost there is a book called the Bible. Not only will it enlighten you, it will reveal the truth to you so that you can recognize, claim and embrace it. Your eyes will be opened to the miracles all around you, yet you will be able to continue enjoying magic as simply what it is – entertainment. You will continue to enjoy laughter and moments of good times that you desire and deserve. But the miracles will make you aware of what is real and enable you to continue your life recognizing, enjoying, and being blessed with miracles and all the good stuff they bring.

We can cause multiplicities of problems by not being able to distinguish magic (fiction) from miracles (divine reality).

CONFUSION

"And be not conformed to this world, but be ye transformed
by the renewing of your mind, that you may prove what is
good and acceptable, and perfect, will of God."
Romans 12:2 (KJV)

To some extent all "normal" human beings become confused at various times in their life. There are myriad reasons for this. Some of them are because of poor hearing, lack of understanding, misunderstanding, and having preconceived notions about what is being said and how it is said.

What is most troubling about confusion is the affect it has on us. This is especially so when what we call "reality" is simply a delusion. We frequently become delusional because we don't take the time to seek the truth. We rely too much on others who are confused themselves. People are more apt to tell you what they think rather than what they know. All of us tend to operate on opinions rather than facts. Why is it so difficult to simply say, "I don't know?" Maybe our ego will not let us admit that we don't know everything. On occasions a person may say,"I don't know, but I think…" Since I seek facts, I don't hear anything past the word know. At that point I am thinking to whom I should go.

What is terribly confusing, annoying and damaging is when facts and fiction are blended into what I call a "sandwich" with a thick helping of opinion, a thin slice of truth and another portion of opinion. When the sandwich is shared with others, they apply their favorite dressing. And there are those who have to add even more garnishing to spice it up a little.

Oddly enough, some people secretly thrive on being the exponent of confusion. Why is this? It's just like the saying, "Misery likes company." Such persons can hide their insecurity while in the company of the same folk. Identification is an ego defense mechanism that helps people to hide with the hope of not having attention spotlighted on them.

People who are hungry for knowledge take delight in researching written sources and searching The Internet. When we get tired of living in a confused state, what can we do? For starters, we can increase our own hunger for learning, knowing that when we know the truth we are free. We can ignore what we are told by simply not "buying" what they have to say (sell).

Life for ourselves and others would be happier, more enjoyable, and less hectic if we relied more on that which is really true and not someone's slant on it. This means that we have to become more cognizant and alert. The only safe haven is to deal with the truth and to know where to find it.

From what you have read so far on confusion, what do you deduce as to what you can do to become more accurate with facts and how to weed out fiction?

Here are a few simple ways that should prove helpful to a large extent:

- Trust people who have proven to be trustworthy.
- Give an ear to people who are upbeat, enthusiastic, the bearer of good news.
- Stay clear of people who spend most of their time complaining.
- Spend as little time as possible with folk who are negative.

Let's look at each bullet for the reason for writing them:

In other words trust those who have the reputation of being honest and trustworthy.
People who enjoy bearing good news have little time for foolishness.
People who are complainers always find something wrong with everything.
Negativism is extremely dangerous and a person can easily be drawn into that pitfall.

Spending just a little time in the company of negative folk can caused anyone to join their cause, whatever that is.

All of us should be winners as we were born to be. We are endowed by our Creator with all we need to be successful, but some of us find ourselves caught up in a web of misunderstanding, misinformation and too much energy and time spent negatively reacting to nonsense thrown our way. If we responded in positive ways, we would be winners. In a nutshell, a positive approach to negativity is the only way our winning can be guaranteed.

People who are hungry for knowledge take delight in researching written sources and searching the Internet.

CONSISTENCY

"A good tree cannot bring forth evil fruit,
neither can a corrupt tree bring forth good fruit."
Matthew 7:18 (KJV)

Unfortunately, there are some persons who are consistent with inconsistency. Because of that they find themselves as losers. Their inconsistencies are blamed on everyone but themselves. However, if they could break the habit and become consistently consistent they would become winners.

Just what are we talking about here? Some people are always late. Some people are always blaming others for their failures. It is never their fault... Some people are always procrastinating. Some people always wait until the last minute which does not give them time to deal with emergencies. What is the consistency here? The answer is the word "always."

To bring this home, perhaps we need a few examples: One classic example is persons feeling they are not liked so they think whatever they do will not be accepted thus, they never put forth the necessary effort to achieve good results.

Another example is people always running late, because they wait until the last moment to even start whatever task they are involved in. They do not allow time for whatever emergency may come up. They lack time management and organization.

What is time management and organization? It is knowing what you have to do and having a reasonable sense of how much time that may be required to do it. This is also allowing for some interruptions and making decisions as quickly as possible what next steps to take in the event something does not work out. It is a sort of schedule yet allowing for some flexibility. It is a kind of stick-to-it-ness until the job or task is completed.

Time management and organization definitely depends on what is to be done first or last. I think, perhaps, an example may help you to understand how time management and organization works. A person preparing a meal would begin cooking with whatever needs to cook the longest and end up with what requires the shortest time to cook.

Time management and organization is not something we are born with. It is a learned skill. Some of the basics required in being able to accomplish this are: starting on time and doing what you have to do when you have to do it. Procrastination is a killer of time management and organization. One has to have an organized mind.

Once this skill is acquired, it becomes second nature and all we do falls right into place because we instinctively know in which or what order each step is to take. Persons who have this skill can accomplish a great deal in a shorter time than most people.

Persons who are brought up in an orderly household where consistency is one of the main rules demonstrated by parents or a parent (in a one parent family) generally learn to be consistent.

Being consistent leads to being organized and conscious of time. We are speaking, of course, of consistency of being orderly not disorderly.

Let us for the moment think about being brought up in a disorderly home where consistency is about not putting things in their proper places and the members of the household feel comfortable in with things being in disarray all of the time.

There are a few exceptions where some children may grow up disliking living like that so when they get their own place, they are neat and orderly. For them the desire for time management and organization taught them to become orderly in their new surrounding.

But for the most part what we learn early in our home we carry to our grave. I am naturally neat and enjoy working under the strictness of time management and organization because my mother and I shared a three room house and neatness and cleanliness were the two words I grew accustom to respect. She was a sleep–in–maid, but when she did come to our little abode on her days off, she better find everything in good order or I would pay dearly.

We who function by excellent time management and organization find great satisfaction and a wonderful sense of accomplishment in completing every task in timely fashion.

Dr. Melvin R. Hall

For persons who do not have these skills, as I said, it is a learned skill and we are never too old to learn. The saying some people like to throw in your face is, "I've been like this all my life, and I'm going to die just the way I am." Then others say, "What's the big deal?" Others may say," It's nobody's business what I do!" Well, that is debatable and perhaps another essay.

The point here now is do you find yourself saying what others are saying to cover up their lack of interest in becoming more orderly or specifically learn time management and organization? Where there is a will there is a way! What do you think you need to do?

**Time management and organization is not
something we are born with.
It is a learned skill.**

COUNSELING

"I, wisdom dwell together with prudence; I possess
knowledge and discretion."
Proverbs 8:12 (NIV)

There are a large number of people in our society in need of counseling. A portion of them do not realize that they need help. Others know and desire it, but they don't seek help because there is an invisible stigma lurking in the darkness of ignorance about what counseling is and who needs it.

Let's examine those who do not know that they need help. Their negative habits and actions (to them) are what they have been used to all of their lives and to them such behaviors are "normal." If questioned you are apt to hear, "I have been like this all my life. There is nothing wrong with me." They are in a "box" and they don't realize that there is a better world outside of the box. They may tell you they are not crazy and only "crazy" people need counseling.

Now let us examine those persons who know they need help to air their problems and to understand why they feel the way they do. They realize that they are not happy, but they may find it embarrassing talking about their home life and of those persons who have contributed to their situation or condition. Not only that, they don't want another person into their family's business.

Counseling is a good thing, but it has gotten a bad name because of our lack of knowledge and understanding of what it is. First, each of us at some point in time needs to talk with someone, and it is not wise to just talk about our feelings to any person we don't know. Even our very best friend may have good intentions, but if the person is not trained, we can be misled and find ourselves in much worse situations.

There are several factors that are vitally important in counseling which are embodied in the training in counseling. An extremely vital component is confidentiality. We have to feel that whatever feelings we express will be treated as confidential. The next vital component is being able to trust the person to whom we are spilling out the "poison" of our thinking, feeling and action. Actually, the trust factor allows us to speak out and share what is bothering us.

In their training, counselors learn to be good, attentive listeners. They not only listen to what is said, but how it is said, and what the body language (accompanying the spoken words) is saying. For instance, a counselor asks how one feels when a particular incident occurs, and the person says, "okay" while tearing. The counselor notices that the uttered "okay" may not be the truth because the tearing may well indicate pain, and pain is not okay. Pain is a good indicator that something is wrong.

The counselor knows how to ask questions to encourage the client (counselee) to express his or her true feelings. Again, the trust factor has to be established so that the counselee feels comfortable.

There may be several weeks of counseling before the counselee opens up. Hopefully, what is happening during those early sessions is that a trusting relationship is in the process of being established.

Now, persons being counseled for the first time often expect the counselor to tell them exactly what to do and how to do it. An experienced good counselor will not do that. The counselor's responsibility is to find out from the counselee what he or she wants. Based on discussions surrounding that, the counselor and the counselee come up with a plan of action to be implemented during their sessions.

Some counselors require homework. There are certain assignments that the counselee has to do. Here is an example. The counselee has not been speaking to a significant other for a long period of time because of something the loved one has done. The counselee holds resentment which is interfering with his or her desire for peace; the assignment may be that the counselee writes a non-accusatory letter expressing his or her feelings, asking for forgiveness for not speaking.

The letter is discussed in a session and the counselor affords the counselee the opportunity to express his or her feelings surrounding writing the letter. The letter may or may not be mailed, depending upon how the assignment helps or not help the client to begin to resolve his or her feelings.

Giving counseling examples is not easy because it depends upon the situation being addressed by the counselor and counselee during their sessions.

The counselor gives suggestions with explanation, not advice. It is the counselor's responsibility to seek from the client what he or she truly wants to do about his or her situation.

The reason for this essay is to allow the reader, who may need and desire counseling, to understand that counseling is a matter of sitting with a trusted guide to clearly think through thoughts that are unhealthy and causing the client pain. The counselor enables the client to examine faulty thinking.

Faulty thinking often has caused people to entertain lots of negative feelings which has caused ill health, emotional problems, and, in extreme cases, thoughts of suicide.

What about you? Do you have a better understanding of what counseling is? Do you truly want to rid yourself of the pain that you are carrying?

This essayist sincerely trusts that you are able to separate what you hear counseling is, and divorce yourself from the stigma too often associated with it; so that you can get the help that you might need. You were created for an abundance of joy, happiness, prosperity and a truly contented life. Why not seek help so that all of this will actually become a reality?

Counseling is a good thing but has gotten a bad name because of our lack of knowledge and understanding of what it is.

DARE TO BE DIFFERENT!

"There are different kinds of gifts, but the same spirit.
There are differences of service, but the same Lord"
I Corinthians 12:4-5 (NIV)

There are no two persons exactly alike. In fact, twins conceived from the one fertilized egg may be seen as and look "identical," but they are not exactly alike.

Each has his or her own distinct personality and behavior pattern. Each is unique unto himself or herself. We are genetically different so why not be different in terms of our individual selves?

Daring to be different requires strong self-acceptance and confidence with not having to be like someone else. We do not have to emulate persons we admire and respect. It is good, however, to adopt some of the good habits and behavior of people well respected and adored, but it is not necessary or wise to attempt to "copy" every one of the person's wonderful attributes. All of us have our own wonderful "package" known as genes.

There is something very special about people being different. Variety is truly the spice of life. Just as everyone does not look the same, it is refreshing to be in the company of people who do not talk, walk and move in sync as if our action was choreographed as in a dance routine or recital.

There are reasons why some people dare not to be different. One is they do not wish to stand out or call attention to themselves. Those persons can be a bit shy and would rather remain "hidden" in the crowd. However, people who make their mark in life are those who dare to be different and are willing to attempt the untried. They are more adventuresome and enjoy doing what has not been done before (to their knowledge). They are the inventors and explorers. They give much to life and, of course, receive much more in return including satisfaction and a sense of accomplishment.

Those who dare to be different (I believe) are happier people because there is always something happening in their lives and each day there is something else to try. As they succeed they feel more and more confident and enjoy a sense of well earned pride while giving credit to our Creator.

Humankind is endowed with many different talents and abilities. The more confidence we gain the more we increase our skills and craft. People who like to try new things are motivated by their failures as well as their successes. The burning question is why something does not seem to work excites the "inventors" to keep trying different things to turn their failures into successes which give them great satisfaction.

To truly enjoy the many talents we have, we should dare to use them. Some talents remain hidden or unknown for some of us because we are too afraid to follow through with some ideas coming from our thoughts and dreams. Sometimes our loved ones see something in us that we are not aware of and try to encourage us to explore the possibility. I applaud those persons who have such positive feelings about you that they are supportive as much as they can be.

However, some people because of their own fear of failure will attempt to discourage others from exploring the unknown or untried. That is why persons should be careful with whom they share their dream.

People who dare to be different usually get quite excited when an idea comes to their mind and heart. Their enthusiasm sometimes causes them to share with the first available ear hoping for encouragement; that is the chance they take. If they are fortunate in reaching the ear of a person who finds their enthusiasm contagious, they will be blessed with the encouragement (and blessing) they desire. Sometimes, that is all they need.

What about you, the reader? What is your feeling about doing something different? Is there something you would like to invent? Is it a subtle feeling or a burning desire?

Do you dare to be different in some way? Don't let anyone hold you back. If God is in the plan, the plan will work. Nothing ventured, nothing gained. It's up to you. Everything made by humankind was once an image in someone's mind.

To truly enjoy the many talents we have, we should dare to use them. Some talents remain hidden or unknown to us because we are too afraid to follow through with some ideas which come to us in our thoughts and dreams.

DEALING WITH PASSIVE-AGGRESSIVE BEHAVIOR

"In everything set ...example by doing what is good. In your teaching show integrity, seriousness and soundness of speech that cannot be condemned, so that those who oppose you may be ashamed because they have nothing bad to say about us."
Titus 2:7 (NIV)

On the surface passive-aggressive persons seemed the sweetest most wonderful and peace loving people in the world. But that is just the surface. They are very apologetic with a "winning" smile. To your knowledge, they never "seem" to get upset with anyone. So what is wrong with that?

A lot is wrong. If you are living with such persons you will know immediately what is wrong with it. You know. But others many not know and they wonder what is wrong with you. Why are you always upset with them? Well, in your defense, let me share with the readers why you are upset most of the time and about to pull your hair out.

First of all, passive-aggressive people are the most selfish and self-centered persons you will ever meet. And everything is all about them. They have no consideration for you or anyone else. It all amounts "me, myself and I." Now if you are not part of the household of such persons, you will not see that.

Sweetness, quietness, smiling faces, and being soft spoken are qualities of some religious folk aren't they? Certainly, you would say these attributes are the behavior of good Christians, at least on the surface, right? So why are people who live with them complaining?

People who live with them or whom they live with are complaining because they are victims. Victims you may ask? Yes, victims because they are very clever and most times they get over on you. They are bent on getting what they want when they want it because "seemingly" there is nothing you can do about it or them. Ah! But there is!

Let us now talk about how they operate and how they affect you adversely. They are extremely manipulative but outside folk cannot see that. Those persons are bent on having their way and being extremely apologetic, they will not do anything you ask them to but, you will always hear, "I'm sorry!" Well, if you are beginning a relationship with those persons, their apology, smile, soft voice and seeming pleasantness get them over and they secretly smile to themselves because they got over on you and successfully elicited and got your forgiveness.

It may happen a few times more over the course of weeks. By this time you begin to notice that they are never ever going do what you asked them to or what they agreed to do. And, most of the time they agree very quickly. But they know they are not going to do it. After a few times apologizing with no explanation, and seeing that you are getting upset, they will begin to give your some rationalization (excuses) why they didn't and they are good at that. So, even though you are upset, you "buy" the excuses.

Then it dawns on you that the persons never ever did anything you requested and this has caused problems and you have had to either do what you had asked them to do it or find someone else to do it. Does this sound familiar to you? Are there such persons in your household?

Although the larger percentage of persons in your home is much younger persons, there are some who are much older. But it seems that the younger people, sharing your bed and board and other extensions of kindness on your part, are your young or older children who decided, with your approval, to come home until they can "get on their feet."

You know what? They are never going to get on their feet as long as you permit them to live with you and do nothing but what they want to do because you are an enabler. Having given into them for so long and accepting their excuses, you are now beginning to react. Your reaction is getting angry, but they "accept" your anger and in their sweet quiet way apologize for their behavior and now you feel sorry for getting angry.

Their behavior continues and you find yourself stressed out because of not getting any cooperation and having to do a great deal more yourself and this is beginning to make you very angry. Others outside of the family do not know what is happening and why you are always upset. (The others are neighbors, friends and family members not residing in your household).

When you finally decide you have to do something, you discover that you need to talk with them because you are now feeling victimized. Well, when you share your feelings *they don't know what on earth you are talking about. They point out that they have forgotten a few thing a few times, but you seemed okay. They have not ever been disrespectful to you so they don't understand why you are getting bent out of shape over nothing.*

This is the time when you are either tearing your hair (weave) out or you throw your very expensive wig in the furnace. So what do you do? First, you have to realize that you created this "monster" initially unaware, and you have consciously allowed it to get out of hand. Now you don't know what to do.

The simple answer is to kick them to the curb and let them fend for themselves. But the problem is you cannot do that. *How will they survive? Whatever happens to them will be your fault.* Every time you think you have mustered enough nerve to tell them your "decision," their quiet sweetness and smiles keep you from doing what you know you have to do. And so you practically give up and the status quo remains. Meanwhile, you are getting angrier and angrier and seemingly you are the only one "out of order" from what others can see.

Although this must be the most difficult task you have ever had to face, you are going to have to face it. Now is the time for you to pick up their traits of passive-aggression and tell them they will have to find somewhere else to live and you must give a date. You have to be calm, soft spoken and looking into their eyes, letting your eyes do the "talking." Your voice must be firm and steady. They, of course, will try their tricks again on you because they are now desperate. You are now also desperate, and playing their game, so they for the first time experience your seriousness. You must not waver. With all the willpower you can draw upon, stand firm. Say what you mean and mean what you say.

The shock will, of course, cause them to become very angry with you, but you are no longer angry because you have found a solution to your problem (yes, it is your problem), but yet, you are the victim. You have to decide that you are no longer going to be a victim. You know, of course, they are going to accused you of all sorts of things and they will "feel victimized." You can't let that sweat you or deter you from what you have to do!

Perhaps, for the very first time in your life you are calling upon **tough love** to see you through and with that you will win. You have to realize that passive-aggressive folk will either wake up and take on their own responsibility or remain the same, but elsewhere.

Let them say whatever they will. I warn you; it is going to be nasty! You will wonder where all of the "fine attributes" went. You will have to do what you have to do, and that's it! Never mind what others (whoever they are) think or say. This is all your business now. Perhaps they will move to another household. Maybe the sympathy of another relative who thinks that you are wrong will allow that relative to take them in. At least when they leave you can either have another weave done to your hair or purchase another very expensive wig in celebration of your liberty.

**When you finally decide to have to do something,
you discover that you need to talk with them
because you are now feeling victimized.**

DECISIONS! DECISIONS! DECISIONS!

"…as for me and my house, we will serve the Lord."
Joshua 24:15 (KJV)

We may never be able to count how many decisions we make each day. Everything we do requires making a decision whether we are consciously aware or not. What I am about to say may be a surprise, but to not make a decision is a decision. Sounds like double-talk doesn't it? Just think about that while reading it aloud to yourself.

Now, my theory is when we make decisions there is an unconscious process in motion; I refer to it as *our three metaphoric baskets.* They are the "file," "hold" and "waste" baskets.

Placed in the file basket is anything that we agree on whether negative or positive. In the hold basket we put anything we are not sure of and we go over when we have more time to make the right decision where it is to be eventually placed. The waste basket is simply that, waste (negative stuff, gossip, lies we hear, and anything that keeps us from feeling safe and secure).

Let us examine carefully what we should or should not put into any basket at any given time. Know that we are using all of these baskets every moment of the day. I feel that I am also doing this while dreaming because I recall a portion of my dreams immediately upon awakening.

What we put into the file basket is immediately fed into the computer (the brain) and it remains there the rest of our life. However, if there is any illness or accident causing brain damage, we suffer from a "computer crash." Because of that we may have a loss of memory to some degree. Therapy is used to help us restore what has been stored as much as possible. Therapy also helps us to correct stored information that should have not been placed in it.

Our computer does not distinguish right from wrong. All it knows is what we desire and it serves to please us by providing ways and means of acquiring it. Another function is to store information and produce or release it when called upon. A small example is if you want to recall a person's name that you have forgotten, just simply say, "I really want to know ..." Switch your mind to something else. Don't push, relax, Soon the name will come to your memory. You must have experienced trying to recall a name but you kept pushing and several times it seemed that the name wanted to slide off your tongue, but it didn't. Trusting your brain (computer) allows it to work smoothly without interference and it will produce favorable results.

The file basket is our God-given computer (brain) Everything worth saving such as knowledge, positive information, facts, thoughts and ideas, beliefs. learning skills and things that melt your heart and bring joy to your soul should be stored there. Nothing should be filed that hurts or harms you or anyone else. Your computer should always bring to mind the things that are uplifting and cause you to be peaceful, joyous, contented and happy.

The hold basket is actually for temporary use, holding things you need to think about so you can make the right choice of what you should file or discard. I must warn you not to clutter this basket. When the basket is cluttered and overflows you will find yourself overwhelmed. Every time you put too much into it, you add to your woes. That is almost like collecting your mail for several months before going through and sorting your personal letters, checks, bills, advertisements, books, magazines and other junk mail. What a mess! Well, cluttering your hold basket is a bigger mess! The result of attempting to weed out the good from the bad may cause headaches, nervousness, depression, lack of energy, confusion and all manners of discomfort. Have you ever experienced feeling terribly overwhelmed? You need to devote time and energy going over the basket's content on a regular basis to keep it down to a manageable amount of work in sorting it out.

The waste basket is the place for all things that do not add to your joy and peace of mind. This is also the place to put junk, garbage, and other waste material. One should be very careful. During certain stages of our life we tend to reject valuable information that we are too immature to understand. Each of us has suffered through "growing pains" and not willing to accept advice from our elders who have been where we have yet to go (you know what I'm talking about). Fortunately, growth, mental and emotional development eventually awakens us and we learn to be obedient to good advice, directions and instructions,

The process does not have to prove disastrous. We (as long as we live) can make changes as they become necessary. If we have put something in the wrong basket, we can always correct it by making whatever changes we have to. It has been said, "It's an ill wind that never changes." As we grow into maturity we become better able to make sound judgment of what we do and say. All of us have had a slip of the tongue at some time or another and wished that we could take back something we have just said. I have! The waste basket action can be changed with an apology and placed in the file basket with the intention of being more careful of what we say and do in the future.

If this essay speaks to you, I trust you will be benefited by reading it. In other words you will place all of this in your file basket and you will govern your life accordingly.

As we grow into maturity we become better able to make sound judgment in what we do and say.

DIPLOMACY

"A soft answer turneth away wrath, but grievous words
stir up anger."
Proverbs 15:1 KJV)

Webster's dictionary defines diplomacy as a "skill in dealing with people." For the purpose of this essay, I would like to expound on that word and how it applies, or should apply to our daily life. And, just for the fun of it, we'll explore how it is seen by persons who do not understand the full and rich meaning of the word.

For starters, let's check how some people thoughtlessly treat others with their tongue. I have heard persons say with a little bragging, "I tell it like it is!" Most of the time what they are "telling" is unsolicited. In other words, they are volunteering information not asked for. Others say, "If the shoe fits you, wear it!" Others may remark, "No one asked me for my two cents, but I'm going to say it anyway!" Such remarks are often said with an attitude and with no regard for another's feeling.

When making a personal statement to or about someone, we need to know if what we are about to say is factual or not. To speak from our own opinion can be damaging, harmful and hurtful. Some of this is unintentional, but much too often, it is the speaker's intention to cause damage, inflict harm, or hurt, and the reason is because the person is hurting himself or herself. The person could care less about diplomacy. If you think about it, a person can only give what she or he has to give. It would be foolhardy to think a person in pain, because of previous ill-treatment, is able to express love, peace, joy or any other good emotion when he or she is consumed with anger and other negative emotions. Diplomacy is not the person's immediate interest and probably not in his or her vocabulary.

When that person is able to reconcile his or her problem by dealing openly and honestly with the person or persons who contributed to the pain, he or she will begin to look into the meaning of the word.

Apparently, the skill of dealing with people is not a forte of the person causing pain. With pain comes anger and it spreads because in every relationship we "share" what we have. When we are angry, we want to let others feel just what we feel. Most of the time we are too angry to communicate directly and honestly about how and what we feel. We show our hurt in myriad inappropriate ways according to the norms of society, but "appropriately" as far as we are concerned because we are hurting.

Getting back to diplomacy: Let's look how diplomacy will help the hurting person to change by using tact (diplomacy) by another person who knows the benefit of this skill and is able to effective communicate. The tactful person is very careful of what and how he or she says anything and is cognizant of body language, posture and facial expressions. This kind of person can elicit information that will enable the hurt person to express his or her feelings. The tactful person showing loving care and concern, perhaps, may be able to help to reduce some of the anger and thereby enable the other person begin to think how he or she is also hurting himself or herself as well. When the person is able to release the anger, he or she will be able to become whole and free of it.

Are you suffering from hurt, pain and anger? Do you want to free yourself of all of this? Is there someone you trust and respect that you can talk to? What about your religious leader? If you are not connected to any religious organization, how about paying a visit to the nearer church or synagogue in your neighborhood or community?

There you will find persons trained to work with situations such as yours or they will direct you to the right source for help. You don't have to live in misery anymore. What are you waiting for? You must be tired of carrying such baggage in your mind and heart. Sweet peace awaits you and it is as new and refreshing as the fresh air you breathe.

> **Most of the time we are too angry to communicate directly and talk about how and what we feel. We show our hurt in inappropriate myriad ways but "appropriate" as far as we are concerned because we are hurting.**

DISAGREEING PEACEFULLY

*"A gentle answer turns away wrath, but a harsh word
stirs up anger."*
Proverb 15:1 (NIV)

When engaging in an argument without facts and we have nothing to rely on but our opinion, the only possible pseudo-winner is the one who out talks the other. That leads to a no winning situation. The shouting match escalates. The loser gets angry and in order to "win," someone gets physical and the other retaliates.

Newspapers and the news media cover far too many stories about incidents of knifing, shooting, and beatings resulting too often in another's death just to prove that someone is right and the other are wrong. In these cases both parties are wrong. Why can't we disagree peacefully?

Everyone has an opinion. Some are right and others are wrong, or both can be wrong. In some cases of a matter of semantics, both are saying the same basic thing using different words, and no one is listening. Usually, when others are standing around taking sides, the "face saving" choice is to "win" A bruised ego may well lead to a fight and fighting never solves any problem. In fact, fighting creates problems and may lead to death.

There is nothing wrong in expressing our opinion. Most people do. But fighting is such a waste and a disagreement should not lead to a fight. We have choices. And if we take advantage of our choices, both sides can win. One of our choices is to listen to the "voice" in our head telling us to *stop talking and walk away because this is not worth fighting over.*

People who are highly opinionated seem to have to "win" every argument. Never mind the facts, they just like to argue. Anyone knowing this and who engages in a conversation with them is just as foolish as the persons who like to argue.

Have you ever listened to "street corner conversations?" There are people who have nothing to do so that is how they use their time. It keeps them from being bored. It is a pastime they enjoy. Normally, they just like a stiff argument, but will not fight. They are out just to make their opponent look ridiculous and they are also welcome standbys who take their side. Facts don't count because there would not be any argument. Although voices are raised, they are not angry... When they "score" there is lots of laughter.

Scoring is being able to make their opponent look foolish or come out with a statement that is agreeable to the people standing by. People standing by may instigate which adds a little fuel to the "fire." This is supposed to be all in fun and, of course, it kills time for those who have nothing else to do but hang out.

This kind of disagreeing even peacefully is not my cup of tea, but it is harmless. It only serves to polish one's ego while damping the opponent's.

I personally enjoy a good debate occasionally, but not often enough to become a habit. A good debate requires having strong and sturdy facts on both side of the pro and con. A good debate has a learning component and requires persons to be able to think and speak well. The ability to win is determined about how skilled the contestants are in expressing the facts and how thorough they have learned them.

If persons who have a great deal of time on their hands with nothing to do would take the time to learn how to debate rather than argue, they could be a real asset in their community. They could, for example, work with and encourage young men and women to learn how to "argue" effectively and sponsor their ability to debate effectively. They may find that constructive action in their community may prove more satisfying than just hanging out looking for someone to argue with.

Audiences enjoy a good "fight" and what better "fight" could there be than a good debate amongst young people in a number of debating teams? In order for the debaters to be successful they would have to study by researching the facts and learning how to speak properly and effectively.

Talking about disagreeing peacefully, what better community activity we can have than to help to motivate, inspire, encourage and excite our young people who have so much time on their hands and very little constructive activities to help them grow and develop into fine young men and women?

We have a natural tendency to argue whether we know what we are talking about or not. So why not use this as a budding skill for the betterment of ourselves and the community? Can you imagine encouraging others to better their life rather than wasting it? I can envision many young people striving to elevate their status as individuals and seeking higher education, study and applying themselves in worthwhile pursuits so that hanging out would no longer appeal to them.

We have an opportunity to show ourselves and the young people in our community that we can be agreeable in our disagreement if we would concentrate on doing whatever it takes to build- up our confidence, self-worth and self-esteem.

What are your thoughts? If you are a young person whose life seems to be aimless and you like to express yourself on a variety of topics, would this appeal to you? Not only would you enjoy discussing issues and subjects within your own community, you may get the opportunity to compete on a larger or greater scale with persons in other communities, locally and globally. The possibilities are beyond your imagination. Not only that, you will find yourselves with increased self-esteem, self-worth and self-confidence.

Having acquired skills of being able to persuade others on a higher level, you will be able to reach out to the very young people in your community and motivate, encourage, and inspire them.

Why don't you take a moment to let this process through your mind and visualize what far reaching effect this will have on the young people in your community. As you think about this looking up into the sky and thinking about there being no limit to what they can do; think about the effect you will have on young people who are just hanging out.

We can be agreeable in our disagreement if we would concentrate on doing whatever it takes to build-up our own confidence, self-worth and esteem.

DIVINE HARMONY

"Do everything without complaining or arguing."
Philippians 2:14 (NIV)

The easiest thing anyone can do in any situation is to complain and argue. Neither requires intelligence. It requires no thinking. All that is required is opening one's mouth. And in opening our mouths we can express our feelings without a grain of thought or a speck of intellect.

Although there is nothing humorous about listening to people arguing, it is awkwardly amusing. This is particularly so when people argue but they don't really listen to what another is saying. Many times they are of the same mind but using different words. In other words, it is a matter of semantics.

When one seems to be losing the argument, emotions kick in, and over nothing, a fight ensues. The loser feels he or she has to "protect" his or her image, without recognizing that the "image" is already tarnished.

Without wanting to appear sexiest and prejudiced, this writer's observations have been more with men standing around with much time on their hands "shooting the breeze." And in additional to not being professionally engaged, they are urged to be conversationally engaged by the use of alcohol or some stimulating drug.

Be that as it may, this essay's theme is not about those persons, but people in general who, for some reason, have a need to present themselves as knowing everything. Somewhere, each reader ought to be able to see him or herself and use this as a wake up call. You may not be one of the men (mentioned earlier) with too much time on your hand, but you may find yourself in the "general" group.

The general group: There are people who are (for whatever reason) plainly disagreeable. They complain about everything and everybody. No one can do anything right according to them. They find fault with little things that most persons would ignore.

Not only do they complain, they seem to enjoy arguing. And it seems they will keep something going on forever. This may end up in someone getting angry and saying things he or she regrets.

People need to realize that there are many ways of doing any task. Of course, there is always an easier way and a harder way, but if the person enjoys doing it his or her way, why not leave him or her alone? Now, when you are doing it, you do it your way. The main thing here is results. I like the expression, "live and let live" as long as it does no harm to anyone.

If you want to know the best way to accomplish any deed, it is to consult with and follow the instructions given to you by the Master Creator. It does not matter how small or big the task. You may get some flack from those who think that they could have done a better job, but the best thing for you to do is laugh (to yourself) and tell them with a smile, "thanks for bringing it to my attention," and keep on stepping. Why? Because you know you have received the best instructions ever and there is no need to get into any argument because of their complaint. You need not waste your precious time.

Divine harmony comes from God Himself. If we practice asking for His guidance, and are obedient to His instructions, we will not only accomplish our tasks efficiently, but many will benefit from what we have done.

People who are less prone to be so critical will compliment you on a job well done. But you will know that it was not you alone who did it. And while you are politely saying, Thank you," you are also saying, "Thank you, God!"

There will always be complainers. There will always be those who take delight in having a good stiff argument. That, however, will not be your problem. You do not have to engage in their discomfort because you have the Master Builder (Creator) telling you what to do and how to do it. So take delight in what you are doing and do not worry in the least what others will think or say.

At all times seek divine harmony, and believe that you did your best, because there is no Wiser Instructor than God.

Divine harmony comes from God Himself.

DIVINE INTERVENTION

"In the beginning God created the heaven and the earth"
Genesis 1:1 (KJV)

Although all of us may not recognize it, our very existence and survival is because of Divine Intervention. If we all knew this, our world would be more peaceful and harmonious. We would also know that there is absolutely nothing we can do solely on our own. Divine Intervention uses people to help others achieve their dreams, ambition, and aspirations.

People, who do not believe that there is a Higher Power than themselves, are operating in the dark, and unfortunately, do not know it. But Divine Intervention is full of grace, compassion, and mercy and that is what keeps people afloat and alive. However, if they only knew about grace, compassion, and mercy, they would save themselves a lot of anguish, difficulties, headaches and worry. This knowledge would help us to deal with life's stresses so that we would not have to depend upon ego defense mechanisms to make us feel better about our mistakes or poor judgment.

Isn't it strange that the one thing that means the most to us costs nothing? Every living creature craves love and love is something we cannot buy because it is not for sale. Yet, we find so many people longing for it. Why is that? The simple answer is that so many people do not believe in anything they cannot see and touch. And Divine Intervention is love personified.

There are so many things going on in this world as we know it that are not physical so they are not touchable. Those very unseen things are what we are depending on for life itself. At this point you may be wondering what this writer is talking about, and you may think I am not dealing with a full deck. Please read on and bear with me.

Some people have reached "rock bottom" in life and discovered that they have reached a point where they need someone to help them to get back on their feet. But they can find no one who will help them. There is unseen help. If they have lost every thing but still have an ounce of trust (as small as a mustard seed) and call upon that trust, it is amazing how things will change. Not only will they be able to stand on their own feet, they will be able to walk and run. The love they desire will find its way into their heart and life. This is all because Divine Intervention uses other people to help those in great need.

Divine Intervention has been a part of this universe from the beginning of time. It was Divine Intervention that created every thing that you can see. And if you had a microscope you would be amazed at the moving organisms you will see too small for the naked eye. So then, for some, seeing is believing!

I have heard persons boasting that they are self-made. What they are trying to say is that they have accomplished whatever "success" on their own and in expressing that, they take full credit believing it is so. But it is not so. It is only through Divine Intervention that we are able to have any degree of success. Divine Intervention has put into the heart of others to help them in various ways...

First of all, we are born with varied abilities. The seed is planted at the time of conception. It remains dormant until our birth. Some of those seeds may be recognized while we are yet infants. Others may be recognized at an older age. But each of us is born with some kind of seed, if pursued, that will come to fruition. But we cannot boast that we are self-made. We did not put the seed into ourselves; Divine Intervention did and is the same Power that is going to see that the seed bears forth fruit - that is if we are determined to work with or on it.

Let me break this seed business down with an example. Let's take little children who have mastered talking and seem to be quite imaginative. They are full of "made up" stories. You have a choice of listening and encouraging them. or you can tell them to stop making up such stories and stifle or discourage them. If you take positive action by encouraging them, you may find they have the making of great writers. The seed of imagination and creativity is there to be used and developed to the fullest.

That sample could have been of any other seed. Some children early on can take their toys apart and reassemble them (at least when they had parts not glued or molded as they are today). All inventors are born with a seed to put objects together or to come up with a different one. Divine Intervention planned all of this at the time of creation and a (or more) seed is planted in each of us to make the world a better place to live for all of us.

Seeds are given and the results of their development are for humankind.

Whether you want to believe in Divine Intervention or not, this power exists and His name is God. Whatever positively productive and loving religion you believe in, **God is the center of it.**

Divine Intervention has been a part of this universe from the beginning of time.

DIPLOMACY AND CONSTRUCTIVE CRITICISM

"The tongue of the wise useth knowledge aright,
but the mouth of fools poureth out foolishness."
Proverbs 15:2 (KJV)

As humble as we try to be (or think we are) our ego may prevent us from accepting even diplomatic criticism. But there is a way in which we can change. This essay can and will help if we will read and internalize it with an open mind and heart.

Diplomacy is quietly and privately calling someone's attention to an error with as little friction as possible. However, some people are very harsh and will blurt out without regard to a person's feelings. Sometimes it is not harshness that propels us to blurt out corrections. Instinctively, we are all "teachers" even though we have not been professionally trained. The teacher in us calls us to speak more often than not without thinking of what we are actually doing.

In most instances, whether the criticism is accepted or not depends on the motive (reason of the person who is providing correction). If the motive is to help the person not to repeat the error, it is seen as constructive criticism and should be very helpful to the person. However, sometimes our delicate ego does not allow us to accept the criticism. Yet if we do, we will find it very valuable to our learning, and it will help us to be more careful.

In many instances, whether it is acceptable or not, depends on the reason why persons are being corrected. If we correct others because we care about them and want them to express or present their best, then our motive is good and the correction is done in a manner that does not offend. This is called being diplomatic.

Diplomacy is best learned in the home. Our exposure to ways and means of being corrected plays out in our adult life. If we were harshly disciplined in our formative years, that is how we express ourselves as adults. In this case we act as we have been taught. Many times we give little thought to how others are affected by our harshness. However, if we allow ourselves to remember how we felt, we would be more cognizant of how others feel because of our harshness.

Since diplomacy is learned behavior, we can always change, but it requires being conscious of what we are doing or treating others. We really don't want to hurt others or do we? We need to examine why we do. Is it because we ourselves are hurting?

People who are truly humble are more often diplomatic. They think before they speak because they do not want to do anything to anyone that they would not want done to them. In thinking, they find ways to soften corrections. They not only think how to do it, but question themselves of the timing. They take into consideration others who are in the presence of the one(s) being corrected. The question may arise, "Should I correct the person now, right on the spot, or wait until we are alone?" If it must be done immediately while still fresh, a suggested way of doing it is to use a little humor. This softens it and the person may be able to laugh and therefore save him or herself from embarrassment.

Since the object of diplomacy is to help people "save face," we want to find and use whatever means that enable us to accomplish just that. We focus on person(s) not ourselves. Humble people are more interested in helping others feel good about themselves, rather than be overly concerned about how people think or feel about them.

In this regard, humbleness and diplomacy work together (hand in hand). If we want to really know if we are as humble as we should be, or think we are, our diplomacy or lack of it, will help us to determine what category we find ourselves.

All of us have been on either side of the coin during some time in our life. If we have been the ones who have been criticized much too much, we become super critical because our ego has been damaged to the point our self-esteem and worth has suffered.

Some people are of the mistaken opinion that diplomacy is keeping their mouths shut and not expressing their informed opinion (which is another subject that I hope to write about). First of all, humble people are not sheepish or fearful but their concentration is on not hurting anyone in any way. Humbleness does not negate their ability or desire to correct wrong. It allows us to smoothly draw attention to a mistake with a smile and without making a big deal of it or getting bent out of shape.

We can learn a great deal about ourselves by becoming more aware of how we treat others. In examining ourselves let's see if we are able to objectively and honestly answer the following questions: (1) Do we find ourselves ridiculing others because of their mistakes? (2) Do we have the patience to wait until the time is right to correct another? (3) Do we point out another's mistake to a third part? (4) Do we correct others automatically without thinking? (5) How do we feel when others treat us without regard to our feeling? Our honesty will give us a desire to make whatever changes we need to make and we will find ourselves becoming the humble and diplomatic persons we truly want to be. Everybody desires genuine love, and the more diplomatic we become, the more we are loved. People love and enjoy being in the company of people who make them feel good about themselves. As we draw closer to positive, loving, humble people, we find ourselves emulating their positive, loving, humble and diplomatic disposition.

Since the object of diplomacy is to help people "save face," we want to find and use whatever that enables us to accomplish just that.

DO YOU LOVE YOURSELF?

"...and now abideth, faith, hope, charity, these three,
but the greatest of these is charity."
I Corinthians 13:13

The simple question, "Do you love yourself?" is a heavier question than one may think. Loving yourself is different than being in love with oneself. In order to love another, one must love himself or herself. We can only give to others what we have to give.

So if love is not in us to love ourselves, how are we going to love another?

Let's clarify what loving oneself is in comparison to being in love with oneself.

Loving oneself is first recognizing who we are and whose we are. We were created by God so we belong to Him. Since we belong to Him we have power in us greater than ourselves. This power allows us to be all that we can be. There is great comfort in knowing that the sky is the limit for our achievements. We have abilities and talents and God's power within allows us to develop our abilities and talents to full fruition. If we love what God has made, we have to love ourselves.

We can feel good about ourselves, yet not put anyone below or above us. We all were uniquely created in God's image. We were fashioned after His own idea of how we should look and what special seeds of abilities and talents we all have to make us different (unique). Loving ourselves enables us to accept others as we find them and not t try to make them over. Our confidence and self-worth are to be at a high level because we are children of God.

Being in love with oneself is actually not love, but a false sense of worth which causes us to think less of others because we over rate ourselves with self-love. Our arms are so tightly wrapped around ourselves that we cannot extend them to others unless we want something from them. This self-love does not allow us the joy, pleasure, and satisfaction of experiencing good, wholesome and pleasing relationships. We see the worse in others rather than the best. Instead of drawing others to us, we repel them. We make them feel ill at ease in our company. We often demand unwarranted respect. We, of course, are not seen as attractive.

The choice is ours. We can choose to spread love to others or we can hold onto ours. The saying is "What goes around comes around." So if we have nothing going from us what can we expect coming back?

Our peace, joy, contentment and all of the good things we hope for ourselves are possible by shared love. When we keep our so called love to ourselves, that is all that we have. I like the expression *"Love isn't love until you give it away,"* The thing about love is we can't give it all away. The more we attempt to the more it comes back to us.

If you love yourself, then you are thinking kindly of yourself, and you are leaving yourself open to be loved by others. What a joy that is! If you love God you love yourself. If you love yourself and others you love God. This is a wonderful unending circle that just keeps going around and around and just think you, too, are part of it. If you were in love with yourself, you would be outside of the love circle watching others receiving what you were born to have and crave for.

Being in love with oneself is not really love, but a false sense of worth which causes us to think less of others and to believe that no one can measure up to us?

Dreams

"I will instruct you and teach you in the way you should go."
Psalm 32.8 (NIV)

There are two kinds of dreams. They are nocturnal (night) and day dreams.

Lets us explore together their similarity and difference. Perhaps some readers will make a major decision to act on their dreams. That will result in major changes in their lives spiritually, emotionally, psychologically and, of course, financially.

Some **nocturnal dreams** are vitally important because they are either warning us about something or attempting to give some instruction or direction. They are not meant to disturb us, but to enlighten us so that we will be prepared to deal with whatever occurs. Their purpose is to alleviate stress and fears. Consequently, we will be able to move on in our life, although something may happen that brings some pain, discomfort or grief.

Most people say that they don't dream. Contrary to that thought, everyone dreams. The thing is that they do not remember their dreams. They are most likely to remember them when the dreams wake them up or they wake up shortly after having a dream.

Speaking for myself, I have several dreams each night. Some I can recall and others I can't. My dreams are usually pleasant but strange. I have had great ideas and solutions to problems come to me as I slept. This often happened when I audibly said, "I am going to drop this for now and get some sleep." Or I would say, "I'm leaving the answer to you, God." What invariably happens is a solution comes and it wakes me up or the problem seems to resolve itself as if it never existed. This is strange but true.

I am not writing about my nightmares. You will find a little about that under the essay titled *The Freudian Mystique*.

Madame C.J. Walker became a very wealthy entrepreneur in cosmetology, learning new ways to treat hair of women of color. She followed the directions given in a dream. I strongly believe that many other inventions were accomplished because persons followed instructions and directions given to them in a dream.

There is an expression that says,"Follow your dream." Although it may apply particularly to your day dreams (your desire for accomplishing a particular something), I think for Madame Walker and others it meant following the nocturnal dream they were blessed to have.

A day dream's true worth is the determination, application and following through to fruition.

There are two kinds of day dreams. One is idle thoughts that we hold onto without doing anything about them. Some persons talk about them openly and others keep them to themselves. Those who talk about them sound so positive, and it is interesting to talk to them, but the fact remains that all they do is talk. However, after a while the listener gets tired of the rhetoric and becomes good at avoiding them.

Ah! The dreamer who is enthusiastic about his dream and is pursuing it with great determination and enthusiasm holds your attention and admiration. Just listening and hearing the person does something to your spirit. It is such a joy to see the glow on his or her face and the light in his or her eyes. It is so contagious that it motivates others to do something about their own life. The listener who thinks he or she has no dream begins to desire one.

The truth and a piece of good news is that each person has some kind of dream, and it is a matter of recognizing it. So which one of the two day dreamers are you?

Yes, each of us is a dreamer. It is never too late to take our dream seriously and move with it. It is amazing what happens when we are caught up in the spirit of our dream. The "impossible" becomes possible and as time passes our accomplishments become easier and easier. We will find others willing to help. Doors will open that we never knew existed. We will find ourselves becoming more positive and gravitating to more positive and motivated persons who enjoy the better things of life. As we enjoy the good life, we find ourselves financially able to give more to others who are less fortunate than ourselves. We will find ourselves giving advice to others who have a dream but doing nothing about them. Before we realize what is happening, we find ourselves traveling and giving motivational speeches to young and old alike. We have truly become not only successful but a living example how one can take his or her day dream and make it a reality.

How can you help but remind all persons to whom you speak that God gives all His people a dream whether it is nocturnal or day, and along with the dream, the wherewithal to bring it to fruition.

Now that you know the deal and are "preaching" it, you may wonder why it took you so long to move from being a doer-dreamer from an idle dreamer. But you know what? You will make a more powerful motivating speaker than the person who was a doer from the very beginning of his dreaming. Why? The reason is because you have a testimony of having been there, done that and done even more than that on a higher level.

You dared to dream. You dared to do!

Some nocturnal dreams are vitally important because they are either warning us about something or attempting to give us some instruction or direction.

EMPOWERMENT

"If you have any encouragement from being united with
Christ, if any comfort from His love, if any fellowship
with the Spirit, if any tenderness and compassion, then
make my joy complete by being likeminded, having the
same love, being one in spirit and purpose."
Philippians 2:1-2

At 3:30 one morning I woke up from a most empowering dream. It seemed that I had moved to California. The city or town was not revealed to me. However, I was looking for a church home. I wandered into a church in the neighborhood looking for a group my age, of "young men" in their seventies or eighties, but I found a much younger group of men and one woman who could have easily been my sons or grandsons and granddaughter.

They were engaged in Bible study, but the lesson although about Jesus, was in comic book form and very colorful. A man and a woman were serving as facilitators. Everyone was standing. I was attracted to the group because everyone seemed so excited and enthusiastic. As the man and woman talked, I got caught up in the lesson as every single person was.

You know how dreams are. You start out in one situation and end up so quickly in another. However, in this dream I had gone to the church alone, but it seems standing next to me was someone who acted as if we had arrived together. Anyway, after the study, the man and I were introduced to the others, and I had never been hugged with so much warmth and acceptance. Also the male facilitator, while hugging me, asked if I knew who the person was of whom we were studying, and I responded loudly and with great enthusiasm, "Jesus!" At that moment, I felt so empowered. I woke myself up saying, "Jesus!"

I stayed in bed for a few minutes thinking about the dream. I jumped out of bed and just had to write this essay. I don't know if there is a story of Jesus' life in a comic book form but there ought to be. If any person reading this essay knows of such, please contact me at hallraymel@aol.com. I would very much appreciate being informed.

Let us look at the word *empowerment* for a moment. What does it mean to you? Does it indicate a sense of excitement, joy or happiness or being able to accomplish something? Does it make you feel that you have the power to do something that will benefit yourself and others?

What a wonderful feeling it is for us to have a sense of accomplishment and to feel that we can accomplish anything we set our mind and heart to. In essence, that is empowerment!

In the dream the group and I learned that we could accomplish whatever we want because each of us has power from the Man we studied. And all we have to do is to embrace and accept Him by simply opening our hearts to Him.

When I think about the hugs I received in my dream, they were as if they were coming directly from Jesus Himself and that was because each person in the group was feeling the same phenomenal great warmth and acceptance.

I can understand how Jesus' disciples felt empowered in His company, although at times when apart from Him, they did not feel as powerful. This was as it is still today when we feel separated from God.

As I think about the wonderful experience, although a dream, I am reminded of the Scripture which says, "I can do all things through Christ Who strengthens me." (Philippians 4:13). This means that we are completely empowered to accomplish anything we set our mind and hearts to.

Being empowered means we no longer have to doubt our abilities because the power to accomplish lies within us. This power is given to us by God through Jesus. We now realize that alone we are not able to accomplish anything, but with the power given to us, we can.

So what does that mean? It means that we all can be victorious in our daily living. We need not entertain defeating thoughts of not being able to do what we need to do, and what we want to do in terms of providing for our family and living the "good life" of prosperity and plenty.

While living the good life, we share what we have with those who have not come to know that they, too, have power. We can also share by action and declaration how to draw from the well of plenty to those who need to know.

My dream can become your dream. In fact, good dreams are given to share. Certainly, this one was. As Philippians 4:13 shows us, we can replace negative expressions with positive ones that are given to us by God, and we can claim our bounty, whatever our bounty is. Empowerment is yours to claim when you embrace the source. That source is God.

**As I think about the wonderful experience,
although a dream, I am reminded of the Scripture
which says, "I can do all things through Christ
Who strengthens me."**

ENERGY: POSITIVE AND NEGATIVE

*"In all your ways acknowledge Him, and He will make
your paths straight."*
Proverbs 3:6 (NIV)

Invisible in our universe are positive and negative energy and we connect to one or the other. And at times we alternately connect to one then to the other. People who consistently connect to positive energy are more successful and seem to have a better life.

Just where is this energy? It surrounds you. It's above, below, to your left and to your right. As your thinking connects to it, you are fortified according to your thoughts.

Even the most positive of persons, think negative from time to time, but they quickly drop those thoughts because they know the harm it will cause and how much a deterrent the energy can be.

Whether you believe this or not does not make it any less true. Although energy cannot be seen by the naked eye, we can see the results of it and we can connect with it by our thinking. Thinking itself is energy and causes things to happen in our life. Thinking causes a chain reaction. First, thinking causes us to feel a certain way, and feelings (emotions) play out into action (behavior).

People are affected by much that they cannot see so unfortunately they don't believe. It is one thing not to believe and quite another to lose out on something that is benefiting just because they do not believe.

Let's talk a little about becoming positive. According to what has been said, in order to be positive we have to think positive. In thinking positive with a great deal of force from the universe, we should visualize what we would like to accomplish. We need to "see" ourselves in action and to feel good about what we "see." As we feel good, we begin to act the part. We should claim success before we actually see or experience it. Miraculously, we will have it.

Negative thinking causes us to connect to the negative energy in the universe; therefore, negative things happen to us. If you want to be a winner or to be successful, you have to think winning, see yourself winning, feel the joy that comes with winning and being successful.

Many persons find themselves in trouble, doing the wrong things, meeting the wrong people and claiming defeat without making any real effort to be a winner or be successful. Why? The reason is they connect themselves to negative energy all around them. Have you ever heard a person say, "I am not going to win so there is no need trying?" Also, "If it weren't for bad luck, there would be no luck at all?" Or "Nothing ever comes out right for me?" It is like self-fulfilling prophesy. Those persons are making direct connection with negative energy. It is like willing something to happen negatively. How can a person hope to win when dealing with losing elements?

Negative energy penetrates negative people and bounces off positive people. Negative energy from other people can connect to our own negative energy. The same is true of positive energy. That is why some people are instantly attracted to other persons.

The magnetism of our own energy connects to the magnetic energy all around us. All of this might sound strange to some, but is well known to others. The reason why it would be well known to others is because they have proof. You can have proof yourself, but it would be most unfortunate if you experienced it as negative.

Do you want to be a winner? Would you like to be successful? Would you like a sense of accomplishment? Decide what you want, and let's get cracking!

Do you want to be a winner? Do you want to be successful?

EQUALITY

"Therefore all things whatsoever ye would that men should do to you, do ye even so to them; for this I the law and the prophets."
Matthew 7:12

On awakening every morning we need to dwell on the teaching as given to us from Matthew 7:12, showing us how to treat others. In so doing, we will not only prepare ourselves for the day's activities and events, we will condition ourselves to love, be joyous, peaceful, patient, kind, good, faithful, humble, and have self -control. This lesson comes from Paul in his letter to the people of Ephesus (Ephesians 5:22).

Can you imagine what kind of world we would have if we would daily concentrate on the simple instructions given to us?

We all know that what goes around comes around. If we simply treated **everyone** as we wish to be treated, there would be less misunderstanding, misinterpretations, gossip, hurt feelings, arguments, fights, and murder.

This does not mean that we like everything about everybody, but we love them (unconditionally) anyhow. That love will enable us to attempt to want to understand what is going on in the persons' life that causes them to act unbecomingly. We will not let them steal our joy. So regardless of their behavior, we will be joyous about our life and blessings.

The peace that we are experiencing in ourselves and our world will perhaps rub off on them because with the peace comes patience. The effort we exercise to understand these persons will enable us to be kind and even enable us to be less offended.

Our kindness will promote being good and being good makes us faithful to our God, ourselves, and to the principle of treating others as we wish to be treated. Being faithful will keep us humble and not lose control.

In other words we show others that responding positively is much better than reacting. Reacting is giving a negative expression to how we are feeling, while responding is giving a positive response to our good feeling.

We all know that what goes around comes around.

EVERYBODY HAS A DREAM!

"...idols speak deceit, diviners see visions that lie; they
tell dreams that are false, they give comfort in vain.
Therefore the people wander like sheep oppressed for lack
of a shepherd."
Zechariah 10:2 *(NIV)*

You can easily tell whether a person has a dream and whether that person's dream is healthy (positive) or unhealthy (negative).Yes, everybody has a dream.

Whether we realize it or not, our dream determines the life we live. Deep down we all desire to be happy, but we don't act on this desire because our negative dream will not allow us to seek the happiness we consciously or unconsciously desire.

By nature we are giving people; and if the only thing we have to give is unhappiness, then that is what we give. Sadly, too much of that is given. Embodied with sadness is a sense of loneliness. When we are lonely we have very little good to share because rather than feeling loved, there seems to be an overwhelming absence of it. So if we don't feel loved, we feel we have nothing good to give, and we condition ourselves not to receive anything that is good. All of this is because our dream is one of loneliness.

Let us talk about how our dream affects everyone we meet and spend a little time and space with. Our lonely condition shows in all that we do. We are not always conscious of what we are doing. What is on the inside shows on the outside. It shows in our walk, in our talk, in our facial expressions and in other non-verbal communication. It shows in the manner in which we dress and how we wear our clothing as well as the choices we make in selecting our wardrobe.

If you have not given any thought to this, you might have at least observed how people present themselves privately and publicly.

This essay is written targeting persons who have been entertaining negative dreams for much too long. All of us were born for greatness, but greatness cannot be attained if we have a negative dream about our life.

Please give full attention to what this essay is saying about the invisible energy in the universe that affects each one of us. Whether we believe this or not, we are definitely affected by the energy surrounding us in the universe which we are an integral part of.

Fortunately or unfortunately, just because we don't believe something it does not mean it isn't true. But lack of belief renders us helpless, hopeless and ultimately powerless. It is a shame because we all have been created with power and the universe is full of power.

Now, for those of us who feel powerless because they don't have a positive dream, we can begin the process of changing our thinking. By doing so we can start thinking about the possibility of acquiring a dream that will better our life. Never mind what has always been. **The time for change is now!** Dare to dream, dare to do. Part of the doing is to believe that change can take place.

The universe holds the power we need to make this change. So as we connect with the powerful forces in the universe, we find that we are slowly changing and life becomes better. We are less lonely, less helpless, and we experience a sense of power so that we can do many things that we once thought we were incapable of.

This gives us a glimmer of hope and deepening our trust in the energy in the universe, we are able to feel differently about ourselves, and that gives us a good feeling. Once we have a taste of the good feeling, we, of course, will want more and we will be able to decide what our dream should be about.

Is this going to be easy? Initially no because we become so set in our thinking of helplessness, hopelessness and powerlessness that we are afraid to even think about making a change. We feel that any kind of power is out of our reach, and we cannot see that all we have to do is to reach out to it and claim what is rightfully ours. Blessed are they who are able to shake off the negative forces and grab tightly onto the positive forces all around us.

The forces in our universe are there by our Creator. Just as the forces are invisible, so is our Creator. If we believe in air and oxygen that keeps us breathing and the many other happenings in our body which we can feel but not see, then we can believe that there is much more going on which we have no control over in the universe. And we are all a part of the universe.

Why then don't we join forces with the power all around us so that we can enjoy to the fullest all that has been placed in our universe for our sense of well-being and happiness? Yes, we all have a choice. Aren't you tired of being lonely, feeling helpless and powerless? We each have a choice. I know what my choice is. What about you?

Now, for those who feel powerless because they don't have a positive dream, we can begin the process of changing our thinking.

Everyone Has a Story!

*"...Live in peace and the God of love and peace will be
with you."*
2 Corinthians 13:11(NIV)

There's a saying that I particularly like, and it says, *"There is so much good in the worse of us and so much bad in the best of us that ill behooves any of us, to talk about the rest of us."*

The topic for this essay came to mind because of a conversation between a dear and highly respected friend and me as we talked sitting next to each other at an anniversary party in September. However, she said, "Everyone has a story to tell." I decided to write Everyone Has a Story because I believe much of our story we really don't want known. Why is that? It is because the best among us have done things we are not proud of that others need not know and we are carrying the burden of our action or behavior.

You can rest assured that someone knows even though most of the people we are acquainted with may not. Another definite certainty is Our Creator (God) knows, and He loves us unconditionally.

For whatever reason (and there can be many) some people take delight in knowing the parts of our story we do not want known. And as much as we may be liked, loved and respected, some of the persons close to us may have less respect for us if they knew the parts of our story we are silent about.

Now, I venture to say some persons who may change their mind about how much they like, love and respect us when they have come to know our story are using our story to feel good about themselves. You see, they too have a story.

Okay, so we all have a story. This could be seen from more than one perspective. For the sake of this essay, I am going to view it from two specific perspectives.

My first view is - as my friend suggested everyone has a story to tell. I am sure she meant that from birth to death we have experienced many things. We have accomplished much. We have done much in our day to day living. We have learned much and we have exercised or used much that we have learned and have been blessed with the acquisition or accumulation of big or small fortunes or material wealth. Based on that each of us has a history (good and bad).If her meaning is different from that, I apologize to her as she reads this essay.

My decision to write this essay from the viewpoint of each of us has some kind of secret which we would rather not let be known. The secret may well be something that we are not proud of. Why do I choose to write from this viewpoint? I choose to write because I want persons who are suffering from the strain of thinking that others are perfect and they are not, to realize they are not any different than the rest of us.

When I say suffering I mean carrying needless guilt. Everyone has something to be guilty of and I used this in the broadest term. I truly mean <u>everyone.</u> Some more than others but all of us need to learn how to forgive ourselves and move on. Others have been able to do just that. And the reason why they have been able to do so is because they realize that we have a God who is high and looks low and is forgiving because of His unconditional love.

If we are not able to forgive ourselves on our own, we have help. All we have to do is to go to Him with a contrite (repentant) heart, meaning we are sincere about wanting to be forgiven and ask to be forgiven. If this is done with all the sincerity we can muster, we will find the burden lifted that we have placed upon ourselves. What a wonderful feeling that is? When you have experienced it, you will never forget it. What is the feeling? It's a peace that passes all human understanding.

The joy of this gives us a different story to tell. The secret no longer exists and in its place we will have a new story, a story that we will not be ashamed to tell anybody who will listen.

So there will be no need to think that you are different than anyone else in carrying your secret all of your life. The burden you bear does not have to be taken to the grave. Embodied in the hymn *What a Friend We Have in Jesus* are the words "Take it to the Lord in prayer."

My heart goes out to persons who are holding themselves hostage. If you find yourself in this situation, it is time you release it to the only Person who can do anything about it. The key is to believe that there is a Power greater than yourself who loves you more than anyone possibly can, including yourself. You are no different than the rest of us. We all have (or have had) secrets we are ashamed of weighing (or have weighed) us down.

Now, if you are a person who only believes because of what you "see", read the Old Testament in the Holy Bible and learn about the secrets of many of the inhabitants in those days. Today is your day to throw off the guilt you are carrying. You and I were not created to be so burdened. Since we are, we have the opportunity to release all and become whole, feel free, and enjoy life to the fullest and be able to share **our story of liberation** with every living soul who will listen. As my friend said, "Everyone has a story to tell." And in your new freedom, you can tell it gladly and others will pick up your exciting, wondrous and indescribable vibes.

The burden you bear does not have to be taken to the grave.

"Exposing Your Button"

"Now may the Lord of peace himself give you peace at all
times and in every way…"
2 Thessalonians 3:16 (NIV)

Do people know how to get on your "last nerve?" Do you find some persons very irritating? Are you trying to avoid some of your "friends"? Are there some people you could just do without? Why do you think you are so vulnerable?

Do you know that you can control all of this and be free of your negative feelings and pulling? Do you want to be free or do you secretly "enjoy" all the attention (though negative) you are getting?

Well, one of the reasons why you are so vulnerable is you are exposing what button to push when it comes to your relationship with other people. People know how to get "under your skin" because you unconsciously tell them by your reaction to whatever they say or do to you.

Unfortunately, you tend to internalize every negative thing that comes your way. Since people realize this and they play you by pushing your button so that they can manipulate you. They know there is going to be a reaction from you. If they didn't get any reaction, they would stop. Now, the question is - how do you stop reacting?

There are two different ways of handling how others treat you. They are: reacting or responding. Reacting is a negative way of dealing with others and responding is the positive way. Reacting includes anger and revenge. Responding enables a person not to retaliate when picked on or hurt.

Unconsciously, our negative feelings about ourselves draw attention and people treat us similarly. The message we send out is "I'm not worthy of being treated decently." So others "dump" on us because they get the impression that is what we want.

No one really stops to think that is not what we really want. We have an unconscious button that says "Push for a reaction." So they push and we react.

If your answer to each of the questions in the first paragraph of this essay is yes, and you want to make changes, the changes will have to begin with you. The first change is to get counseling or join a workshop with other persons similar to you.

As you compare past experiences of what happened when you were younger, you will see why you act the way you do.

There are many workshops. It would be wise to join one that deals with the positive rather than a continual discussion on what happened. A positive workshop works with what is happening **NOW** and not so much **THEN**.

Your desire should be to move on so that you and the other members can begin to respond to situations, removing yourselves from the desire to react.

The right workshop would allow you to see the good in yourself because you and each member will be able to point out your positives. While each of you is helping each other, all of you are internalizing your good points.

Amazingly, when your transformation takes place you will like the person you become. People who used to push your button no longer "see" it. They will learn how to respect you and treat you respectfully. Why? This will be because your behavior now demands respect. You will consciously and unconsciously demand the best from people in relationship to you.

At all times our internal qualities are shown externally. The anger, shame, discontent, and negative feelings which caused as to frown, argue and behave badly are all gone. Our smile and wonderful new sense of humor replaces the negativism we used to display.

People we used to avoid may become an important part of our life. We will also have a better understanding of why they treated us the way they did. The old us will be history and the new us will be what will make our life more interesting, happy, enjoyable, peaceful and loving.

We began this essay with questions and we end with questions: Do you recognize that you have a major part to play in your condition? Are you willing to make whatever change is necessary in your life to become the happy person you secretly long to be? Have you sought the help you need? The final question is – are you now the person you have always wanted to be?

Amazingly, when your transformation takes place, you will like the person you become.

FACING PROBLEMS

"For as a man thinketh in his heart, so is he."
Proverbs 23:7 (KJV)

Facing problems is not the easiest of life's tasks, but it is easier when we tackle each one as it is presented to us. We create bigger festering "monsters" when we let time pass without resolving them. We do it to ourselves with the cooperation of others.

Our tendency to blame everyone does not make it any easier. Let us take a look to see what happens when we do not face our problems immediately and straight on.

The stress that we put on ourselves can be overwhelming. Our imagination takes off to such an extent that it affects us physically, emotionally and psychologically. This can cause a mental breakdown depending upon the problem. Procrastination neither cures nor resolves anything.

Our imagination alone can bring on more problems. We began to think thoughts that are not related to the problems, thereby making the problems grow to the point that they require a great deal more attention and harder to resolve. Had we taken care of the matter while it was much smaller, it would have been resolved and forgotten about.

To bring this home, let us suppose the problem was a small matter of miscommunication. Let's say we were told that a falsehood had been stated against us by a person very close to us. It was made by a much loved significant other, blaming us for having lied about him or her. This is a "he said, she said" sort of thing which should have been ignored from the moment it reached our ears. Ignoring it would have been the immediate thing to do, but we didn't. So what did we do? Without confronting the person in a calm manner with the intention of getting the facts, we retaliated by really saying things against the person that we will later regret. Wow! What a mess!

You, the reader must find this quite confusing. Have you ever found yourself caught up in such a mess?

Let us examine how we can avoid this problem by "nipping it in the bud," Then we will look into ways the mess we have gotten ourselves into when the "bud" becomes an "embittered bloom."

Nipping it in the bud:

One way of doing this is to ignore it completely. If it is true, you will find out sooner or later and the friend you thought you had will probably miss you more than you will miss him or her. The person will have to live with the guilt. Meanwhile, you are free of a false friend. Have you ever not noticed that an enemy cannot hurt you as badly as a person you are very fond of?

Another way to nip a situation in the bud is to calmly inquire into the matter with your friend. Your approach should not be an accusatory one, but a matter of asking for clarity and understanding. If he or she "blows off steam," it will probably be the way he or she expresses guilt. If your friend has been falsely accused, his or her anger will be expressed toward the "news bearer" and not toward you.

Having the bud become an embittered bloom:

Now, perhaps you have allowed yourself to get "bent out of shape" by retaliating. But later, you want to straighten the matter out and put it behind you for your own sake and peace of mind. What should you do? Let your friend know what you are guilty of and apologize. If the friend is also guilty, he or she will also apologize to you. After forgiving one another, it is up to you and your friend how you will treat the friendship from then on.

Whether you face your problems early in the game or later, the important thing is to resolve it once and for all. After that, you will experience your own unique and sweet sense of freedom whether the friendship remains or not. If the friendship is equally important to the both of you, it will become stronger and both of you will have learned a dear lesson.

Whether you face your problems early in the game or later, the important thing is to resolve it once and for all.

FACTS VERSUS OPINIONS

"Seek and ye shall find"
Matthew 7:7 (KJV)

We have a tendency to confuse opinions with facts. They are as different as night and day. Facts can be proven and carry a great deal of logic. Opinions can be extremely harmful and carry a multitude of negativity.

Let us examine both of them. We will start with opinions so that we can end up on a positive and happy note when we observe what happens in a family that uses facts in its daily existence.

Opinions at best are lucky or unlucky guessing. So what families would want to spend their lives hoping they are right rather than get the facts and be right? Opinions sometimes serve as a poor means of covering up for a lack of knowledge, understanding and belief. They cause disagreements, arguments, fights and to some extent death. It is sad to say that even some families become dysfunctional because members do not want to expose themselves as being unaware of how to handle certain family issues. So they attempt to cover up their lack of knowledge by having a temper tantrum; when their opinions are contested, they flare up in anger.

What happens is that some families cannot have positive conversations so there is no communication. When there is a lack of communication, the family suffers because members are afraid to express their feelings. When feelings are not expressed, there is a build up of powerful negative emotions and no means of ventilating pent up feelings; eventually that leads to some sort of explosion. So opinions override facts because facts are unknown in this family. No one seems to seek it because they seem to be caught up in negative emotions.

All this results in hurt feelings, excessive fear, feeling of being unloved and no one cares about the other. One day if a professional does not intercede there will be a very damaging explosion within that

118

family and if there are any children involved, I have great fear of what might be the outcome.

Just writing this gives me an awful and most disturbing feeling of doom. Because of that I am leaving that family as it is and moving on to a family that operates on facts as best as it can.

Facts are undeniable truths. When family members insist that they will deal with life problems with as much facts as possible, homeostasis exists. Homeostasis is a state of harmony with all of the positives such as love, peace, joy lively and free conversations associated with their harmonious existence.

Being able to converse with one another without fear of having to prove anything is healthy communication. Not only is it healthy, it's enjoyable. Family members cannot wait for family gathering in order to share what's happening when they are apart from one another in their various day to day activities. The family operates on factual information and because of that, they have a sense of security and well-being. Sticking with the facts enables them to be believed and it gives validation that we all seek as persons and family members. Validation is demonstrated by recognition, acceptance and agreement.

Family members not knowing the answer to any question asked feel free to say "I don't know but let us look it up." Can you imagine what a joy living in such a household is for this family? Hopefully, the family includes children. Why? The children have the opportunity to grow up in a peaceful family and they would want that to continue with their own individual families when they become adults and start their own families. History has proven that we bring whatever attitudes we have from generation to generation.

Being factual sounds good, but most of us are highly opinionated, and attached to that is we are very emotional. There is nothing wrong with strong emotions as long as they are positive. In comparing the two families we can see the importance of being factual as compared to being opinionated. The mode in family operation is extremely important and the reader can see the night and day comparison.

May peace find itself at your door and in your heart every day of your life.

Facts are undeniable truths.

FORGIVING AND FORGETTING

*"In Him we have we have redemption through His
blood, the forgiveness of sins, according to the richness of
God's grace...."*
Ephesians 1:7 (NIV)

The words "unforgiving " and "not forgetting" are words which can
be called Siamese twins because they both thrive on the same bloodline.
People say, "I can forgive but not forget." This is not possible. Both are
stuck together. As long as one does not forgive, one cannot truly forget.

Looking closely at this we will be able to understand. Forgiving
gives us the power to move on with our life, and to free us from anger
and resentment, which eats at us as a cancer. Negative thinking plays
in our mind and keeps us from being productive and free. It robs our
confidence. As we think, we feel. As we feel, we behave. Complete
freedom begins with forgiving. When we are able to forgive the person
who harmed us in any way, we no longer have to harbor feelings about
someone who has wronged us.

In actuality, we never forget, but the forgiving takes the sting,
anger and resentment away. Remembering is no longer a daily thing. It
gradually allows the memory to be less and less frequent until we reach
the point where casually remembering is without pain. The infrequent
remembering is good because it guards us from allowing ourselves to
be in a situation where we can get hurt again.

Each one of us is subject to someone's thoughtlessness, carelessness,
or insensitivity. And because of any one or all of them, we get hurt. We
as a people are vulnerable to others. And we are most vulnerable to those
whom we love and respect, some of us more than others. Whatever the
case, we cannot allow ourselves to get caught up in anger to the point
it affects our mental or physical health.

Our ego is easily bruised. However, we are not helpless or powerless.
We do not have to let our ego be damaged beyond hope. We have the

power of control. We can use this control to free ourselves from what others may say or do.

When we hold on to others' negativity we place ourselves under their control because we give them license to control our emotions and actions. But when we forgive them, whether they accept our forgiveness or not, we are free and the forgetting process begins and eventually will be put on the "back burner" of our memory.

There are many choices we have to make in life. The choice of forgiving is a noble act which ultimately frees the victim and the culprit by lessening the memory of both.

You are worth the freedom and peace of mind as a result of your forgiving and forgetting.

**Forgiving gives us the power to
move on with our life.**

FORTUNATE OR BLESSED?

"And you have been given the fullness of Christ,
Who is the head over every power and authority."
Colossians 2:10 (NIV)

When good things happen to you do you consider yourself fortunate or blessed?

Most persons consider being fortunate and being blessed as the same; however, they are as different as night and day. How so, you may ask.

Being fortunate implies coincidental happenings when there is no such thing as coincidence.

Every good thing that happens to us is done on purpose. It is the Master's plan. If we have to ask who the Master is, we are missing more than we can possibly imagine. We miss recognizing ourselves as being blessed. Why? The more we believe we are blessed the more we want to continue to be blessed. And the only way this can happen is to recognize and be obedient to the most subtle instructions. The source of our blessings is God. And He has a plan for all of us because He created us, and our blessings are embodied in our creation. We were all created for greatness. God put the best into His creation. Please take a few minutes to read the book of Genesis.

It is most unfortunate that some people claim not to believe in God. If they did they would recognize, receive and appreciate even more blessings. Let us do a little testing to determine the possible times we missed out on some of our blessings. As we do it, let us think about how better off we would have been if we had done something that "out of the blue" has come to our mind. **There is a correction here** because nothing comes "out of the blue."

We have very creative ways of expressing what we don't understand and the saying "out of the blue" is one of them. Another one is "coincidence." There are also those who say they believe in God, yet, they seem to have a lack of trust starting with themselves. When we don't trust ourselves, we cannot have much trust in others. Without trust we miss out on so many wonderful things in life. Success or failure has a lot to do with trusting or not trusting.

Let us get back to the testing. How many of the following questions can you answer "Yes" to?

Have you ever had a thought to call someone and you didn't? Have you ever had a thought to visit a shopping mall or area and you didn't go? Have you had a dream with some kind of instructions and you didn't follow through? Have you ever met a stranger and had a strange desire to take his or her telephone number but didn't because you were too embarrassed to ask for it? Have you ever had a desire to strike up a conversation with a stranger and didn't because you didn't know how to start it? Have you ever needed or wanted some information but was too embarrassed to ask for it? Have you ever needed or wanted something tangible but was too ashamed to ask? Has someone offered you something that you really wanted but you did not accept it? **For every answer "yes" you missed out on a blessing simply because for whatever reason you were not receptive.**

The more we trust ourselves and others the more we will enjoy our God-given freedom to express ourselves. The more we trust ourselves the less concerned we are of what others think about us. The truth is if we are doing the right thing, we don't have to worry about what others think or say. If we can truly say to another person who likes to hear himself or herself talking, "Talk about me all you want to, but just tell the truth," you will feel free and comfortable in the company of all people without fear of their thinking or saying.

The point that I am making is that we must know when we are blessed as compared to being fortunate. The beginning of our many blessings is life itself. That is God's gift to us. What we do with our life is our gift to God. Ultimately, recognizing our blessings places us in a unique position to receive many more and it is not by chance or whatever co-incidence means.

Often in sermons we hear, "When the praises go up, the blessings come down." This is true! The more credit, honor and praise we give to our God, the more He blesses us.

The more we trust ourselves and others the more we will be able to enjoy our God given freedom to express ourselves.

FREUDIAN THEORY ON
HUMAN BEHAVIOR

"And God said, Let us make man in our image, after our
likeness".
Genesis 1:26 (KJV)

Sigmund Freud (1856-1939 Vienna, Austria), the father of Psychoanalysis may not be every day reading even for the most avid reader, but I believe you will find this topic interesting and very different from my other essays. You may want to discuss this with someone. I hope you do!

Why am I writing this particular essay? I'm writing it because this topic affects every human being and it will give you insight for further study and an explanation of how you and I "tick" as unique and interesting individuals created by God.

If you have been following my writings in *Our Times,* you should have noticed that I prefer using words easily understood without your having to go to the dictionary. My intention is to reach your heart more than your intellect. However, this may well be an intellectual piece. Nevertheless, if this were a scholarly essay, I would have to use "million dollar" words rather than the "ninety-nine cents" variety. Having said that, I shall now get to the heart of this essay.

For more than 15 years, I have worked as an adjunct professor at Touro College after retiring from New York City Department of Social Services. I find teaching Theories of Counseling one of my favorite courses. It not only enables my students to get to know themselves better, it helps me to work on keeping myself in check. I am hoping that you, the reader, will also be inspired and encouraged to be the best person you can possibly be so that life will be more rewarding and most enjoyable for you.

Freud's Id, Ego and Superego

Learning Dr. Freud's theory of the id, ego and superego helps students to understand conscious and unconscious motivations that stimulate our thinking and behavior. The forces of the id, ego and superego directly affect our day to day behavior. They are unconscious inherent forces of our nature that remain active every second of our life from birth to death. These forces work differently as we grow and mature into adulthood. Each stage of our development brings appropriate and more sophisticated changes in our behavior.

Starting with infants, the id takes over and prompts the baby to make demands for his wants and desires. There is no reasoning because immediate gratification is the infants' sole desire. When they are satisfied, depending upon how many months they are, they will play, coo or sleep. It may surprise you to know that the id stays in an operative mode until we die.

We will not go into the results of functioning under the influence of the id, ego and superego with the other childhood stages of development. Instead, we will move to the adult stage.

Strangely enough, adults of all ages functioning heavily under the id's influence may find themselves committing all sorts of crimes. Why? Because they want and desire to satisfy their craving whatever it may be. They simply take what they want. The thought of paying for it or getting it legitimately does not cross their mind. They take it simply because they want it, whatever "it" is.

The next force is called the ego. This has to do with our reasoning power. This unconscious force finds ways to satisfy the id by legitimately acquiring what the id wants.

The superego is the unconscious force that stresses morality (the conscience) what is right. So the ego and the superego work together to help to satisfy the id. The superego reminds the id of what is right and the ego uses that to find a way for the id to get what it wants the right way.

Let us talk about this a little and move on to the adult who wants to operate from the id even though he or she has been taught morality, the right thing to do and know that in order to acquire anything you just don't take it. You either purchase it or negotiate to get it. But the adult functioning on his id ignores the ego and the superego and you know what happens to him or her when he or she gets caught.

Ego-defense Mechanisms

Another of Freud's theory is ego-defense mechanisms. They serve to help people save face, reduce embarrassment and cope with life stresses. This is, to some extent, like a "survival kit." I will explain some of the mechanisms so that you will get an idea of how the individual mechanisms work.

Denial is the first one that we are going to talk about. You have heard people say, "He is in denial." That means if you are in denial you are not taking ownership for your action. So if you don't "own" it you don't have to do anything about it.

Let me give you an illustration for this one that I use in my classes: A father is a weekend alcoholic. He drinks from Friday night to Saturday night recuperating on Sunday so he can be ready for work on Monday. He has never missed a day of work or is never late. He is a good supporting father and his children and wife want for nothing. Based on his record, he denies being an alcoholic. The man is in denial so he does not have to do anything about his drinking he says because it is purely recreational. That is an example of denial. For your own enjoyment and edification, why don't you run this by a friend and discuss whether he is an alcoholic or not. If you happen to talk to someone whose situation closely resembles this example, you know what the person's answer is going to be because he, too, will probably be in denial.

I am going to mention several other ego defense mechanisms with examples before bringing this essay to a close.

Rationalization is offering excuses. The person reduces his responsibility because of a handy excuse. He hopes his excuse will make him less responsible.

Projection is another which places the blame for his action on someone else. Another person caused him or her to do something he should not have done.

Identification enables a person to not be singled out. He was with a group so he feels comfortable and less embarrassed.

Displacement is taking out frustration on the wrong person because he is afraid to confront the right person. Example: A man is angry with his boss so he takes out his frustration on his wife and children,

Compensation allows a person to mask perceived weakness by highlighting strength.

Example: A failing college student is a star basketball player at his college.

All of us have to deal with the id, ego and superego on a daily basis – some of us more than others because of our propensity to do the wrong things. We cannot avoid them. And our ego and superego have saved us from getting into trouble many times. Our ego-defense mechanisms have helped us not to look foolish at times, but hopefully they have helped us to get a reprieve and we have learned from the use of them.

I trust that you found this essay interesting and, that you are inspired to do more reading and expanding your mind. There is a world of good stuff to learn. Be informed!

Each of us is unique and our uniqueness makes us special!

"From A Caterpillar to A Butterfly"

*"Be not conformed to this world, but be ye transformed
by the renewing of our mind."*
Romans 12:2 (KJV)

Unless one understands the metamorphic process of the transformation of the caterpillar, one would think it is impossible.

We are going to examine this kind of transformation from two points of view. The first is the physical (metamorphism) such as described in the first paragraph and the second will be a spiritual transformation, the changing of one's thinking (mind), feeling (heart) and behavior.

Physical (Metamorphic) Transformation:

I hardly think anyone would much enjoy holding a caterpillar in his or her hand. In fact, it makes me shiver imagining it. But when the transformation is complete, the joy of having a butterfly land on ones hand would be delightful. Now as you observe this magnificent change, you have to believe there is a God. Reading about the creation in the book of Genesis should also convince anyone that there must be something greater than him or her embodied in the creation of the universe.

Spiritual Transformation:

Metaphorically speaking, just as the "ugly" caterpillar can be transformed into something magnificently beautiful, we as creatures of God can change. I apologize to anyone whom I've offended by the adjective "ugly" describing the caterpillar. Your see, some persons may find the caterpillar attractive (no insult intended).

On the other hand, some of our readers may be able to cite some persons (like the caterpillar) that they would avoid as they would the bubonic plague because of their attitude and behavior. But, because we love God, we know that we are required to love them anyhow. So we love them at a distance. We love them but do not necessarily like them.

Regardless how annoying, disturbing, revolting and dangerous some persons are, they can change from their "ugliness" and become as beautiful as the butterfly." How so" you may ask? The same love that we are required by God to give has to be deeply intentional and cannot be given from a distance. Without God our human condition will not allow us to assert the energy needed in order to begin the process of neutralizing people who are so full of hate and anger. First of all, they don't trust anyone to get too close to them. In fact, they act up in order to avoid anyone attempting to get close. Secondly, they, as everyone, want a healthy and wholesome relationship, but they are afraid of being hurt again. Can you understand that?

This situation calls for prayer and our unselfish giving of empathy after getting some semblance of understanding. We have to remember that no one is born evil. Some become that way because of the negative things that have been meted to them through life. Bad experiences can destroy us just as good experiences can motivate us to do the right thing to others.

The persons suffering from the wrongs that have been dealt to them have to be, to some degree, convinced that you are not one of those persons who will harm them emotionally, psychologically or physically. It is usually a long process. Their condition occurred over time and cannot be changed overnight. Only long term unconditional love can make it possible. But first, if anyone attempts to transform someone who is bitter because of his or her experiences, he or she has to prove unconditional love. That person will be tested because of the lack of trust. The vulnerability of the person seeking help is acute. The good news is that unconditional love and patience will definitely bring about transformation from the "caterpillar" stage to the "butterfly" existence.

Let's pause and think for a moment. Do you know someone who has made this grand transformation? It is utterly astounding when you have not seen the person in a number of years and then have the wonderful opportunity to see him or her as a renewed beautiful person.

The person, no doubt, will tell you with much enthusiasm that he or he was not able to change without the unconditional love of God in the heart, mind and soul of the person working with him or her. That love was demonstrated by another human being who had taken the interest and time to let God's light shine through him or her.

If you, the reader, happen to have been caught up with bitterness, hurt and anger, what about your transformation? Have you always been the sweet person you are now? My guess is that you have had more than your share of "put downs" and the trials and tribulations associated with the negative experiences you have endured. If this is the case, you are readily agreeing with me. Despite all of that, you have become a beautiful butterfly and your world is better and so are the lives of the people you continue to touch.

For you, this message serves as a reminder of what is possible. So, it is conceivable that you are helping others make the desired transformation. For those who have forgotten the "cocoon" from which they have been delivered, it is time to let your love be shown, known and demonstrated in full measure. You know, of course, the more you give (of anything) the more you receive in kind.

To all the butterflies, may the joy you give be returned in such abundance that you will have much difficulty trying to count your blessings because they are as amazing as the miracle of the transformation of a caterpillar becoming a butterfly. As you move from shoulder to shoulder and hand to hand, the joy you spread will be most appreciative by all who have the good fortune to be in your path.

Regardless how annoying, disturbing, revolting, violent and dangerous some persons are, they can change from their "ugliness" and become as beautiful as the butterfly.

From Self-Rejection
to Self-Acceptance

"If you fulfill the royal law according to the scripture,
thou shalt love thy neighbor as thyself, ye do well.
James 2:8 (KJV)

You may be surprised by the number of persons who loathe themselves. There are many reasons for that, and I am not going to attempt to explain why to a great extent. I would, however, like to say that we must be very careful how we talk to and treat our children from infancy through young adulthood and/or adulthood.

Parents and care- guardians daily interact with young children and they are impressionable and internalize the negatives as well as the positives. It is safe to say that children who grow up being put down on a daily basis or very often tend to not accept themselves as worth loving or respecting. So it begins with not loving self and finding all kinds of problems dealing with self.

I am disturbed by the way some adults talk and treat each other, and I get very angry when I hear parents cursing their children, slapping them in public and calling them all kinds of names. Does it happen? Surely you must have seen this on the street, in stores, and in their homes. What are we teaching our children? We are teaching them to be self-haters.

All of that negative programming takes years and years to get rid of and it is not going away on its own. It is too ingrained. Negative programming causes great of damage. Everyone who comes into that kind of interaction will be affected by the negative programming of negative persons.

It stands to reason if persons do not like and love themselves, they will not love anyone else. And they definitely do not trust but a very few persons. Even then they have to "test" those few persons to determine who are trustworthy and who aren't.

Personally speaking, I have been tested so many times by emotionally disturbed adolescents when I worked for ten years in Social Services as a live-in counselor in group homes.

The need for testing is easy to figure out and understand when you think about what I am about to say. If you can't trust your own mother in whose womb you lived for nine months and upon your birth began to experience not only negative behavior but downright evil now considered abuse, how then can you trust the persons with whom you are not genetically connected to? How can you trust other people in your life in order to feel safe, comfortable and cared for?

So what do you do? For some reason that you may not be able to articulate, you are attracted to certain persons who are your new (temporary) caregivers because they seem to be nice. Now, the question is how "nice" are they going to be when you do something you should not do? How will they discipline you? What are they going to say? What are they going to do? The only way to find out is to purposely do something wrong. You are then testing if they really care as you hope they will.

All children unconsciously want discipline. They also need to know how wide and broad are their boundaries. In some households (including foster care) they are too narrow and others too wide. Wise parenting and counseling requires that the size of the boundaries should be according to the maturity (not always age) of the children.

How much space does each individual child need in order for the children under your supervision to grow and mature in positive and acceptable ways? Let us go back to the testing. In order to pass the test with children who have been taken from their homes because of abuse or negative influence by their parents, the new caregivers or guardians must be truly caring, fair, consistent, and a very good listener. Very importantly, the persons have to be as less judgmental as they possibly can even with a child who lies at the "drop of a hat" and will look you in the eye while lying. Such a child can be very dramatic and when caught in the wrong will cry and say that you don't love him or her. The child is testing your consistency. If you fall for the drama, the child will spot a weakness. All children look for strength along with your fairness, caring and consistency. When they plainly see and feel it coming from you, they will begin to trust you and you will be able to "save" that child from self-destruction,

If you continue being that trustworthy person even into his or her adulthood, you will not only have a friend for life, but can see your wonderful role modeling. The child will undoubtedly emulate you in many ways. Not only will your name be on his or her tongue the rest of his or her life, his or her children will reap the benefit of good parenting. You will have enabled that child to be transformed from self-rejection to self-acceptance.

Sounds easy, doesn't it? It is not but, **this is the key**, you must be a person who believes lives and trusts without any reservation that there is **Power** beyond your own being. You must know that there is a **Force** within you that is not of your making which gives you the desire, the will, and the strength to deal with any and every thing that comes into your life. You should not be surprised to know (after reading my essays for the last four years) that the **Force** I am referring to is **God Almighty, Himself!**

It stands to reason if persons do not like and love themselves, they will not love someone else.

Functioning From the Heart

"Now fear the Lord and serve Him with all faithfulness."
Joshua 24:14 (NIV)

What distinguishes people's quality of life is whether they function (operate) from the head or the heart. Someone may ask what the difference is. The result of how we live our lives depends upon what motivates us to do whatever we do. And the motivator determines the quality of life. Who is your motivator?

When we speak of the quality of life, for the purpose of this essay, it has nothing to do with wealth, education, social position or power. Rather, the quality of life this essay refers to is personal happiness, joy, peace, love, contentment, confidence and a general feeling of well-being. These are the things not even wealth can bring. If wealth could, only the wealthy would be the recipients of the best quality of life.

Let's look at functioning (operating) from the head and the functioning (operating) from the heart.

The Head:

In one of my essays I referred to our brain as our God-given computer. In the same essay I referred to making decisions using three baskets – the file basket, the hold basket and the waste basket. If you remember reading the essay what I'm about to say will enable you to tie in that essay with this one. If you have not read the essay, that's okay because I am going to bring you to a realization you may have not given any thought to.

Very succinctly, the file basket is the one from which you get information to put in your computer. The hold basket holds information you are not sure what to do with and you have lingering thoughts about, and your waste basket is where you put garbage (things not worth even thinking about or dealing with).

Many things come to our heads every moment of the day. Whether we are conscious of this or not, we are processing thoughts determining whether to accept them as factual, hold them to think about later, or discard them.

The trouble, much too often, is that we delay the process and by doing so we function from our heads. We don't always take the time to think through the thoughts that are swiftly coming. When we function from the head, we make a lot of mistakes because we are using thoughts that are not always factual. Opinions are also in our heads and they influence our emotions, and our emotions cause us to act up accordingly. Did you know that facts usually have a more positive effect on us than opinions? And the reason for this is that facts deal with what one can prove and that gives validity. When something is valid it leaves no room for argument. When it is just an opinion it goes against other opinions and there we have a problem. Embodied in the problem are other negative thoughts causing persons to have hurt feelings, anger and sometimes bitterness.

For this reason we cannot trust our heads to give us the right information. Have you ever heard the expression, "talking (speaking) from the top of my head?" I have learned to take what a person says from the top of his head with a grain of salt. A wise person would not give a second thought to what a person said coming from his head (top, middle or bottom). Another way of knowing that an opinion is being shared is when a person says, "I think." What does "I think" mean? It means a person doesn't know. Now, would you accept what a person doesn't know as factual information? **The only thing factual is that the person doesn't know.**

We sometimes find out too late that we didn't hear "I think." Not hearing that, we may tell someone, "so and so said...." After much talking and the information is spread to heaven knows where, someone (hopefully) says, "But I said I think!" Unfortunately, this misinformation gets out of hand and causes too many problems when people are operating from the head.

The Heart:

The only way to function (operate) from the heart is to be centered on God. When we are centered on God, we process information differently. God teaches, advises, directs, and instructs us on how we disseminate information so that we would put things in their proper perspective by placing them where they belong. He tells us what to put into our file baskets and waste baskets. Sometimes in our stubbornness (that is another essay), we decide that we don't want to place the information where God is telling us to put it so we put it in the hold basket for a time. When he nudges us enough we transfer it to where it actually belongs. Because we decided to put something in our hold basket for a time, we get into a little problem, but as soon as we place it where it should have been in the first place, the problem is dissolved.

I think this call for an example, don't you? Suppose some information came to you which was wrong. Instead of putting it directly in the waste basket you put it in the hold basket which caused you to keep "messing" with it. While you were messing with it, it caused some disturbance. Seeing the disturbance you finally place it in the garbage. After you did so you no longer had any problem and you could breathe easier. Had you done that from the beginning you would have not had any negative feelings.

Working from the heart allows you to function without fear. It makes you feel good about what you say and do. You have the right answers and do not have to guess. Working from the heart gives you the wonderful opportunity to act in love. Even when there are minor or major corrections to be made because persons are pulling out their garbage and treating it as if it were true or factual, the heart will direct you and me how to handle it.

And in doing so, the heart enables you and me to help persons to correct their errors without putting a heavy label on it. They simply made a mistake and we go on from there.

Can you imagine how that would have been handled with the head in operation? Man, you would have the biggest mess you ever saw! A little mistake becomes a huge mountain when it wasn't even a molehill. You see it all the time!

There is really a simple answer and that is to let God into your heart. You know Satan plays with your head, don't you? If you are one of the many persons who do not believe he does, you are fair game for him because he's got you fooled. Even with God in your heart, Satan still tries to get to your head, but you are protected.

Dr. Melvin R. Hall

What quality of life do you wish to have? Even the best has its headaches and heartaches occasionally; otherwise, we do not appreciate the good times and all of the blessings that come with having God in our heart.

Joshua says, "Choose you this day whom you shall serve. As for me and my house, we will serve the Lord. "What do you say?

You know Satan plays with your head, don't you?

GENUINE FRIENDS

"A man that hath friends must show himself friendly,
and there is a friend that sticketh closer than a brother."
Proverbs 18:24 (KJV)

There is a saying, "True friends are hard to find." I agree wholeheartedly. I also believe that in order "to have a friend one must be a friend." And even deeper than that, genuine friendship is something we have to work on. It is not automatic; one learns what being a friend is all about when one truly wants to be close to another as a friend.

Most close friendships are with the same sex. When there are genuine friends between male and female, it requires a real understanding and appreciation for engaged, married, or intimate couples to understand the relationship between persons of both sexes as genuine platonic friends.

Regardless as to what combination the friendship is, in order for it to be genuine; persons have to be real with each other. What does that mean? As you read this essay the meaning will unfold.

Some people are confused as to their friendship with others. I find that friendship develops because of certain variables such as geographical proximity, similar likes, working together, religious affiliation, sports, academic studies, and other situations where people are placed together and they find that they have something in common.

When persons become friends, they should want the best for each other. Because of that, depending upon how close they become, some friends may exhibit a tendency to exceed some boundaries. For example: When we are afraid the person is going to do harm to himself or herself, we may become the "rescuer, feeling that it is our responsibility to "save" the person " from himself or herself. "Actually, there is nothing wrong with that except when we take it further than we should. Part of taking it too far is to "harp" on the issue every time we meet. The friendship is then in jeopardy because of the "nagging."

Part of genuine friendship is learning what is annoying to our friends and to avoid trying to make them over. When we begin to see their imperfections and attempt to "help" them, we sometimes try to make them more like us, not realizing that no one is perfect, and we, of course, are not.

This happens because we try to get our friend to conform to our "standards." There is nothing wrong with in casually giving attention to a matter of importance that may reflect our friend in a bad light. How important or high strong is our friendship will help us to determine the worth and value of the friendship. If it is highly valued, why let small things get in the way?

Genuine friendship is on built, trust, respect and patience. Love is also a component. The mutuality of all those ingredients makes for a strong, deep and genuine friendship. A genuine friendship brings a deep spiritual feeling that transcends human understanding, and that is somehow we know when our friend is in trouble, or is ill and needs help. Sometimes the urgency to communicate with the person is so keenly strong it cannot be ignored.

In friendship, female to female in the American culture is more demonstrative than male to male. Men are taught not to be too emotional in public. Different forms of handshaking are acceptable and that seems to change overtime. Hugging between males is accepted with upper body pressing except on the ball field where even smacking someone on the derriere (one smack only) is accepted and sometimes expected with or without close body hugging.

True, honest, genuine friendship is priceless and cannot be bought. The only cost is trust, unconditional love, patience, and respect. If you have one genuine friend in your life, you are blessed beyond measure. Enjoy the friendship!

**Part of genuine friendship is learning what is
annoying to our friends and to avoid trying to
make them over**

GO FOR THE GOLD!

"...the Queen of Sheba came to Jerusalem with a very great train with camels that bare spices and very much gold, and precious stones, and she was come to Solomon, she communed with him all of what was in her heart."
I King 10:2 (KJV)

Achievers usually are those persons who early in life set their sight on a particular goal. Their goal is real to them. They have a strong desire for achievement and the fruition is never a matter of "if" but when.

A prime example of this is a cousin who resided in California. When she was eight years old I visited her family and she said to me, "Cousin Raymond, I'm going to win gold medals in the Olympics!" I responded with, "If that is your dream hold onto it and you will." At that time I was honestly thinking, "Fat chance." Well, that little girl as an adult in Seoul, Korea in 1988 was a winner of three gold relay medals and one silver. Prior to her Olympics fame, she was known as "Dee Dee." Her actual name was Florence Griffith-Joyner. She proved that her conversation with me was not idle talk or a "pipe" dream. When I learned about her achievements, a very clear picture flashed in my mind of a little girl with very bright smiling eyes telling me about her dream of winning gold medals.

This multitalented gold medal winner came from humble beginnings as she and her family of ten siblings were recipients of social welfare in Watts, a section of Los Angeles, California. In addition to her achievements in the Olympics, she was a graduate of UCLA, a fashion designer, a cosmetologist, a painter, a poetess, an entrepreneur. She was also a writer, and a lecturer and the founder of Flo-Jo International (a youth organization still to this day promoting youth relays, motivation, inspiration and academic excellence to its young participants). There is a strong possibility that I have left out something. The executive director of the organization is her sister, Elizabeth Griffith-Tate (Cissy).

With all of those achievements to her credit, she remained a very humble person who gave credit and ownership to God. This was seen by her falling on her knees at each winning and giving thanks to God which I personally witnessed on television.

Another verbalized declaration of her faith, trust, belief and dependence on God was when she was driving me to the airport. This was on one of my many visits to California for my flight home to New York. I asked her if she was in anyway fearful of being shot as she jogged with President "Bill" Clinton as a co-partner of his Physical Fitness Program. She quickly reminded me that she was not jogging with the President, but walking with God.

One of the many demonstrations of her humility was of her chasing a lady's hat that the wind had blown off. Florence retrieved it and returned it to the lady with one of her bright, captivating smiles. When the lady learned of Florence's fame, she was surprised that Florence would come to her aid.

In my eyes, and the eyes of many, Florence, although now residing in Heaven, will always be a role model. How so? She proved that anyone can be an achiever. All one needs is a goal grounded in the belief that, "All things are possible to those who believe." She believed that whatever one sets his or her mind to can be realized.

The following is her Dream Statement: "I dream big, and I dream wide. I dig deep to bring out what's inside… I give my all, on all my tests to achieve my goal. I do my best…Sometimes I fall short of my dreams, I lose my focus, unfair life seems. But I don't quit. Nor do I give up that way; I thank the Lord for each day. I set higher goals, never looking back, learning from my mistakes, performing new acts… I believe in me, and my dreams are real, because they're mine from inside, what I feel."

Flo-Jo left a legacy and as a role model lets us know that all of us can be achievers. All we need is determination, belief in the power of God and self. We can win anything we set our mind and heart to. One hundred percent belief and one hundred percent humility all add up to one hundred percent gold.

Going for the gold actually means putting everything we have into action, and, at all times, stretching it to the maximum. There is no room or place for negative thoughts. Surely, there are going to be moments of a little despair. But it must not last more than a moment. After the moment is spent, we have to reinforce ourselves with affirmations, to rid ourselves of our momentary concerns.

A person going for the gold cannot afford too many moments of being overly concerned about not achieving the smaller goals as he or she moves toward making the largest and greatest goal, which, of course is the gold.

Whatever is that you are striving to obtain or become, your chance of winning is great, as Flo-Jo has shown. She was a prime example of humble greatness. What about the older or younger you? She is encouraging you from her Heavenly home to be all you can be as you strive for that desired and ultimate goal. Whatever it is, your ultimate goal can be your gold, go for it!

In my eyes and the eyes of many, Florence Griffith-Joyner, although in Heaven, will always be a role model.

"God is For Real, Man"

*"God is Spirit and Those who worship Him
must worship in spirit and in truth."*
John 4:24 (KJV)

*"Blessed is the nation whose God is the Lord;
and the people whom He hath chosen for His own
inheritance,"*
Psalms 33:12 (KJV)

Seventy five years ago I was not able to tell you this story that I'm about to tell you because I was so caught up with Father Divine and his banquets when he came to Harlem.

But later on in life I met God. No, I didn't actually see Him like I saw Father Divine. But I met God through His Son. I call Him JC because of our relationship.

Let me tell you about our meeting.

Well, I met this Cat. He was about 30 years old. And He hung out with 12 other cats That He called his Disciples. And while JC talked, those cats would seem spellbound, listening to His every word. Well, I was, too.

I had never seen anyone who could rap like He could. He told us about His Father, and of course, the things He said were hard to believe. He said His Father created the universe. Part of me wanted to laugh and the other part sort of encouraged me to believe Him.

I was so taken by him. I had a dream one night that I actually shook His hand and I felt like electric current was going through my body. His eyes were piercing as if He were looking through me and could read my thoughts. Then he hugged me tight. I thought to myself, "What a strange man He is!" No man goes around hugging folk like he did.

But then, everything he did was strange including His talk. I could not conceive of His Father creating the universe and owning everything. But JC said that His Father would give us anything we wanted. We only had to ask through JC.

Being a curious child I wanted to know why. His answer was that His Father loved us regardless of the bad we do and have done. He said His Father would forgive us if we confessed our wrong doing and are sorry for them. You know what? He said this with so much sincerity and love that I could not help but believe Him.

And being a child, I at that time believed that seeing was believing. As time went on I recognize that everything I have ever needed I got. So then I began to believe even more... Some say people should not ask for their wants, but I tested that too. With little reservation, all that I have wanted I have received as far back as I can remember. So as I got to talk with JC more and more, a relationship developed.

I found that He was available to me 24/7. Any hour of the day and night I could talk to Him. And I learned that if I remained still and calm, he would answer in so many different ways. It is only through a relationship this is possible. Why? Because of our relationship, I came to believe everything He said and I would obey Him.

I learned, too, that he accepted me as imperfect as I was and that He would help me to become a better person. I, of course, was willing to make any changes He made me aware of. I began to think about my day just before drifting off to sleep. I thought about the conversations I had had that perhaps hurt someone's feelings. I thought about my actions and behavior that were not right and I was encouraged to speak to persons asking for forgiveness because I was sorry for my behavior.

That led to many strange things happening in my life which are too numerous to relate at this time, but it makes for good conversation to those who believe or do not believe.

I have given my thought to our conversation and to the book which tells us all about God, His Father, and the Holy Spirit. Sometimes it is hard to comprehend the book, but I learned that studying the book with others who are truly interested in learning about JC and His father and the power of the Holy Spirit, much would be revealed to us.

Another rather strange happening is the more we study, the more we realize that the same passage of the Bible will give an even broader understanding at each reading. And when we read the Bible alone, all we have to do is ask for understanding of what we are reading. And here is another strange experience, at another time something said or done will occur in direct relationship to a question we may have posed in our mind as we read.

One dear lesson I learned is that God doesn't just speak to me, but to others. And we should not argue our understanding of a passage, but share and leave it. We should not try to convince others of our so called "smarts." Leave that up to so called religious folk.

One day they will be enlightened to the truth. We know that some religious folk think they are the only ones who know how to get into heaven. But we must keep our unconditioned love alive and ask God to let them be less argumentative while the process of enlightenment is trying to take place.

Yes, God is real! And the only way I found this for myself is to keep an open mind.

JC warned us about becoming so religious that we miss out on the messages sent by God. He tells us of his awkward relationship with the most pious religious folk during his life on earth the three last years of His life. He tells us in the Gospel of how the religious leaders were more concerned with laws and appearances and power than they were about human relations. JC was all about human relations. In fact, much of the Bible talks about how we should relate to one another and about unconditional love.

JC was, and still is, a role model. I found out if I take the time to question what Jesus would do in a certain situation in my life, and then ask Him what should I do, I would save myself and others some heartaches.

JC never said the journey with Him would be easy, but it is easier than doing it on my own. It was not easy for Him. So how do I think it is going to be easy for me? I know that I have Him as my friend and His Father has both our backs, so how can we lose?

Thanks be to God I found a friend so I don't have to worry about today or tomorrow as long as I listen to Him, internalize what He says to me and obey Him..

I learned …He accepted me as imperfect as I was, and that He would help me to become a better person.

GOD IS UTTERLY AWESOME AND GREATLY AMAZING!

"Now to Him who is able to do immeasurably more than all we ask or imagine, according to His power that is at work in us, to Him be the glory..."
Ephesians 3:20-21 (NIV)

Even though there are some people who claim they don't believe in God, they are still unconditionally loved, protected and provided for by Him. Why is that? It is because He is utterly awesome, and greatly amazing.

No one can explain Him. No one has seen Him. No one can imagine His greatness. His vastness (thinking, love, and caring) is beyond anyone's ability to comprehend. His depth is beyond human understanding.

Believing in Him enables us to recognize our blessings and be even more blessed because we are able to rely on Him rather than to depend on ourselves. People who trust God and remain strong and steadfast in their faith are recipients of more miracles than they will ever be able to count.

Unfortunately, people who do not believe in God have to depend on themselves and they miss out because there are some things humankind just cannot do on their own. Humankind can invent and make new things using what God has already created, but humankind cannot create anything from nothing as God has done and continues to do.

For any human-being to think he or she is self-sufficient is a farce and he or she is fooling him or herself. That would mean he or she has the power to create and needs no one other than him or herself to survive. Anyone thinking he or she has this kind of power is operating under the spell of delusion or self-deception.

One of the reasons why it is hard for some people to believe in God is because they confuse religion with God. When they speak of religion and God in the same breath they are judging God by the behavior of people who claim to love God and yet their behavior is contrary to God's way of doing things.

Once people are able to see the difference between God and religion by reading, learning and internalizing the Word as written in the Holy Bible, they will see the difference and realize that religion is simply a method of exercising what one believes. But when people gain knowledge from the Word of God; practice what they learn by committing themselves to God by following His teachings, instructions and directions, they will find how awesome and amazing He is.

Speaking of religions, there are many kinds. Some are sun worshippers, idol worshippers, satanic worshippers, to name a few. So we have to be very careful when we say we are "religious." Persons who truly believe in God do not have to brag because action speaks louder than words. People determine what we are; who we are and whose we are by the way we carry ourselves, especially when times are rough. If we have to "prove" to others that we are "religious," there is something missing. And what is missing is not having the love of God in us. Love has it own talk and walk. The talk is about God and the walk is doing what God will have us do.

True believers in God act a certain way and their action is motivated by love, God's love. That is why the Bible says to let our light so shine before men that they will see our good works and glorify our God Who is in heaven.

People who claim to believe in God and boast they are "very religious" often are very judgmental. Non-believers observe us more than we may be aware. And their observation causes them to want to learn (or not learn) about the God we serve simply because of how we conduct ourselves as believers. We don't have to argue what we believe, just live it and we will attract more persons to want to believe because of our conduct in difficult situations. An example of this is how we treat persons who mistreat us. How forgiving we are, how we treat trivial matters as well as very complex and difficult situations, and how we conduct ourselves in public and in private.

We who believe should like all persons to get to know God for themselves but "preaching" to do them may turn them off. What are visible and obvious are our disposition, behavior, loving-kindness, respect, patience, attempt to understand, listening, and our ability to love unconditionally and genuinely care about others. Those traits show that God lives in our hearts and if we want to introduce anyone to God, it begins by showing His living in us.

Everyone has equal opportunity of embracing God and finding Him utterly awesome and greatly amazing. It is just a matter of reading and studying alone or with true believers in Bible reading and study groups. Life is a great deal more rewarding and wonderful when we truly get to realize that God's light surrounding us, His love enfolds us, His presence protects us, His presence watches over us and wherever we are, God is.

One of the reasons why it is hard for some people to believe in God is because they confuse religion with God.

Godparents Are Very Special People

"Obey your leaders and submit to their authority...obey them so their work will be a joy, not a burden"
Hebrews 13:27 (NIV)

You have heard the saying 'it takes a village to raise a child.' often two members of that 'village' are the child's godparents.

Usually godparents are selected by parents for their children. They are apt to be very close friends of the parents. Some of us believe that godparents are chosen by God even though selected by parents, sometimes even relatives (a sibling, an aunt or uncle, or a cousin). Oftentimes, godparents are selected because they have financial means to help raise a child in the event that the parents may die.

Despite, this 'selection' process, some of us believe that godparents are chosen by God even though they appear to be 'chosen' by parents. The Holy Spirit has a hand in this process, and if godparents truly live up to their high calling, the godparents and the godchildren will be blessed beyond measure.

There is a rarity in the selection of godparents, however. It is so rare that some people may be unaware that it even exists. Just know that this is still the hand of God working with the godparents and the godchildren. The rarity is when an older adult elects to be a godparent to another adult. In most cases the godchild is young enough to be an offspring of his or her godparent.

Regardless how a godparent is selected, it can be an awesome relationship. In addition, the role of a godparent does not in any way replace the role of a parent (living or deceased). It is a special role with its own set of responsibilities.

When godparents are chosen and appear at the Christening of the young infant, the godparents promise to nurture the child in the belief and love of God. In some instances should the parents (because death or circumstance) not be able to rear their child, the godparents will fill that role.

Other than this, a godparent is one who should be available to be a good listener and offer sincere and honest advice when asked for. The godparent should be kind, considerate, empathetic, compassionate, and able to understand his or her godchild. The godchild should feel comfortable in sharing (sometimes) intimate details with his of her godparent. In the case of adult to adult, the godparent may also disclose intimate details with his or her godchild. This may bring about closeness in their relationship.

Above all, the godparent should be nonjudgmental even when offering advice. Best of all, being a good listener is one of the best advantages to a wonderful godparent-godchild relationship. Communication is definitely a must. The medium of communication will, of course, have to be mutual.

Godparents are very special people when they take their role seriously, but not too seriously. Godparents are not responsible for the decisions and actions of their godchildren. Nor should godparents place themselves in an adversarial role with their godchildren's parents. Rather, godparents can always offer a listening ear and varying (difference) perspectives (or opinions) to their godchildren. Godparents have to be especially careful when their godchildren are adults and the godparents feel strongly about the direction their godchildren are taking which may be harmful to them.

The godparent's role may well include being a consoler rather than a disciplinarian. The role of disciplining is a parental one and that depends (most times) by the age of the godchild. Unfortunately, some parents do not know how to let go and let the adult child make his or her mistakes.

The role of the godparent may also be that he or she should remind dad or mom to back off at times. On the other hand, godparents must also be wary of too easily taking the 'side' of their godchildren without fully listening to the concerns of the parents. Godchildren sometimes may try to pit their godparents against their biological parents. This is not good; all must work together.

Godparents usually find their role very rewarding and pleasant. The love factor is different in that the love is unconditional. While having unconditional love, the godparents want the best for their godchildren as they rejoice with them, mourn with them, and cry with them. Their very special bond causes them to be emotionally involved with them, pretty much as their parents are, and sometimes more than their parents.

Godparents who truly fulfill their role are blessed in many ways. One of the ways is the love and devotion received from their godchildren. That in itself is priceless!

Regardless how a godparent is selected, it can be an awesome relationship.

GRATIFICATION:
IMMEDIATE OR DELAYED

O Lord, our God we will wait upon Thee for Thou hast
made all these things."
Jeremiah 14:22 (KJV)

A simplistic definition of the word gratification is to be pleased or satisfied. One feels this in one of two ways; one is immediate, the other is delayed.

According to Sigmund Freud, a psychoanalytic therapist, a part of our nature known as the id craves immediate gratification and that starts in our infancy. Whatever a baby wants, he or she wants it "right now." As we mature we supposedly learn to wait, which I call delayed gratification.

You may be surprised by the number of persons who still function from the id and that is why we have so many problems in society. Persons functioning from the id do not have much patience, if any. Those persons find themselves going through life getting caught up in problem after problem. Crimes are committed just because people cannot wait for something to happen naturally. A good example is when people want something but do not have the money to purchase it; they take it as if the thing belongs to them. Their only interest is to satisfy their desire for it. Based on that example you can use your imagination as to other ways that people satisfy their craving immediately without having the least conscience about the rights of others.

Let us look at immediate gratification that is harmless. I would imagine that you will find yourself in the scenario I am about to give. Let us say that on your birthday you are given two gifts, one of them is in a very large box and the other is a very tiny box. You are told to open the larger box first. Guess what your desire would be? It would probably be to open the box you are not instructed to open just yet.

And, which is more; you will not get much satisfaction opening the bigger box because your concentration would be on the smaller one. This is supposed to be a time of enjoyment and happiness because of being gifted, but you will lose out on the intended joy because you would want to hurry and get to the small box. Actually, there is no harm in so doing, but you will shorten or reduce your own joy and delight.

Now if you are the kind of person who enjoys delayed gratification you would open both gifts with the same amount of joy, and being told which gift to open first would not matter with you as you will be happy and the giver would also feel delighted because of your happiness.

Let us talk more about delayed gratification and how that spices up your life and gives greater appreciation, joy, happiness, and gratitude. Those of us who enjoy delaying the special feeling we experience by waiting find ways to make delayed gratification a daily experience.

Permit me to share how I do it. I love personal letters so I write quite a bit. When my letters are responded to, I wait until just before retiring for the night to read them. I then think about my answers and most likely send my reply the next day. But all during the day I am thinking about reading my letters and it gives me a great feeling. I have something to look forward to at the end of my day. This is especially appreciated if I have a rough day. As I experience my rough moments, I say to myself, "At least tonight I have something pleasant happening. It feels good having my letters to read later.

When I receive catalog ordered packages and unexpected gifts, I save unwrapping them until I have time to really enjoy opening them, and I then vigorously tear into each one.

You may wonder why I have such a propensity for delayed satisfaction and gratification. It is because at an early age I was taught to wait. My mother and my financial situations were such that I had to learn to wait until we could afford whatever I wanted or thought I wanted.

I have found that I am more appreciative when I have to wait for something. What I am about to say may be an extreme for some people, but for me, I find being less affluent has a great advantage for me. I suppose it is nice to be able to buy all the furniture in your house or apartment at one time, but being able to furnish one room at a time by purchasing different pieces of furniture piece by piece makes it especially wonderful for me. And when I have finally furnished my apartment there is such joy and feeling of being so blessed that mere words are not sufficient to explain how good it feels and how grateful I am.

To each his own, but the main point of this essay is to find what gives you the maximum joy without harming or hurting another person because we are placed on earth to bring a maximum of happiness to others and to ourselves. We have the ability to control our lives more than we think. No one can make us happy. The choice is ours to make. My choice is delayed gratification, what is yours?

I have found that I am more appreciative when I have to wait for something.

GREAT EXPECTATION!

"Ask, and it shall be given you; seek, and ye shall find;
Knock and it shall be opened unto you."
Matthew 7:7 (KJV)

It is most unfortunate that some of us wake up each morning expecting the worse. The fact is every day we find ourselves in the land of the living is a blessing. And it is the beginning of many other blessings throughout the day. What is your expectation - the worse or the best?

Whichever one you expect, I hope this essay will be one that you can relate to with great interest. I trust it will enlighten some persons who need to know that the sun shines on them and blessings are overflowing. They may or may not be able to see, recognize, recall or count but it is happening.

As you read this you will become more aware that you are blessed and you will be able to feel better about yourself and begin to look forward to good happenings in your life. Great expectations are yours to pull and to claim. You may wonder how one pulls blessings. It begins with thinking.

Thinking has powerful magnetic energy and can make things happen. Have you ever heard of self-fulfilling-prophecy? This happens when we hold onto thoughts and begin to believe them whether good or bad. Some people, unfortunately, think that they can do nothing right. Consequently, they end up messing up even simple things. This is also found in physical activities as well as sending or giving messages. They name themselves "screw-ups." These people sometimes find themselves making purchases they regret because invariably they find something wrong with the merchandise or furniture. They believe in the so called "Murphy's Law" and that is the possibility if something is going to go wrong, it will go wrong. Their expectation of failure becomes a reality.

Those persons can use the benefit of a motivational workshop which will give them an opportunity to see life in a brighter perspective and dispel the negative thinking that cripples them. Persons in their group all entertain the same type of negative reasoning. With a trained facilitator, each can help the others to change as he or she changes.

Let's think about those persons who only believe what they can see and hear. If you are one of those persons, please read very slowly and seriously ponder what you read. As persons without medical training we cannot see what is physically happening internally in our bodies. We cannot see the production of new cells replacing worn-out-diseased cells causing healing and allowing us to wake up each day. Along with that, there are multiplicities of happenings we cannot see that were designed and created by God. For example: We cannot see oxygen, yet it keeps us alive and without it we would not be able to breathe.

It is hoped that persons who find themselves waking up every day expecting the best will try the impossible task of counting their blessings. That will keep them ever grateful to our God for the multiple blessings He bestows upon us. I hope that others who have been expecting the worse will be able to take necessary action so that they too may be able to experience God's compassion, mercy and grace and will be able to enjoy each day to the fullest.

Ponder this philosophical thought: Whatever happens could be worse. So let us be grateful when it isn't. This will encourage us to dwell on positive thoughts enabling us to get past the bad times and help us to be aware that nothing remains the same forever.

Great expectations are given to us by God and the Scripture tells us that God desires the best for us and He can make the seemingly impossible, possible. All we have to do is to ask, seek and knock. In other words communicating with Him will bring desired results that are truly benefiting to us according to His will. The key is to believe and trust while taking Him at His word.

> **Within our universe there are multiplicities of happenings we cannot see that were designed and created by God.**

Harmony

"And the fruit of righteousness is sown in peace of them that make peace."
James 3:18 (KJV)

When you define harmony according to the dictionary, you have not learned what it truly is. The word actually defies defining because it lives within the very soul of a person. It is an indescribable feeling that everyone experiences at sometime in his or her life. But the dictionary cannot give you more than interesting sounding words.

Harmony is a word that expresses something so deep that it can only be explained by attempting to express how you feel. Even then you don't know what you are feeling Let us suffice to say it is a deep, smooth, warm feeling connecting to another's like feeling.

The only persons who have been able to come close to describing the word are musicians, especially when another brother or sister in music is able to feel the music at the same time, yet not feel it the same way. The feeling is, of course, intense, but not felt with the same intensity. If it did, it would be beyond any earthly feeling.

Those of us who have fleetingly felt harmony cannot explain it to someone else. However, that should not keep us from striving to obtain it for ourselves and others. One thing is sure, and that is unless you attempt to bring it into the life of another, you will never have it for yourself. It is somewhat like love, only stronger. Love you can explain in so many ways. Harmony is as contagious as love and lovely to behold.

Let us do this. Think along with me and honestly answer the following questions to the best of your ability. Have you ever felt so good that you felt a separation from your body? It cannot be physical. A physical body cannot separate from itself so it must be a spiritual part of you that no one can see. Have you ever suddenly felt that you had chills running down your spine? Did the chills feel good as if something wonderful is happening but you don't know what? The only thing you can say is that feeling the chills was awesome.

Moving on with the questions: Have you ever felt far removed from a dangerous person or situation that is physically near yet, you felt immune and safe? Have you ever "heard" a clear voice telling you to do something like getting away from where you are? Have you ever had a dream of a person you don't recall ever meeting and you actually met the person later?

At this point you may think I'm nuts and you may want to skip this essay. But if you happen to be a person who just happens to know what I am talking about because you have had the experiences, count yourself as blessed beyond measure because you have experienced a form of harmony that most people do not talk about because it is not understood too well.

Harmony dwells in the heart. It gives the feeling that everything is alright even though the appearance of what is going on is not alright. While others are feeling scary, you are calm. This has much to do with your spirituality and although spiritual persons may be in your presence, each one's spirituality is different. So it is something also hard to describe and talk about, and you certainly cannot argue about it because it is not arguable.

The reason why it is not arguable is because it possesses harmony. Actually, harmony is a feeling beyond human understanding and connected to the heart and spirit of a person.

If anyone who is Heaven bound has not experienced harmony during his or her lifetime, just before he or she closes his or her eyes the final time, harmony is definitely felt. At that moment everything impure washes away and ones soul is cleansed. It is a last minute reprieve that our Creator gives us because someone has been praying for our soul.

To a very large extent, mothers pray for the souls of their wayward children asking for harmony to come into their life. Children (of all ages) are saved by God's grace, compassion and mercy because of their mothers' prayers.

Mothers might have said to their wayward children, "I'm praying for you." And the children may have taken it very slightly without giving much if any thought about it. So do not underestimate a mother's prayer. This is not to leave out fathers. But it is believed more mothers pray for harmony for their children than fathers. A father's prayer is just as effective, but there is something about a child having been in the womb of his or her mother. There is a certain attachment that began when the seed was fertilized in the mother's body.

Just as mothers and no one else can explain why mothers feel the way they do about their children, harmony cannot be explained.

Children (of all ages) are saved by God's grace and compassion and mercy because of their mothers' prayers.

"Happiness"

"...for the joy of the Lord is your strength."
Nehemiah 8:10 (KJV)

All the ingredients for happiness are within oneself. No one can make us happy. When one makes a definite decision to be happy, things will automatically trigger in the mind of the individual that will cause that person to feel good, happy, and joyous and at peace with his or her world.

Happiness cannot be bought. When we attempt to buy it, we find ourselves in misery. The price is too dear. It gets higher and higher and will eventually reach a point where we cannot afford it. The good news is it's absolutely free! Helping others to feel good is very contagious. When we spend time thinking how to make others happy, we cannot help but be happy ourselves. Yes, happiness begets happiness!

One way of being or making ourselves happy is to plan little or big surprises that are going to help a significant other feel excited. It can be an unexpected telephone call, a small gift hidden for that special person in your life with whom you live. If the person and you do not live together, you can mail it. But for the person you want to surprise with whom you live, hiding the gift can be fun for both of you. After you have hidden the gift you tell the object of your love that there is a surprise hidden in the house somewhere. As the person looks for it you can let him or her know when he or she is near or far from the gift by saying he or she is "either hot, cold, warm or freezing." Of course, the closer the person gets to the gift, the more excited you are and that pleasantly excites the person.

While you are purchasing the gift, your joy in this game begins. And, as it is played, both of you get caught up in the fun. This will be a great and most appreciative surprise if you can afford to purchase what you have heard your lover say he or she wanted for quite awhile.

On the other hand you can be as creative as you allow your mind to expand. For example you can hide an announcement that the baby you both want is in the womb and waiting to meet his/her dad. The announcement can be in the form of a "Dear Dad" letter stating that he or she is starting the 9 months journey in preparation of "my birth." Can you imagine how excited he will be when he finds the letter? After hiding the envelope, you can say it is something he has been wanting for quite awhile. I suggest that you do not say something you both have been wanting because psychologically he would be a bit more excited if he thought what he was looking for would be exclusively his. We men are sometimes "selfish." Again, knowing your man helps you to expand your imagination in making him happy. What goes around comes around. Do not be surprised when he springs his surprise on you – for you.

What helps to bring happiness to a relationship is child-like (good) behavior and not forgetting being a "child" at appropriate times. The key is that it has to be appropriate.

If you are in the mood for a nice sexual evening here are some tips. Taking the role of being the initiator, you can plant little seeds by complimenting the object of your affection via phone call or text message while she is at work. Women should know that men like for their women to be the initiator at times. And they ought to know what to do. If she is recently married and do not know what to do, there are books in the library on enhancing a couple's sex life. If you are seen reading the book by a female friend, do not be embarrassed. The person looking on may need to check the book for herself.

Whether we are trying to increase the possibility of happiness to or with a loved one, a stranger, a friend, a family member, or someone we just care about, allow yourself to be appropriately creative. Happiness is contagious. The more you are instrumental in causing it, the more it will come to you because the receiver will want to be the giver as well.

What helps to bring happiness (and spice) to a relationship is child-like good behavior and not forgetting being a "child" is appropriate at times. The key is to be appropriate.

Healthy Thinking and Physical Condition

"As a man thinketh in his heart, so is he…"
Proverb 23:7 (KJV)

There is a definite correlation between the way we think and our physical condition. What is healthy thinking? Healthy thinking is being able to see good even in the worst scenario. We have the freedom and the choice to think as we please. But if we want to enjoy life to the fullest, we have to sift through our thoughts and decide which ones we will keep. Whatever we select goes into our belief system. So as we think, we feel and act on our emotions brought on by what we think.

Personally, I prefer to look on the bright side and put that into my belief system. It is unfortunate that bad news seems more appealing than the good that is happening all around us. We tend to thrive on the misfortune of others. Why is that? It could well be that bad news is played up more than good news. It lends itself to gossip more and can be quite "spicy."

We all like "spices." They do much in making our meals delicious and tasty which plays games with our palate. Now the spicy things we hear about others whets our appetite for more gossip and our ears for what is put into them. And not only that, our eyes like to pick up spicy stuff, too.

Just as we select good spices to season our food, we can be selective as to what is good for us or not good. Since our physical well-being is greatly affected by the things we accept and believe, it makes good sense to me not to put stuff in my head that is going to cause me discomfort, pain, grief or minor or major problems.

It is a given that persons are going to talk about people. If you remove that, there would be little to talk about. Now, what they say about people depends upon how well the people are liked. Based on that, it stands to reason that people who are not liked are going to be talked about negatively, while people who are well liked will be complimented and spoken well of.

Why do people talk about others in derogatory ways? The prime reason usually is jealousy. Some unpaid gossipers unconsciously wish they could measure up to the person. They don't realize they can if they had the desire and put forth the time and effort. But they are too busy trying to put others down, not being cognizant of two things. One is they are just as capable if they believed that they are, and the second is that as they put others down they draw negative attention to themselves.

The old expression says, "A dog that brings a bone is looking for another bone to take back." A gossiper cannot trust another because he or she is looking for spice to take to another pair of ears. Granted, it is quite difficult to not lend your ears to spicy news. It takes great effort to avoid persons who actually do not see themselves as gossipers. They are the other people. Gossipers, who do not classify themselves as such, consider themselves "sharers." They have a lot to share, but when you do not make yourself available they will soon find some willing ears. You can be sure that you will be talked about more than ever.

People can say what they want (and they will), but we cannot let what they say bother us. We just have to make sure to the best of our ability we are doing what we are supposed to be doing to please God.

Since we are not listening to gossip and not adding to the spicy tales, we can concentrate on thinking healthy thoughts which will enable us to feel good about our world and ourselves. This will lead to behavior worthy to be talked about. What is going to happen is that other people will see the light of God in us and will speak up saying something to the effect that all they know about us is better than what they are hearing.

Have you ever noticed that most gossipers are always complaining about their health, aches, pains discomfort and problems? They don't realize the bad seeds they are sowing are coming back to them. We can always "justify" anything when we are in denial because we are blind to our own faults. However, we can very clearly see what others are doing wrong.

We, of course, are always going to have some kind of pain. That's life. But the pains can and will become worse as long as we continue with faulty thinking. Frankly speaking, we are going to die with something. Even what is called "natural causes" must have been brought on because of something.

We cannot live forever, but as long as there is life, we ought to be able to live it to the fullest. That is bringing all the joy we can, to everyone we can, in all the time we can using a minimum of facial muscles by smiling since it takes more muscles to frown than to smile. A smile lifts the spirit of the one receiving it, and it adds to the external beauty of the giver. Besides, a smiling person feels good when he or she shares that expression of love, respect, recognition, and peace. A smile is a good way to "pass the peace" of God.

What stops us from doing that? We stop ourselves by our intake of negative stuff which makes us feel emotionally drained, unhappy and sad. Then we justify our condition by saying, "There is nothing to be happy about." But I say, "Yes, there is. And there are more blessings than we will ever be able to count!" If we believe healthy thinking is a direct correlation to physical health, we are blessed indeed!

What do you believe? How blessed are you? From whom do your blessings come?

**Just as we select good spices to season our food,
we can be as selective to what is good for us or not
good for us.**

165

How to Be Distinguished
and Important

*"Be clothed with humility, for God resisteth the proud
and giveth grace to the humble."*
I Peter 5:5 (KJV)

Deep down in the recesses of our being is the desire to be distinguished and important in the eyes of others. The more one says he or she doesn't, the stronger the need. It is an unconscious need and desire from the time of birth until death.

Let us examine this statement together, and after doing so, I trust you will agree. Just keep an open mind. Many strange and very benefiting phenomena are happening in our lives that we reject by calling them "unreal." That is why we miss out on many blessings or good fortunes that we were born to receive and enjoy.

June 27, 2007 (Daily Guideposts 2007 from the book *Spirit Lifting Thought for Every Day of the Year* included a brief story about a famous lawyer serving on the Governor's Council at the Boston State House. "The family was greatly impressed by his humble demeanor: quiet, almost shy, and his propensity to express his appreciation and gratitude for services rendered. After each meal he would tiptoe to the kitchen to express how much he enjoyed his meal."

The author of the story is Oscar Greene, one of Guideposts writers. His family as entrepreneurs ran a boarding home. His parents received a letter from a gentleman named Joseph H. Mitchell, Jr., who was unknown to the Greene family.

Now, that was a true gentleman who was distinguished and important. Mr. Mitchell without any doubt demanded without asking for it. He simply was respectful to all persons without considering their "status." He was then, indeed, distinguished and important. Whether he thought he was or not was not important. He simply was.

Education, social and professional status, wealth, positions and titles have **absolutely nothing** to do with being distinguish and important. What has to do with it is the person we are and how well we express ourselves from the heart. People who are truly distinguished and important are those who are more concerned about how others feel about themselves, than they do about themselves.

Let us talk about how we can become distinguished and important. All we have to do is to follow Mr. Mitchell's example. Apparently, he was a humble man, a secure man, a gentle man, and an appreciative man among his other attributes. Being a gentle man makes a gentleman.

It is believed by many young men today that being a "man" is to be loud, seen, and domineering, saying nothing about displaying colorful underwear with their pants hanging "hiplessly" down. It is unfortunate how this has been instilled in their mind. There is nothing distinguished or important in that kind of appearance or behavior. The core point to Mr. Greene's story was that Mr. Mitchell was able to see and appreciate the good in others, and he shared his observations with the persons from whom he received service.

Let us now begin to look at ourselves as we interact socially and professionally with others. Do we look for the good in others? Do we let others know how much they and their services are appreciated? Do we say, "Thank you" for every kind remark or deed? Do we extend ourselves to others by helping whenever we can? Do we smile or are we frowning most of the time? Do we smile and greet with a nod the people we meet in our neighborhood or smaller community? As I pose these questions I realize that I, often enough, fail to do what I am asking of you the reader. But I shall do something about my own neglect. I do find most of the time that the persons I pass seem caught up in their own thoughts, and they are not cognizant of anyone passing. However, I am going to make it a conscious effort to at least nod with a smile, and if there is any recognition of any kind, I will speak.

In keeping with our need and desire to be distinguished and important, let us concentrate on doing the right thing so that people can speak well of us rather than despairingly. Everyone draws attention to herself or himself by his or her behavior. When people can see we truly value conducting ourselves in a manner that demands respect, they simply give that earned respect. In our humbleness we are not only seen as distinguished and important to everybody, we feel so to ourselves as well.

Actually, persons, who think themselves as being so important, are operating under the delusion of grandeur.

JOY

"...do not grieve, for joy of the Lord is your strength."
Nehemiah 8:10 (NIV)

We are not always joyous. However, we experience various degrees of joy during our life's journey. Simply being human can be joyous when we are grateful for life and the blessings that come to us.

Joy comes directly from God and it lives in our soul and it finds its expression in the heart. Without God, it is impossible to have joy because God is love and without love there is no joy.

Life was not guaranteed to be joyous every minute of the day. There are times we have to experience disappointment, grief, sadness, and maybe failure of some kind, but when those things pass, there is pure joy to replace them. That is why the Bible tells us "Mourning endures for a night, but joy comes in the morning."

Mourning is a sad feeling experienced because of death, separation, disappointment, or failing to obtain a desired something. Because of joy replacing negatives experiences, we feel the replacement of them through joy and our joy is even greater.

When we look all around us we too often find many people wearing sad expressions. Those expressions show our inner feelings. We don't have to harbor negative feelings. We can release them by giving them to God. All is required is a simple conversation with God. He, of course, already knows, but He does nothing until we release them to Him. Just talking to Him is not enough because if we are not willing to release the negative thoughts and feelings, He will not be able to take them unto Himself. A simple example of this is when you are handing something to someone, that person cannot take it fully into his or her hand until you release it completely.

Now, when you are attempting to give something to God and still holding on to it, you may change your mind and take it back. So God cannot and will not do anything with it until it is fully released. That makes good sense. We cannot be "wishy washy" and expect anything to happen. We have to be very definite about what action we want others to take or what we are to do. God does not play games. Further, when we ask others to do something for us we have to be clear and definite what we want, otherwise, they will not be able to do anything. It is as simple as that.

The opposite of anything cannot coexist with what is. What is has to become what was and then, it can be replaced. In other words, a bad habit cannot be removed until we replace it with a good habit.

There is nothing in our environment that can bring us joy. No person can give us joy. The only place it comes is from God through power of the Holy Spirit. So we have to be ready to receive what every one craves. And that is finding joy in life, along with joy; we want peace, contentment, happiness and a sense of value and worth. Since no one can give us any of these, no one can them away from us.

If you have no joy it is because you have not asked; therefore, you have not received. We were created not only to receive, but to let the world know that we have it in our soul.

Joy comes from God and lives in our soul.

JUDGING OR NOT JUDGING
A BOOK BY ITS COVER

"The way of a fool seems right to him, but a wise man listens to advice"
Proverbs 12:15 (NIV)

You must have heard not to judge a book by its cover. And if you heard it as a little child, it might well be that you didn't understand the meaning. Now that you are an adult you may have found yourself judging a certain book by its cover and to your disappointment found the book not being at all related to the cover. What an eye opener that must have been!

Some books are cleverly illustrated with beautiful pictures and when you start reading the book you wonder how on earth could the author select or authorize the printing of the cover.

In order to really get to know what is in a book one has to read it with an open mind and sometimes read between the lines. Doing that even has it throwback because we can read too broadly between the lines by forming our own opinions, and our opinions may be so different from the author's that we don't get what the author intended. We might become disappointed with the book and blame the author.

Just as we judge a book by its cover we judge strangers. None of us will truly know a person fully even if we live with the person a hundred years because no one reveals him or herself completely. To do so means that we have to share every thought, and who does that? Some thoughts are best left unsaid. There is a saying, "It is best to remain silent and be thought a fool, than to speak out and remove all doubt."

By outward appearance (cover of the book) what was hoped to be a wonderful romantic relationship ended up as "sour grapes." Usually the person will utter how "fine" the object of his or her attention is. On the first few pages of the book one finds flowering expressions that tend to make the attraction even stronger. While others who have not read the book and could care less are able to be objective and might or might not tell you, "You better read that book slowly and carefully for what you are telling me seems too good to be real." Of course, since the reader is so smitten, he or she quickly comes to the book's defense. With his or her "captured heart, soul and mind" he or she thinks that the person who is trying to give warning signals does not know what he or she is talking about.

Even before reading further, do you know what I am talking about? If you can confirm what I'm saying then it must have happened to you and, of course, you have learned how to read other books waiting to be read.

For those who have never misread a book, perhaps reading this will enlighten you so that if you ever come across a book that seems so beautiful on the cover and the first few pages, you will be able to know what to do. You have probably guessed by now that the "book" that seems good reading is about a person one finds "just too fine to be real!"

Some books require slow reading and checking to see if what you are reading really relates to the cover. After reading several pages you need to question if both cover and those pages are congruent. If they appear to be good, now check between the lines. Do you think you are getting what the book intends to say or are you reading what you want to read?

Perhaps we ought to reserve judgment so we can be objective. Most of us are too inpatient to attempt to do what I am about to suggest, but those looking for a good book for life, it will pay to develop patience for the real thing or the real deal.

When you come across a book that you seem to have a little interest in and it appears to be fine, why not read slowly and just become friendly with the book. Read the book page by page and observe what you like about the book or maybe not like. Then you can determine if what you don't like is minor or major. If it is minor and you like what you are reading, and it is as fine as you first thought, then move on to the other pages and become romantic. Warning: if what you don't like is serious and really gets under your skin or your "last nerves," put the book down and leave yourself open to check out another one.

Whatever you do, don't stop reading. There are many good (fine) books waiting to be read and taken to heart.

Let us say you are truly enjoying your book, and you have moved to the romantic stage as previously suggested. You find that the book's cover not only complements the book, it has some very good reading and you like and very much enjoy what you are reading; then the next step is engagement. Whether you carry the book to bed depends on your own personal values, morals and ethics. The book's personal values, morals and ethics may suggest waiting until you and the book become legal lifetime partners.

The problem for most persons, as alluded to earlier, is they do not want to take the time reading the book. Some are so caught up with it having the "finest" cover that they want to take the book to bed immediately, and before one knows what's happening there is the making of little books for others to read later in life. Those books may be read carefully or hastily and we may find the little volumes carrying messages that get someone in more hot water than a tea bag. It may turn out with or without the little volume; they may find themselves alone again without anything suitable to their taste to read for awhile.

Do you have the patience to read slowly and carefully? You may never get to know a person 100%, but that isn't necessary as 99 44/100 will do just fine! This is what happens when you do not judge a book by its cover. It is best to read, wait and see if the cover truly gives us an accurate account of what the book is about. If it complements and compliments the pages in the book, we can then decide if it is to become a lifetime partnership experience.

Just as we judge a book by its cover we judge strangers. None of us will know a person fully even if we lived with the person a hundred years.

Just Beyond the Darkness

"The light shines in the darkness, but the darkness has not understood it."
John 1:5 (NIV)

Just beyond the darkness there is light that enables us to survive and thrive. Unfortunately, some people give up before reaching the light. All they see is doom, despair, problems and disaster which causes them to feel helpless, powerless and hopeless. Every person experiences such moments but most of us know that there is light just beyond our own personal situation of darkness.

Persons who feel that they have to depend on themselves alone have great difficulty shaking these feelings; the truth is believing that everything rests upon their shoulders is a myth and myths do not have any power. Each of us alone has no power. That is why the world is populated with people and that is why we should do all we can to help others. We can be the light beyond the darkness for people in many ways.

Let us make ourselves aware of some very simple ways that cost us nothing but a little energy and time, and not too much of either. A kind word of recognition in passing, for example, is "You have such pretty dimples." Of course, you wouldn't say that to a person who has no dimples. But if you recognize a good or pleasant feature, say something nice about it. The object of this is to help to lift someone's spirit so he or she can look on the bright side, just beyond the darkness.

Some people are preoccupied with the darkness. They don't allow themselves the opportunity to look beyond their failures, shortcomings, and hard times. If they would share some of their childhood experiences, you would quickly know why they are in a "doomed" existence.

We recognize people's low spirit, self-esteem and self-worth and we say to ourselves, and sometimes to others, "I wonder why so and so seems so down?" Well, you can find out if you will just take the time.

Verbalizing that question to them probably will make them clam up more. However, there is a way and it is simply starting a conversation with a simple sentence with positive facial expressions. An example is, "Aren't you glad the weather has changed for the better? I thought it would never stop raining, but I'm glad it has." Do not be surprised by the person's response. "Yes, it sure has been lousy weather!" You, of course, will not know where the conversation will lead to, but at least you will get some sort of response, which is a beginning.

Your next statement should be as cheerful and inviting with eye contact if possible. Leave your expectation out of this encounter. Remember your attempt is to let this person know she or he is not alone and someone cares. Don't expect to be fast friends but a friendly seed is sown. And with time and continued small talk, the seed will germinate and take root. Why? Because your genuine interest is the light beyond the darkness.

When a person has been in the dark for a very long time, a bright light can be overwhelming and he or she will have to blink awhile in order to get adjusted to the light. Once the person gets used to the light, he or she can move with more confidence. One day the person will feel free and comfortable enough to share with you his or her experiences which have caused him or her to take refuge in the dark.

When it becomes a habit of yours to help people see the light, you will find many wonderful things happening in your life. Many of the wonderful things will be your own happiness in helping someone to be happy. It cost you absolutely nothing, but so much can be gained in your investment of self. Your "bonus" may well be that you have found a friend who will begin to enjoy life looking and living on the bright side.

Of the many persons we casually pass daily, we don't know how many are caught up in darkness without the will or belief that they can penetrate the darkness to the light. There are an awful lot of people in the dark about life. Many long for peace, joy, happiness and the confidence to accept and be themselves. People who can bring the best out of others will never know their greatness but they will know how great they feel about themselves and their world.

Since no one is an island unto himself or herself, we are all created to help one another. Some of us are too independent to ask for help, but are more than willing to offer and give help.

What a joy it is to finally break through the darkness and see the light. Anyone responsible for making this happen should feel blessed. I am reminded of the scripture that says "It is more blessed to give than to receive." Based on that, I can understand why a person is more willing to be of help than to receive help.

The world is populated with people and that is why we should do all we can to help others. We can be the light beyond the darkness for people in many ways.

KEYS TO ACHIEVING YOUR "IMPOSSIBLE" DREAM

"But Jesus beheld them, and said unto them, 'With men this is impossible; but with God all things are possible'"
Matthew 19:26 (KJV)

The word *impossible* is enclosed in quote marks because too often we consider anything very difficult as impossible. And we base this on our own limitations without regarding that there is help for that which we find too difficult to achieve on our own.

No major achievement has ever been accomplished by any one person on his or her own. So when we have a dream we need the appropriate "tools" to accomplish it.

The tools I am suggesting are actually eight (8) keys. They are (1) **visualization**, (2) **internalization**, (3) **decision making**, (4) **preparation,** (5) **believing in yourself** and in the possibility of your decision coming into fruition, (6) **willingness to take the proper action** required, (7) **trusting yourself and** (8) **trusting God** to do whatever is beyond your own ability by letting go and letting Him take over.

Let us talk about each key so that you can see the possibility and not become overwhelmed by viewing any task too difficult to be accomplished. The Bible tells us that "All things are possible to those who believe."

First, realize that every good dream is given to you by God who will help you to accomplish it if you will just follow the 8 keys explained in this essay.

Visualization is having a clear picture in your head. Everything humankind has made was once a picture in the head of the dreamer.

The dreamer can "see" the end result. To a large extent the dreamer can describe how the thing or activity will look upon completion.

Internalization calls upon your emotions. When you visualize what you want to achieve, you feel so good' about it that you will not be able to fully verbally express your feelings, but everyone you talk to will know that you are excited and enthusiastic about your dream. And your enthusiasm and excitement will cause them to share some of your feelings. You have to see yourself working with it or using it. Your enjoyment will be so great that you cannot help but want to share your joy with others. If it is an invention, you will see it being used by others and how happy they are using it. If it is a ministry of helping others, you will see yourself in action and how good those that you are helping feel about receiving your help.

Decision is extremely important because without it – it is just a dream. You have to make up your mind that you want whatever it is, and you want it badly. Your strong decision will give you the determination to get started on the project (invention, activity).

Preparation has to be made in order to learn how to go about beginning the task. It may require specialized training. It may require a college degree or several degrees. It may require an apprenticeship. It may require some reading. Whatever is required has to be met and accomplished.

Believing in yourself and that your dream (goal, or desire) is possible is another strong **must.** You also have to believe that you are equal to the task and can accomplish anything you set your mind to.

Willingness to take the required action is a big part of your beginning. You must have a willingness to take and complete each step in an orderly fashion. You also must have patience with yourself and other persons that you may have to call upon for physical and other assistance.

Trusting yourself and others is so important because if you don't trust yourself you will begin to doubt your own capabilities as well as the capabilities of those who may be assisting you. Self-doubt has caused many persons to give up either in the beginning or midway of the task or just about when the task is about to come to fruition.

Trusting God is of the greatest importance because you will find there are some things you just cannot do and you have to believe there is power greater than yourself. That Power has proven Himself as the Creator of the universe, and certainly if God can create a universe, whatever problem you may face that is too big or complicated for you can be accomplished by our Creator with amazing ease.

Taking an honest assessment of yourself will enable you to become cognizant of your own weaknesses. Which of the tools mentioned in this essay do you need to work on? Strengthen it by asking God to help you with it so that you can be successful in your dream, goals or desires. Strangely enough, some of us need the courage just to be able to honestly assess ourselves. For some reason we don't really want to know what our weaknesses are. But the only way to gain strength, confidence and ability to be achievers is to learn what our weaknesses are and do what we have to do in order to feel good about ourselves and our ability to become achievers.

Everybody has a dream. God gives us at least one and some have many. Those dreams are given to us so that we can contribute to our world and at the same time live well in the land of great abundance. We contribute by making life better for others by sharing a portion of our bounty that we are able to acquire because of the realization of our dreams.

No major achievement has ever been accomplished by a person on his or her own.

LADIES AND GENTLEMEN

"Let your conversations be always full of grace, seasoned
with salt so that you may know how to answer everyone."
Colossians 4:6 (NIV)

I don't remember how old I was when I first heard the words, "Ladies and Gentlemen!" But I do remember I was greatly impressed. My earliest recollection is that of a little boy, and the words were music to my ears. I Might have been at my first circus or the county or state fair in the southern town where I was raised.

Although I try hard not to be judgmental, I find myself placing people in such categories as being either ladies or gentlemen according to their behavior and manner of speaking. My mother's demeanor, style and mannerism cemented my thoughts and feelings regarding those words. To me, my mother was definitely a lady.

It is such a joy to me to see a woman being a lady and a man, a gentleman. Please pause for a moment and view the picture that comes to your mind and what feelings you engender.

Now let me share with you my thoughts and feelings. Perhaps we will enjoy a kinship.

Ladies:
When I see a lady I see my mother well groomed, walking and talking with dignity, thereby demanding respect and positive responses from others and me. I see someone who I cannot help but love and be kind to. I see someone whose company I feel I would enjoy. I see someone whose encourages the best from me, and it makes me feel good about myself and my relationship with her. Sadly, my mother passed away when I was thirteen years old, but she left me the blessing of desiring and knowing how to be a gentle man and a gentleman.

In addition to my mother, I have had great pleasure of meeting other ladies. Some of whom were in my family and others were not, but a kinship was established in my heart. I found myself "in love" with them and especially my English teacher.

Gentlemen:

When I think of the word "Gentlemen," I actually see and feel the word as two words, "gentle men." To me gentleness enables men to be both gentle men and gentlemen. Because of my mother's teaching and influence she saw and referred to me as "her little gentleman."

My father passed away while my brother and I were under 4. Fortunately, there were other gentle men and gentlemen in our lives whom we admired, respected and emulated... Unfortunately, my brother passed away at five years old.

We have defined the term "ladies," so we need to determine who are gentle men and gentlemen. Both are male figures who demonstrate their masculinity through the fruit of the Spirit as instructed in Galatians 5:22 saying the Spirit produces love, joy, peace, patience, kindness, goodness, faithfulness, humility and self-control."

Men displaying such attributes are worthy of the title "Gentlemen" and they are gentle men. As young boys witnessing and experiencing their behavior, they too, desire to become gentlemen. It may not be grammatically correct to capitalize the word when it is not the beginning of a sentence, but it is so important to me to give such respect to it because it makes a great deal of difference in relationship between Ladies and Gentlemen.

Ladies and Gentlemen:

Children learn very quickly how to show qualities of becoming ladies and gentlemen. They learn by example and give rapt attention to what they see rather than what they are told. Children emulate their elders and particularly the ones they love. Later in life we often hear adults repeating something that their mother or daddy had said as well as grandparents.

Is there a guide or a formula to follow in achieving our desire to be Ladies and Gentlemen? **You bet there is!**

The Bible gives all the needed instructions and if we followed them as closely as humanly possible, we would succeed in being Ladies and Gentlemen and will be duly respected as such. If we read, internalized and followed Galatians 5:22, we would definitely be on the right track. Your conversations and behavior would not only be full of grace, but people will see the qualities of being a lady or gentleman in you.

**When I think about the word "Gentlemen,"
I see and feel the word as two words. "Gentle men."**

LIFE CAN BE SWEETER

"Trust in the Lord with all thine heart; lean not unto thine own understanding.
And in all thy ways acknowledge Him and He shall direct thy path."
Proverbs 3:5-6 (KJV)

Too often in many seemingly close and happy families the decease of the last parent creates a major problem in terms of relationships. Perhaps the word "seemingly" is the key. Have you ever noticed how some families seem to split up when the last parent departs to meet his or her mate in our home beyond the skies?

Sometimes it is over an overrated heirloom, or it can be an insurance policy, a little money in the bank, a house, or a piece of furniture, Before the deceased can be buried or whatever the wish for his or her the remains, family members are at odds with each other, and in some cases, remain so for the rest of their lives. The natural emotion that comes with grief blends with other emotions that may have been hidden or denied.

In such cases one wonders what was taught in the family about togetherness, love, peace and harmony amongst the siblings coming from the same womb and resulting from the same sperm. I am not talking about step-siblings. The ugly emotion of pure hate surfaces and persons are not speaking and each one talks badly about the others. In large families some of them take sides against the others as if there were no blood connection.

How sad this is. Parents do not always consider what problems may arise after their departure from their earthly life. There must have been some sign or clue. What is hidden during life sneaks out at death and it makes it so hard for loved ones who are mutually grieving their lost. It is at death when they should come together in love and help each other to work through their bereavement.

All is not futile. For those who wish to work through their pain, anger (and sometimes hate), they can connect to a workshop that brings God into the midst. Some religious institutions provide such a ministry with trained professionals.

Let us think about avoidance of the behavior we find ourselves in. How can this be done? First, parents have to be completely honest with their children. Unfortunately, favoritism (although denied) rears its ugly head in families. Parents have to be careful how they show it. Some siblings take unfair advantage of this and when death comes, it becomes crystal clear by the will how assets are distributed. Parents have been known to make statements which should not have been made. Those statements are seeds that start to germinate as soon as they are made and come into full bloom at death.

Promises are sometimes made and never kept and that creates problems. Too often we hear, "Mother promised me…." "Dad said he was giving me his tools." Parents do not realize that they are setting in motion a means of splitting the family after their death. Also, another terrible thing is to talk badly about one child to another at any age. But it seems a bit more destructive when the "children" have reached adulthood. Life is tough enough without having to deal with family discord to the point of anger for the rest of the siblings' life.

Just as in all of my other essays (hopefully) that you have read, when an ill is mentioned a panacea is offered. In this writing of life becoming less sweet because of incidents leading to family discord, what offered here is for family members involved to seek appropriate professional help. Life is too short to carry unwanted and undesired baggage of anger. It destroys not only the family as a unit, but it destroys each person individually and often flows into the marriages. Who in their right mind wants that?

Life is meant to be sweet. We should raise our children to be sweet. We should do all in our power to not only keep the sweetness, but make sure that we add a little bit more sweetener. How can we be so sweet to others when we find we can't be sweet to our siblings? I can't imagine leaving mother earth and not speaking to someone (sibling or not).

If this essay is also your story and is bringing tears to your eyes, why not reach out and get the help you need to get your life back on track so you can enjoy life's sweetness while still on earth? None of us knows how much time he or she or anyone has. Let us waste no more time!

Life is meant to be sweet!

LIVING WITH REGRETS

"Refrain from anger and turn from wrath; do not fret –
it leads only to evil."
Psalm 37:8 (NIV)

I dare to believe (and say) that everyone in his or her life time has at least one regret. And many of us have many but they do not have to keep us from pursuing our hopes, dreams and goals.

This essay is about those of us who have several regrets that crop up from time to time and we find ourselves saying, "should have, could have and would have." This means we didn't do something when it was the right time to do it. This was, perhaps, negligence on our part and we have no one else to blame but ourselves.

The blame, however, should be short-lived. Why? It is wise to know what should have been done, but after knowing we have to move on and not be stymied by an opportunity that has passed. It is never too late to rectify any negligence. One example is not continuing ones education at an earlier age. Well, it is never too late to go back to school. Another example is completing a project. All we have to do is pick up the pieces and continue working toward its completion.

Suppose you miss the companionship of a friend because you said or did something that offended the person and he or she has cut you loose. Why not get in touch with that person and apologize. What's wrong with saying," I'm sorry, I made a mistake and I want to correct it and clear the air. Will you please forgive me?"

There must be some regrets that you have procrastinated correcting over the years. Clearing the air will not only help to restore the relationship we used to enjoy, but it helps us to feel good about ourselves and the person whom we have neglected.

Living with regrets dampens our spirit and makes us feel badly about what we have done or not done. By commission or omission we may have hurt others, and as long as they are hurting we are also hurting, consciously or unconsciously. Whenever we are in their presence or their name is mentioned, we feel pangs of guilt.

Most of the time we try to stay away from them as much as possible, but if we had a good relationship before, we miss them. We also miss the good times we had with them for whatever time we have spent together.

The feeling (baggage) we carry in our hearts can be released and we can once again enjoy their company and fellowship. It will feel good being back in the good graces and company of loved ones.

As strange as it may sound, entertaining regret for a very short time can serve a useful purpose. It serves to remind us that no one is perfect and all of us are subject to err. The more active we are the more we err because the more we do the more mistakes we make. Have you ever noticed that some mistakes have proven beneficial and a blessing? The term *serendipity* means something good is realized as a result of a mistake. Some people refer to this as "lucking up" when it is actually being blessed. See my essay "Lucky? No, Blessed? Yes."

If anyone declares he or she is perfect, he or she is in denial. Denial is one of the ego defense mechanisms introduced by psychotherapist Sigmund Freud that keeps us from admitting a wrong we have committed. Being in denial means that we do not have to do anything to correct our fault because we are denying it. However, not admitting does not save us and the fault will not vanish but will remain forever with us and the person to whom we committed the fault, if we do not make the necessary correction.

As long as we have breath we have the opportunity to right our wrongs. In doing so we become free by the power on the Holy Spirit to accomplish anything we wish to. No one is powerless. Anyone thinking he or she is powerless reminds me of an electric cord not plugged into an outlet where it could get its "juice." Our "juice" comes from our Creator who empowers us to recoup from any situation we either place or find ourselves in.

As long as we have breath, we can muster the strength, but living with regrets is disastrous to our and my quality of life. So let us pick up the pieces, whatever they are and make whatever corrections we need to make and move on.

We deserve to be happy and free of regrets. Let's face it, all of us have done things we regret and as long as we live, this will crop up again and again. But the human thing to do, for the sake of continuing our friendship with those we love, is to do what we have to and move on. The buck stops with us!

The feeling (baggage) we carry in our hearts can be released.

LOOKING ON THE BRIGHT SIDE

"The desire of the righteous is only good,
but the expectation of the wicked is wrath."
Proverbs 11:23 (KJV)

A life lesson I learned as a child was based on the words, "This too shall pass!" My mother said that every time she ran into a problem. I internalized not only the words but her feelings when she uttered them. And, guess what? Whatever it was always passed... Things were very difficult for my mother but I never realized it until she passed when I was 13 years old. She never told me of what she was going through. I realized, however, that her cancer was often very painful, but she always smiled in my presence. We were poor but I never heard the word spoken.

Life teaches many dear lessons. One of the best lessons is knowing what to do when things happen that are not under our control. That is why I love the prayer: "God, grant me the serenity to accept the things I cannot change...the courage to change the things I can...and the wisdom to know the difference."

We agonize over many things unnecessarily. Sometimes we dwell on the moment and we keep that moment lingering without realizing that "This too shall pass."

I learned those words for myself because I got to know God in an intimate way through His Son, JC who has become a very close friend. It is so wonderful to have a Friend who does not judge you, who understands you thoroughly, who knew you when you were just a seed without a name, who loves you unconditionally, and has such compassion, grace, and mercy.

Don't you sometimes wonder what would happen to you if God withheld His love, His grace and His mercy from you? Because of God we can always look on the bright side. Why? Because He promises that He would be with us at all times, through the good as well as the bad. Whatever we are going through shall pass because He will see that it passes. When we are wise enough, trusting enough, faithful enough to place every thing into His loving care, we have nothing to worry about.

You may wonder why I never give a particular verse in my essays when I talk about His goodness. The reason for that is I am hoping that you will search the scriptures for yourself. If I told you the book, the chapter and the verse, you may read it and only that. But my hope is that you will do your own searching because in seeking you will find.

As we all know, there is nothing greater than finding out for ourselves. As we raise our children we try to show them the pitfalls so they can avoid some of the heartaches and disappointments they will run into. But you and I have learned that everyone has to find out for him or herself. "In this case seeing (for themselves) is believing."

We agonize and worry what is going to become of our children. We have taught them well, but there comes a time when we have to let go of the reins we have on our adult children and let them make their own mistakes and learn from them. As much as we may want to "save" them from making the same mistakes we made, because we love them so much. We cannot. We have to trust them.

We have to trust that our teachings took root and will manifest themselves in their daily lives after they have ventured into unfamiliar paths and experienced heaven knows what. They have to have the trust and faith in the same Heavenly Father who created them as well as us as parents. Whatever befalls them, "This too shall pass." Along with our teaching, we need to teach them those words with conviction. It will definitely make a difference in their lives and will pass on to other generations. And, while we are teaching, introduce them to the Power beyond ourselves that created us and every thing in our universe. That is all we as parents can do. My mother did and I am eternally grateful that she taught me whatever happens, "It too shall pass." Knowing this enables me to stay focused and always looking on the bright side, regardless of whatever physical appearance or situation I am forced to deal with.

We agonize over many things unnecessarily.
Sometimes we dwell on the moment and keeps the
moment lingering without realizing that this, too,
shall pass.

LOVE, COMPASSION, GRACE AND MERCY

"It is the Lord's mercies that we are not consumed,
because of His compassions fail not."
Lamentations 3:22 (KJV)

Some people may be in denial, but each and everyone was created with the desire for love, compassion, grace and mercy. Others may not be aware, but there is no mistaking it. As we give these gifts, we receive them. They are a part of love that is returned in great abundance.

The more we say that we don't need them, the more we hunger for them. The body, soul and mind cry out for love. Love is not easy to define. One cannot actually see it because it is not visible, but it is deeply felt. The absence of it causes all kinds of problems beginning with problems one has with oneself.

The deepest form of love comes from the One who created us because we were made in love. The wonderful and extraordinary thing about love is that you can't store it and hold it unto yourself. The word love is both a noun and a verb meaning action. The more you give, the more you receive. Trying to withhold it also causes problems because everyone and everything that lives desires love. People, plants grass: animals require loving care in order to strive.

Let us examine this a little. (Most of this essay will be about people so we will hold that until a little later.) Plants that are given proper care coming from love grow and bloom. When we have green leaf plants you will find that their coloring is rich and shiny. Some people have what is called a "green thumb" because they love their plants so much they spend a lot of time working with and on them. The plants respond by "smiling" showing their appreciation and ultimately displaying radiant colors.

You may get a "kick" from what I am about to say, but plants love to be talked to as well. A study was done at Duke University quite a few years ago. Plants that were talked to regularly as compared to other plants not talked to seem to have thrived better looked prettier and lasted longer. If you have any plants, I suggest that you try it. See for yourself.

Grass appears greener and thicker when properly cared for. Animals just know when they are loved and well treated, and they respond. I am especially fond of dogs as pets because when they are happy their tails wag "a mile a minute" and they usually like to kiss. When they are especially pleased about something their tongue (if you let them) will wash your face. Again, every living thing thrives because of love.

Now, getting to the basis of love of and from humankind, the more we feel loved the better we feel about ourselves. The reverse is true, but this essay is about the positive effects of love. Love not only makes us feel good about ourselves, we feel the same about others. Love prompts us to help others, to help make them happy, and to ease their pains. Love enables us to be sympathetic and empathetic. It enables us to grieve with those who are grieving, to cry with those who are mourning and to laugh with people who enjoy wholesome laughter.

Love encourages us to be the best that we can be, and love from others enables us to love, respect, and take the best care of ourselves. Happy people love themselves. As mentioned earlier, the love we feel cannot remain exclusively ours. It is impossible to keep it to ourselves and just for ourselves. Love is very inclusive.

The first thing a baby looks for immediately after birth is love. The infant's attention is drawn to the caregiver and is very much attracted to the voice he or she heard while in the womb of his or her mother, developing and preparing for the grand entrance into this wide wonderful world.

What infants do as soon as they can focus their eyes is to make eye contact. All through our years on earth, the greatest joy is to look into the eyes of someone we love while talking to or with them. Another attraction infants have that really makes them happy is for us to smile and speak when eye contact is made. Watch them wiggle and kick their feet showing their happiness. That is the beginning of their ability to feel loved and comfortable in their new world.

As we grow and age into the difference stages of our development, we find that the more love we have in our life, the better we are emotionally, psychologically, and physically. Just being loved by those we love enables us to be more patient, understanding, and compassionate.

As compassion, grace and mercy are a large part of love, let us examine each of them. Embodied in compassion is a feeling of understanding and deep caring... As we age, younger persons should be able to understand our slowness, lack of energy, forgetfulness, and nonsensical remarks and conversations. Loved ones understanding will enable us to feel still wanted and loved and a part of their life. As we age we need our younger loved ones to have more patience with us.

Understanding is so vital and important because it is so easy to take something someone says the wrong way. We may not hear what is being said in the way the speaker intends it. Or we may not use the right words. We all make mistakes in speech and action. So we need understanding to avoid needless arguments and disagreements. Many little things said or done can be taken out of context and cause heartaches and hurt feelings. Understanding allows us to not do anything that will hurt another as much as humanly possible. We all do not think alike or on the same level. We must be tolerant and believe that loved ones are acting out of love and in our best interest.

No one is perfect. We understand that, but as best we can, let us be always cognizant of how much we love someone and whatever interactions we are having, keep that love in the forefront and act on it. This way we will remain loving, compassionate, and full grace and mercy. By so doing we will do unto others what we expect and love to be done unto us.

The more we say we don't need love, compassion and mercy, the body, soul and mind cry out for them.

Love Personified

*"The eyes of the Lord range throughout the earth to strengthen
those whose hearts are fully committed to Him…"*
2 Chronicles 16:9 (NIV)

Most of us may not think about it, but we were born in love and that love is so great, so wonderful and so powerful, Best of all it is unconditional. The greatness of the love we were born with is personified. It comes with the "package" of life itself. Whether we consciously acknowledge it or not, it is a part of each of us and completely determines our success or lack of it until the end of this life as we know it. And it will carry us into the spiritual (eternal) realm of life.

The reason why we do not recognize love is because things happen to us that seem to separate us from the love which still remains but not shown by humankind for whatever reason. We many not know what happened because we were too young to know what was happening, but whatever it was, it left painful impressions into our adult mind and heart. Believe it or not, the pain and hurt do not have to remain with us forever.

When love seems missing we feel helpless, powerless and hopeless. Love gives us a feeling of hope and a sense of power so we can obtain whatever we want and become what we desire to be.

We weren't created (born) to just drift through life, hitting or missing. We were born for greatness. To be completely honest, my heart actually "aches" when I see young people drift and not doing anything with their potentials … just "hanging out." We all pretty much observe that doing nothing constructive leads to being destructive.

The manner in which people dress, talk, walk, act says much about themselves. What is inside a person is shown on the outside. One unconsciously "advertises" who he or she really is as body language is strong. One may not be aware of what message he or she is sending to the world, and that in itself is so sad because many act if they don't care, but deep down they actually do care.

Love is not lost forever. That in itself is a blessing. All we have to do is sincerely and earnestly ask to be able to put it to good use. It is a pity that some persons pass through life thinking what they have is all they are going to get. And some feel that they have to take what does not belong to them in order to have. There is more than enough for everybody if we would just apply ourselves. Developing and using the potentials embodied in our genes enables us to obtain or acquire whatever things we desire. This is so because the sky is the limit.

The only limitation is what we place on ourselves. You see, the One who gave us productive genes is the only One who can keep us from using them. And He wouldn't. No one else in humankind can stop us from being productive or acquiring what we strive for. Humankind can talk a good game and may be successful in hindering us from accomplishing our goals only because we listen to their negativism and internalize it. If we put and keep our trust in the One who gave us life and our genes, we cannot avoid being winners.

As an octogenarian I have read much, seen and experienced much, and consequently learned about human behavior and what experiences have made negative impact on our life. The only way to change is to seek professional help and one form of professional help is counseling. However, counseling is successful if only persons want to make a change. Often through counseling we learn that most of our behavior is a result of negative influences others have had on us.

Counseling on the part of the persons seeking it can be successful if the persons really want to put themselves in the position of accomplishing their hopes, dreams, desires and goals. Do they really want to make the change is the important question. When the persons being counseled can hang tough and move beyond denial and accept the fact that their thinking has gotten them in trouble. And if they are able to admit they have wronged others as well as themselves, that's half the battle. They can then begin to make the necessary changes in their thinking, attitude and behavior.

The love we were born with gives us strength. Some people may not want to admit it, but there is a difference between persons feeling loved and persons feeling unloved. When we hear someone saying, "I don't care whether you love me or not," it is an actual cry for love. The person is hurting and has a great need and desire to feel loved, especially by the one he or she loves. But what usually happens is we respond unkindly and argumentatively not recognizing the person is crying out. This is the time he or she needs to be reassured that he or she is indeed loved. Apparently, we have not through speech and action shown the person that he or she is cared for and loved.

Feeling unloved by someone we love is very painful. Unrequited love is the term used for this situation. A person can feel not only unloved, but hated. and that compounds the pain. We think we find ways to hide, but it is demonstrated in our striking back at the ones we love. So we end up making matters worse. In trying to spare ourselves pain, hate becomes a weapon we use to combat our false thinking of being hated.

There should never be a need for this kind of pain, and the need for a weapon because love personified is a part of our birthright and each of us should let our love flow freely, be felt and do all we can to effect peace, joy, happiness with the ones we love.

The manner in which people dress, talk, walk and act says much about them.

Lucky? "No" – Blessed? "Yes"

"Blessed are those who hunger and thirst for
righteousness for they will be filled."
Matthew 5:6 (NIV)

I'm beginning to think that most people use the words *lucky* and *blessed* interchangeably, but they are not the same. The dictionary tells us that *blessed* means "hallowed, sacred, consecrated, holy and beatified." *Lucky* means "having good luck, fortunate, prosperous and successful." Of course, the larger dictionaries give many other synonyms.

Let us closely examine those two words for a moment: As the dictionary states such words as *hallow, sacred, consecrated, holy and beatified* indicate that God is in the picture. God blesses us so when we unite with Him. The well known saying to believers is, "When the praises go up, blessings come down." To some degree, then, we have some input into our being blessed.

I would think the implication of being lucky is a chance experience and everyone is not lucky. We have a choice in what we think concerning being lucky and being blessed. My personal choice 24/7 is being blessed. In order to be blessed I send my praises up daily so that my blessings can come down. Everyone, whether he or she is cognizant or not, is daily blessed in some form by our Creator. We could cite many blessings that we take for granted, but the joy of it all is to recognize when and how we are blessed and thank God for the blessings. So-called charms are worthless. All we have to do is ask God to bless us. Life itself is a gift (blessing) from God. What we do with it, is our gift to God. Be blessed!

HONESTY

Some people think that to be honest is to utter every thought that enters our heads. But silence is golden, and before we speak we should process our thoughts to make sure they heal, not hurt or hinder. In other words, we should make sure our thoughts are positive and not negative.

Some people rationalize their speaking by saying, "I speak the truth and if it hurts, too bad." Many otherwise nice, fine persons are caught up in such thinking and it takes away from their niceness and fineness. We need to question our motive.

Sometimes it profits us nothing to express our feelings. Other times it is vitally necessary to express what we feel. The key is to know when it is or isn't the time or place to have the courage of ones conviction to speak up without malice, but with love and respect.

I think when criticism is given it should be constructive. If the aim is to help then it should be given sweetly and not harshly. People appreciate honesty. Ones integrity comes from being honest. An honest answer to a question does not always require a litany of words. Speak the truth with a sweet tongue. Lemonade without some kind of sweetener is too sour (if not bitter). I just happen to love lemonade when the bitter rime is left out.

HELPING OR HINDERING

As strange as this may sound, we are not always helpful when we "help" others. Before you become perturbed by what I've just said, let me haste to explain myself (smile).

Most people desire a sense of independence. When we are too helpful by not letting persons do what they are capable of doing, we "cripple" them and they become unnecessarily dependent. Giving loans may appear helpful, but it can turn out to be a wrong move in the name of helping. How so, you may wonder. Some answers follow:

Let us talk about lending money to friends or loved ones. After a while, if too much "help" is given, the borrowers become resentful instead of grateful. And we wonder why they turn on us. A good example of this is seen in the court shows on television.

Hiding behind the "gift or loan" dialogue, the defendants are so resentful they become down right nasty. Of course, the plaintiffs, who are suing for payment, are disturbed by the fact that they are not only unappreciated, but are disrespected. To add insult to injury, the defendants expose present or previous behavior of the plaintiffs which has nothing to do with the loan.

I think we do not listen to our inner-selves. Most of the time we ignore the feeling that we should not give in to the request for another loan. But our desire to be "helpful" outweighs our common sense and feeling that we shouldn't give in. This is not helping persons to establish ways and means of becoming independent.

Some people act as if they expect to be given whatever and whenever they ask, and we are the ones who have taught them that expectation by meeting their requests. If our intention is to help, we need to do it with empathy instead of sympathy.

EMPATHY VERSUS SYMPATHY

People take negative advantage of persons who operate from sympathy rather than empathy. There is a vast difference between the two. Sympathy is simply feeling sorry for someone. It renders the giver vulnerable because the desire to help is so strong that it overrides common sense. There is a feeling of guilt on the part of the giver because the thinking is that not helping a person in his or her predicament is wrong. The pathetic part of this scenario is the receiver knows how to place the giver on a guilt trip.

Empathy, on the other hand, causes one to respond to a call for help, but being rational in the helping. Being empathetic allows the person to be able to understand (to some degree) why or how a person is in a certain situation. Empathetic persons find ways to give assistance without the persons being helped becoming dependent on them. In responding to a crisis, the givers do whatever they can with assisting the persons in crisis to help them become more independent. This reminds me of a saying, "It is better to give a person a fishing rod and point out where to fish than to keep giving fish."

To be able to be independent is a blessing. One does not "luck up" on anything. We who are strong believers know from whence our blessings come and many times we have an intuition which we follow and it leads us to the blessing or it brings the blessing to us. Those who depend upon luck are not guaranteed any "luck." But blessings are guaranteed because the Bible tells that if we ask we will receive; if we seek we will find and if we knock, the door will be open to us." So why depend on luck which in an uncertainty?

Be blessed!

Sometimes it profits us nothing to express our feelings. Other times it is vitally necessary to express what we feel.

MAGNETISM:
THAT SPECIAL ATTRACTION

"And whatever you do whether in word or deed, do it
all in the name of Lord Jesus, giving thanks to God the
Father through Him"
Colossians 3:17(NIV)

People who have the same interests seem to find each other with little effort; In fact, they do not have to look. It is my belief that like energy travels from person to person. People of the same interests find each other; therefore, there is a potential connection.

Have you ever had the experience of seeing a person for the first time, and instantly there seemed to be a kinship which made you want to get to know that person?

This has happened to me more times than I can count. It happened to me one Sunday morning as I was walking to the home of the person with whom I ride to church. A person approached me on his bile. He introduced himself with a smile and asked me a simple question. I gave him my business card and we both hurried off. This encounter stayed on my mind and then I received a call. We have been corresponding ever since. Our kinship is sharing the same interest in journalism. The forthright gentleman happens to be the editor of *Our Times* (a community newspaper) in Queens, New York.

Having the opportunity to share this very subject with others, I find that many persons have had similar experiences, which resulted in acquiring new friends, obtaining a job with upward mobility possibilities, joining a church or Synagogue, deciding to continue higher education and sharing other interests in keeping with their values.

Since we as people do not function in the blind, we know that negative magnetism attracts and works as well as positive. I am only sharing the positive concept of magnetism because my propensity for positive outcome is foremost in my mind at all times. I have to have a sense of accomplishments with every task I tackle.

It is indeed a wonderful feeling when positive energy meets and connects to another's positive energy. In working together with another person who has like goals, dreams and aspiration, the synergy is most powerful. The question of this being wrong or right never enters the head of either one of the persons. One just instantly, instinctively knows that the connection is a right one. It is actually a blessing. Most persons recognize blessings and they know from whom they come.

Magnetic energy presents itself as a pure unadulterated manifestation and it connects with the magnetic energy of another in the same manner two magnets connect to each other. Just bring two magnets into close proximity to each other and feel them very quickly drawn together.

When persons are seeking to find their significant other for a lifetime commitment, it would be more expedient if they frequent places they really enjoy. There they will find others who have the same interest in such places as places of worship, museums, art shows, dance halls, self-improvement seminars, sport events, motivational lectures, etc.

Some people rely on the internet and the many dating clubs which is really taking risks in meeting strangers with myriad interests and values not necessarily to their taste or interest. People are good at saying just what you want to hear after asking a few questions.

Actually, some persons looking for that genuine special person have found them where they least expected to. Some of those places were bus stop, subway, at a play and places of business at the very moment in time when they were not actually looking. I tend to believe that such connections were made through the power of the magnetic energy. Such encounters require purposeful pursuit in order for a genuine, steady and permanent connection to come into fruition.

I strongly believe when you send your vibes (energy) out and relax; it will attract the right person because magnetism causes you to be initially connected to the right person. Of course, the rest is up to you. When you meet initially, remember nothing ventured, nothing gained.

Magnetic energy presents itself as a purely unadulterated manifestation of you and it connects with the magnetic energy of another in the same manner two magnets connect to each other when brought into close proximity.

Mapping Our Lives with the Power of Love

"Many are the plans in a man's heart, but it is the Lord's purpose that prevails." Proverbs 19:21 (NIV)

Love is a spiritual ingredient in life that one cannot see but deeply feel. Love is a motivator. It inspires us to do good things. Doing good things begins with us and we share and spread them to others.

We are all influenced by love, and without it we suffer all kinds of pains. Some of the pains are loneliness, despair, depression, and worthlessness. All of these can lead to feeling that we do not belong to anything or anybody. This is faulty thinking because we all belong. We belong first to the Creator who made us and He is the common denominator of all of us. Everyone He creates is related because we are made in His image and He loves us more than we can ever imagine. Next we belong to the family in which we have been a part of since birth.

If you happen to be one of those persons who can be described as feeling unloved, know that you are loved. Love is the reason for your being able to still breathe the breath of life. The mere fact that we are living shows that Someone greater than ourselves cares deeply for us.

When we get rid of the feeling that no one loves us, we are able to do things that bring even more love to ourselves and others. As this continues, we will find love springing up all around us and we will be able to see the beautiful of even the small loving things in our lives.

That is enough talk on the absence of love. Let us begin to seek it. Let us seek first the One who is all about love. He freely gives it, but we don't always recognize it. We sometimes falsely think love is something tangible. It is nothing that we can physically touch or see. Love takes root in the heart and begins to spread throughout our being, and then it reaches out to others.

When we plan (map) our lives based on the love we feel and enjoy, we find ourselves giving and receiving more love. It is the one thing that we have that the more we give the more we have. It is powerful and it keeps coming.

It changes our outlook on life. It evens affects our feelings about ourselves and others. When it takes over, we feel that we can conquer the world and there is nothing that we cannot do. So as we map out our lives, love makes us feel that the sky is our only limit. All we have to do is make up our mind what we truly want in life. Then we can start mapping which is another word for planning. With love we are able to plan with the confidence of being able to achieve anything we want.

Love helps us to believe the "impossible" can become possible. When we believe that we can accomplish the impossible, we are not afraid to step up and take whatever steps that are necessary.

Feeling loved keeps us from doing destructive things and wasting our life. Life is actually too precious to waste. Every minute given to us should be filled with something good and rewarding to us and the people around us.

We have a responsibility to ourselves to do all that we can to make this a better world. If each one of us would concentrate on just that, we cannot imagine how great our community, our city, our state, our country, and our world can become.

Love dispels evil and is attracted to all that is good around us. As we map the course of our existence in the world and determine what we shall do to promote love, peace and tranquility within ourselves and others, we will find a great sense of peace and happiness. And this will have a boomerang effect throughout the universe. As we map, we live. As we live, we make it possible for others to live. As we make it possible for others to live, the good life becomes contagious, fulfilling, enjoyable and very much rewarding.

If you happen to be a reader who needs the encouragement this essay offers, why not take on the challenge of beginning to love yourself? Loving others will come easily after you have successfully begun to love yourself.

If you are not involved in some positive pursuits and you are letting time pass by with no plan for changing your feelings about self and your situation, you have some mapping to do. In order to enjoy the blessings of life right in your grasp, start with filling your heart with love! Then with certainty you can map out your life for what you want to do, and how you plan to do all of the things placed on earth (with love) for your enjoyment.

Loving others will come easily after you have successfully begun to love yourself.

ME, MYSELF AND I

"…God opposes the proud but gives grace to the humble"
James 4:6 (NIV)

The tile of this essay sounds egotistical, doesn't it? The three-fold purpose of this writing is (1) to how living alone can be a happy experience, (2) how to ensure happiness in a household of two persons and (3) making everyone happy when there are more than two living together.

The Single Dweller

Happiness in a household of one can start with doing small things which pleases the dweller. One of those things is letter writing which does not have to be long but positive and cheery. What does this do? The anticipated responses will give you something to look forward to. If the closing line of your letter states something a bit mysterious, you will find yourself getting an immediate answer. Another point is to be genuinely complimentary by letting your loved ones know high highly you admire and respect them. Moreover, let them know how you enjoy hearing from them. Your personal letters will, hopefully, exceed the bills, advertisements and other junk mail.

If you have a computer, there is much you can do to bring joy and happiness to yourself and into your home. There are all kinds of games, unlimited information on just about any subject. If you love to read, there are books that are interesting and so suspenseful you would hardly want to stop reading to do other things you have to do. Selected television programs of your interest will make time fly fast!

When you are grateful for your life and try counting your blessings, you will find yourself praising God for His goodness to you. And in praising God, you will have blessings overflowing into your heart, life and home. Do you have a hobby? Be creative! Let your positive imagination run wild! The biggest motivator for your own sense of peace and happiness is always thinking the best even in the worse situation, It's up to you. Isn't it better to be happy than to be lonely?

A Couple

In a couple-household there are many things both parties can do together in order to bring happiness into the home. Some of the things are cooking, playing cards, once a week hiding inexpensive gifts each of you likes, dancing, viewing TV and discussing what's happening, reading the Scriptures together and discussing what you are reading. Have light conversation with a little light teasing just before going to bed. That will add spice to the bedroom activities (umm). When both persons have a sense of humor, laughter fills the home. When we do all we can do for ourselves happiness is ensured. Using your imagination will enable you to bring great ideas that would be fun for both of you.

In a Home of Many Persons

In a home in which there are many persons dwelling as a family (extended or otherwise), there are many things that all can do together. When older persons are a part of the household do not neglect them. The younger ones (children of any age) should share some time with grandmother/grandfather or whoever the elders are. Let them feel a part of the activities that can be shared. Older persons like to talk about the past and younger ones can encouraged them and enjoy good times together. Be good listeners, Show genuine interest. Surprise them with little inexpensive gifts - something you know they may like. Never be too busy to include them in whatever activities you can. I don't know about you, but I love to hear people of advanced age giggling and laughing. It is so good for them when they aren't afraid of being a little silly.

Younger household dwellers have their own "programs." I hardly think they need any suggestions from this writer. I just want to make sure that the older dwellers are treated with the respect and interest they deserve.

It is rare today to see three generations living together even though people are living much longer than years ago. Because of poor health many much older persons are in nursing homes. In such cases we can make our visits interesting and enjoyable. A gift is always welcomed. Sharing pictures of other family members at a gathering would be nice. Reading to them and light positive conversations are welcomed by them. Singing familiar hymns and songs brings joy to their soul. If possible give them a portable CD player with their favorite CDs.

Whether you are a household of one, a couple or many, the decision to add spice to your household is up to you. Loneliness can be experienced in either of those households but it should not be an invited "guest." It should not be allowed to stay more than second, if at all.

Stretching our imaginations will result in good ideas that the entire household can enjoy and appreciate. Each member can contribute something. What about having as many meals together as possible without the television? In some households each one eats alone while watching television. What a pity!

Let us enjoy each other as much as possible the few years we have together. There are some things we enjoyed back in the days that can be a part of today. It is hoped that everyone in each household shares his or her time and interest with other members of the household. You will find this most rewarding. And while we are at it, let's do whatever we can to laugh so hard at least one a week (more times is better) that the belly hurts. Humor is good medicine!

Life and family is more than just one person concerned with just himself or herself. It actually should be "we, us and our." That way we will have a maximum of amount of joy and happiness living together in our various households.

Whether you are a household of one, a couple or many, the decision to add spice to your household is up to you.

MIND OVER MATTER

"Cast all your anxiety on Him because He cares for you."
I Peter 5:7 (NIV)

I would guess that most people know what the phrase means, and I would think whether we know what it means or not, it would be a subject catchy enough to get anyone's attention.

It speaks of our ability to not give too much thought to simple matters and how to cope with the day to day encounters that either seem to bless us or hurt us, and it also speaks of the bigger problems that we have to deal with each day. Mind over matter in simpler terms means how we think influences not only our decisions, but also what emotions are invoked by our thinking. We can think ourselves into a "bottomless pit," and we can think ourselves into becoming so ill we can be near death. In some extreme cases, we can become mentally unbalanced.

While reading this book of essays, you have probably noticed that, although I mention the negatives that occur in our lives, I am primarily focused on the positives and various panaceas or ways to become positive. It is so vitally important to learn how to override or change our negativism that destroys us or keeps us separated from the best life has to offer.

Those persons who have their "heads in the sand" attempt to stay there until everything blows over, but nothing is going away until it is acted upon. We cannot afford to fool ourselves by thinking that if we ignore"it," it will go away. We have to realize negative thinking, feeling and action cause negative things to happen and that it takes positive action to send these negative things on their merry way.

Everyday that we can get out of bed is a blessing. We have another day filled with other blessings and challenges. Now, how we deal with the challenges speaks to our mind over matter. When we realize that we are not alone and that we have Someone who guides instructs, directs and leads us, we are able to get through each day with a minimum of anxiety. The Scriptures say, "Trust the Lord with all of your heart and lean not into your own understanding. In all your ways acknowledge Him and He will direct your path." (Proverbs 3:5-6)

For those who do not believe in God, I can honestly say I for pray them because they are carrying burdens that they don't have to carry. Their lives are beset with anxiety, fears, worry, uncertainties, hopelessness, helplessness and all of the other negatives feelings that cause them to think they are alone in all decisions.

Believe or not, I can understand why some people do not believe in God. One reason is because some very "religious" people can turn others off. This is heavy so I have to take my time expressing this deep feeling I have about some "religious" folk. I speak from experience and not from the top of my head.

Some religious folk I have observed are so "righteous" and judgmental that they are an embarrassment to God Himself, They are quick to "quote" the Bible and they have their own narrow interpretation and will spend endless time "arguing" (not discussing) their point of view. If you don't believe this, read for yourself about the Pharisees Sadducees and Scribes found in the Books of the Gospel: Matthew, Mark, Luke and John.

This is important for us to know because those who seek a way of life that will bring joy, happiness, peace, contentment, and a quality of life that is satisfying are influenced by us. They need to know that there is Someone who can supply all of their needs according to His riches in heaven.

Let's make it clear. Very religious folk are not necessarily godly people. Who are godly people? They are people who try as best they can to live up to what is expected of them according to the Scriptures. Godly people know that they are not without flaws. They do not condemn others with flaws but try to help them rid themselves of them. Godly people are always seeking to be better and do better. They do not place themselves on a pedestal because they know the meaning of humility.

If you want to know other distinguishing traits of godly people from self-righteous religious folk, take note. Truly godly folk are humble, loving, kind, forgiving understanding, and ever trying to withhold judgment as much as possible. That is not an easy feat to accomplish

211

even for godly folk. Godly people are pleasant and make you feel good just being in their company. They smile more and there is something contagious about their personality. We are drawn to them and yet we do not know why until we are engaged in conversation with them.

Very religious folks have a tendency to preach rather than talk. There is nothing wrong with preaching, but when people want to know about God, they also want to witness the conviction we claim to have as believers.

In cases where people are physically hungry and at the same time starving for comforting words and greater understanding of what life is supposed to be, the godly person sees that their physical needs are taken care of first, and then they address their spiritual needs. The very religious start preaching about sin. I have actually witnessed this. We have to show by our actions what God is about; then persons will be more receptive to what we have to say so that they can become believers, too.

Mind over matter determines how we think and how we process our thoughts. We are either negative or positive. Every situation is to be treated so that we get the best results. Yes, there are going to be problems in our lives, but when they occur, we should be able to work with them in a manner that reduces our fears and anxieties.

Mind over matter is letting go and letting God guide us through the maze of our many trials and tribulations. He will put the right thoughts in our mind and the right feelings(s) in our spirit and hearts so that we have less to be anxious about.

We cannot afford to fool ourselves by thinking if we ignore "it," it will go away."

MISPLACING THINGS!

*"There is a time for everything, and a season for every
activity under heaven: A time to weep and a time to laugh"*
Ecclesiastes 3: 1, 4 (NIV)

Surely, you are not blaming yourself for things that are being misplaced in your home. It cannot be you. I have come to the conclusion that when I unlock my door and walk into my apartment, invisible people rush in and make themselves at home. They don't live with me.

The first thing they do is to hide my keys. As soon as I put them down on my dresser they snatch them. It has to be them because I always place my keys on one spot so they are either on the dresser or in my pant pocket. One time they had the nerve to take them from my pocket and put them on the dresser. It's downright annoying!

As annoyed as I get, if it were just my keys I could tolerate their antics by using my spare set, but sometimes while working on papers, I find pages temporarily missing. I know that I could not have misplaced them in such a small area as my desk is small. But you know what? After much agonizing, I found the papers were on the floor on the other side of my desk. I wouldn't have any reason to put them there. You see what I mean? Another time papers were in the kitchen. How on earth did they get there? They had to be taken by someone, and I didn't do it.

I thought this sort of thing happened to seniors only, but it happens to children, too. In fact, I don't think anyone can escape them. Children lose their shoes, boys their caps and sometimes they find their lunch money missing. These invisible people apparently have nothing to do but play all day. I'm too old to play around with them and I wish they would leave me alone. But instead of leaving me alone, they visit every day. Can you imagine that?

213

They are very quiet or they talk in whispers, and I don't hear a sound. The only disturbance is playing with my things. If they talked to me what on earth would we talk about? Here are some possible topics: Current events, other people's business? No, I have my hands full taking care of my own business. Beside I never was interested in what my neighbors or anyone else did or do.

Strange as this may sound I was on the bus the other day and I happened to look down at my feet. I had on one black shoe and a brown shoe, but they were the same style. Don't you know when I took my shoes over to my favorite chair to put them on; they switched a shoe on me. I never noticed it until I was on the bus. I was so embarrassed I hid one foot behind the other.

Have you experienced these people in your house? Tell me, how does one get rid of them forever? I once asked a friend and she told me to talk to my doctor. She is so foolish; my doctor does not make house calls. And if he did why would he come to see my invisible visitors?

I have gone into a room to get something and while in there I wondered what it was. But the minute I stepped out of the room, it came to me what I was in there for. Do you suppose those folks are messing with my head as well? They must be because the second I stepped out of the room it came to me what I went in there for. They must have had a good laugh on me. I supposed I should be thankful that I don't hear them laughing. I would be really mad!. But I do wish they would stop coming around. They are at everyone's home I understand from what I hear.

At the check out counter at the supermarket, they had the nerve to take a bag of my groceries. I discovered when I got home that I didn't have everything. I went back to the store and they had the bag waiting for me. I told them that invisible people were playing with me, and I got such curious looks. I wonder if they have that problem too. Can you imagine them in the supermarket changing food on the shelves during the night? They must drive them crazy when customers ask where so and so is. The store people, of course, wouldn't know. Well, my problem with my house guests is nothing compared to what they have to contend with.

So I am not going to get bent out of shape worrying about my little problem. I do find it a bit strange that I do a lot of thinking, perhaps out loud. When I find myself speaking out, I think they put the words in my mind and I spit them out. That's a little too much for me though.

At least they are not around when I take my showers. They may hide my towel. Let me let you go. I have too many stories about the two of them (husband and wife I presume). I'm just glad they didn't bring their children if they have any. I have not been formally introduced so I know very little about them or their other activities.

Do you think I should leave well enough, alone? How do you get rid of your unwanted guests?

I don't know what to do about my things being misplaced.

Much Ado About Nothing!

*"Finally, brethren, whatever things are true, whatever
things are noble, whatever things are just, whatever
things are pure, whatever things are lovely, whatever
things are of good report, if there is any virtue and if
there is anything praiseworthy meditates on these things."*
Philippians 4:8 (KJV)

Wherever people gather (families, social organizations, churches, political gatherings and the work place) we find arguments, and disagreements.

Sometimes the most innocent statement is blown out of proportion. The most trivial statement becomes "snowballed" into such controversy it is difficult trying to get to the truth. Significant others in your life begin to move away from you and join little groups called cliques.

A clique huddled together in whispered conversations stops talking when you happen to walk pass. The expressions on some faces might let you know that you are somehow included or connected to their conversation.

Your inclusion could be innocent, but because of your friendship with the person who made an innocent remark causes you to be ostracized along with your friend.

Now the clique causes no small amount of disturbance and everything that happens is placed on you and your friend who are the "outsiders" when you have not a clue as to what the clique is up to except the talking.

Ironically, the clique is quick to place anything that the group dislikes on you. This is because you are not a part of them. The behavior of this group is more often very mean and demeaning. If a person interested in conflict resolution were to look into the situation, he or she would find that the "controversy" developed from something that was not even a mole hill, but the clique has made it a mountain of confusion and misunderstanding, innuendoes, opinions, misinformation and too much imagination going awry.

Of all the settings (families, social organizations, churches, political gatherings, and the work place), the most damaging seems to be in the churches. Why? Because the church should be the very place where we should surely find love, peace, unity, harmony and a loving togetherness. The church is the one place we should not allow any act that is not of love to occur.

The question then is why is there so much ado about nothing in the church? The church is the one place we should be able to find reconciliation and a coming together in peace and harmony. The church should be the one place where the truth reigns supreme. Why is this not so?

One of the reasons is that church becomes (to some people) a place of formality, where form and fashion is displayed, and where outward appearances count more than what's in the heart.

Let's look into this. You will find "loving souls" whispering about the way others are dressed. The whisperers become "temporarily" distracted by the dress a worshiper is wearing. They are some members of a church who feel strongly that a woman should not wear slacks to church.

There are some men who will not dare come to church without a tie and a suit-coat. The there was a time when a woman would dare not attend church hatless. So in some ways we are moving away from old traditions, and that's good.

Since from generation to generation many changes take place, we hope and trust that people will place more value in love, peace, and harmony rather than judgment of outer appearances. In so doing we don't get upset over insignificant matters, but put our efforts in matters of the heart.

Love should be the prevailing factor in every place of worship. We should do all that we can to try to understand human behavior and do all that we can to either alleviate or obviate inhumane behavior.

Whether we are aware of it or not, gossip plays a major role in cliques. Cliques strive on false information and the sharing of it is detrimental to any sense of well-being, and the love we proclaim for each other in church is often an expression without actually being genuine love.

There is nothing under the sun that cannot change. Certainly, much ado about nothing does not have to be. We must be more tolerant of others who are different than we are and accept the fact that each of us is created to be unique. Our diversities make us special, and as we come together as people of God with the love of God in our hearts, we will find no need for cliques. We all don't have to think alike, and we do not have to persuade others to our way of thinking.

However, it is most important to respect others for whom they are. We don't have to like what everyone does, but loving unconditionally will make a big change in all of our lives.

If there is to be any kind of "clique," let it be one big body of people from every corner of the world loving one another with the love of God and bringing all together our multicultural differences and ethnicity. We must always remember that we are all children of God with our various customs and ways of interacting based on our culture.

If there is any kind of "clique" let it be one body of people from every corner of the world loving one another with the love of God.

Nipping It in the Bud

"If my sons forsake my laws and do not follow my statues
and fail to keep my commands, I will punish their sin
with the rod...but I will not take my love from them."
Psalms 89:32-32 (NIV)

All of my life I have heard the expression, "Nipping it in the bud." This actually means trying to stop whatever is happening while it is still a small problem.

My mother, a very strong woman and a firm disciplinarian didn't believe in letting anything bud, because if there is a bud, the problem exists. She believed in pulling the plant by its tender roots which means, there would be no budding.

What is the difference? The difference is when a plant has buds it has already rooted. The strong root gives nourishment and allows the plant to strive. My mother made sure that anything I did had to meet her approval. If it didn't, it was stopped immediately. So she stayed on my case like "white on rice." She felt if she didn't I would develop bad habits. Had she let me get away with anything, it would have become a habit. There was no outsmarting Martha; she watched "her plant" with diligence.

As I grew toward manhood she must have somehow known that she would not live to see me ripen into manhood. She died when I was thirteen years of age. As an adult I am so glad that she believed in destroying the roots while still tender.

Children will be children and as such with so much time on their hands, they think of things to do to avoid boredom. I pulled a stunt at twelve years old that I vividly remember to this day, even though that was sixty-eight years ago. I decided on my twelfth year that I would give myself a party as I never had one. My mother worked as a sleep-in maid and I stayed part-time with a cousin who later became my foster mother. I told my cousin that my mother said I could have a small party.

I purchased my party goods at a neighborhood grocery store where my mother had an account so I could purchase whatever I needed while living by myself in our little house. My guests had been invited and everything was in place for my party at my cousin's house. Around the time I expected my guests to arrive, I answered a knock on the door. I prepared to greet my guests by grinning from ear to ear. Guess who it was? It was my mother! Seeing how I was dressed in my party clothes, she asked what was going on. I told her that my cousin was giving me a party.

She went to my cousin and told her how nice she thought it was to give me a party. My cousin told her that I had told her that she had given me permission to have the party and to purchase what I needed .You can guess how my party was celebrated with the only arriving guest was my mother. Now, sense my mother believed in tender roots pulling, I was not allowed to have even a mouthful of any party goodies. I was ordered to take the goods in my little cousin's wagon and serve my guests at their homes.

My disciplinarian mother made sure that I got a suitable long switch and she administered my birthday present as soon as I had made my deliveries. Did I Learn my lesson not to lie? You bet I did! After disciplining me, my mother said she realized that I had never had a party so she asked for the day off to surprise me with something for my birthday.

I learned two things that day - one was not to lie and the other was having patience. Even though something may appear not to be, if you want it badly enough, believing and having patience will make it a reality.

Children do not think of the consequences for their action, and the only way for them to learn is for you to be a good overseer as parents or caregivers.

When our children are very small and begin to express themselves, we too often think they are so "cute." That cuteness becomes a little plant of behavior. Instead of pulling it by the tender root, we let it root even more and it becomes a habit which we no longer find cute but undesirable. If allowed to grow any more, parents or caregiver are going to have quite a problem pulling the roots that are no longer tender. If something isn't done and the law is broken, the correction authorities will step in and handle the matter.

Let me give an example with my little daughter when she was going through her amazing discovery period as a little tot. When she was told not to touch something, she would give me the prettiest smile while backing up to the object and touching it with her hand behind her back. She was actually testing my authority and to see what she could possibly get away with. But what I did was to continue to look at her and remind her in a firm but authoritative low key voice and say without smiling, "Didn't I tell you not to touch ...?" The first time she pushed to see what I was going to do and she touched it anyway. Her little hand got a little smack and from then on I had no problem.

We tend to under estimate children at that age. They know exactly what they are doing. And do you know, they are looking to learn what their boundaries are and they will test your authority until they learn that you say what you mean and you mean what you say.

Temper tantrums are designed consciously or unconsciously (depending upon their age) to test you and to get to know their boundaries and what they can or cannot get away with. Parents, guardians, and child caregivers have to learn about nipping it in the bud or better still, pulling it by the tender roots. Martha (my mother) believed in tough love even before the phrase was probably used.

Today, it takes tough love to raise our children because we are overwhelmed with competition from the street, society, the law makers, psychologists who over stress child abuse on one hand and the authorities whose responsibility is to investigate alleged child abuse do not have enough workers to adequately check and keep checking and take immediate action of possible child abuse cases. Can you imagine what would have happened to my mother and me had those days been these days. With my roots so strong on doing "my thing" it would take strong action by the authorities and I might have ended up with a criminal record. Who knows, but the possibility is certainly clear.

We have awesome responsibilities during this time in history in raising children. And it is more than biological clocks ticking and we want to have a baby. In today's world children are spoiled with all kinds of gadgets and toys and their room look like "play land." There is nothing wrong with that if we can afford them, but along with that, they need to know boundaries and what acceptable behavior is and what isn't.

Parents who cannot afford some of the things children want are doing their children a disservice and sending them the wrong message when we buy them what we cannot afford. The lesson we are teaching them is not good. That is the standard they will carry all of their lives into the next generation. Teaching them the benefit of education and professional training will enable them to be able to afford for their children, the things you could not afford to give them. And guess what? Their value system and level of appreciation would be high and they will respect you even more.

When the time comes (if it does) when you need assistance from your children, they would be more apt to be there for you. But if they lack appreciation for all you have done for them, they will not be there for you. Why? The reason is (unconsciously) you have taught them to become selfish, unappreciative and it is all about them. In your time of need, it will still be all about them, not you. You may not believe this, but it will be a sad state of affairs if you get to learn this at a time when you are late in years and need them in some way to be supportive and loving to you as you were to them.

My mother, a strong and firm disciplinarian, didn't nip anything in the bud. She pulled the thing by its tender roots.

Not Complaining – Just Explaining

"A soft answer turneth away wrath,
but grievous words stir up anger."
Proverbs 15:1 (KJV)

When we love and care for the people who mean the most to us we want the best for them. But the problem is we have to know how to give constructive criticism and how often. Even though we may mean well, trying to correct another is not always taken well.

Quite frankly, I don't care how much persons love me; I don't want them correcting me every time we are together. As it turns me off, I am sure it turns you, the reader off. How often it is done and how it is done may place it in the category of complaining.

We all know there is no one is perfect so why do we try to perfect others when we aren't perfect ourselves? A wise person would overlook insignificant behavior, meaning it is not worth having a discussion about. It seems the more imperfect people are the less tolerance they have for others.

The more I try to do unto others as I would have them do unto me, I find that my sometimes lack of patience makes me speak sharply. The minute I do this I regret having done it. I know full well that I do not like someone speaking to me in a sharp tone.

Although we know we are imperfect, we should pay attention to any behavior that is unbecoming and is an annoyance to others that is brought to our attention. That is why explaining is better rather than complaining. What is the difference?

I think we all know what complaining is, but we may not be aware of our voice tone and body language. First, complaining is negative. We see all that is wrong and the use of "I" seems to dominate the conversation. We sound self-centered as it is all about "me." That, of course, becomes boring to the listener after a very few minutes. Not only do we complain to our friends and loved ones, but to everyone whose ears seem willing. Well, their ears may be willing the very first time, but, depending upon how much time the person sat and pretended to listen, you can bet they will attempt at all possible to avoid us. And then we wonder how is it that no one wants to have a conversation with us. Ever noticed when friends always seemed to be in a hurry and cannot stay on the phone too long or always having somewhere to go or something to do when a complainer wants a "Little" time with us?

Explainers (as long as they don't overdo it) are people we can learn from and they can subtly help us to correct or change our thinking and behavior without offending us. Now, there are too kinds of explainers. One is long-winded who never seems to get to the point and is quite repetitive. But that one is not as bad as a complainer.

When we find a loved one who is a longwinded explainer, we can complain to them about their habit. Complaining to them is not going to help them to change, and if we do it too often, we will find ourselves without their company. If the persons are the ones whose company we normally enjoy, but just wish they would get to the point sooner, we would not want to discourage them from conversing with us. So we have to find a way to get them to become more cognizant of their speech pattern without complaining. An example of how we can help them without complaining, but explaining is to say," When you initially explained it to me I was quite clear of what you were saying, but I am now confused." Another example is when you are receiving an answer to a question regarding a direction of a place you are traveling to, you can say, "The first direction you gave me seems easy enough, but I'm confused by the alternate route. May I repeat the one I think you said initially?" Hopefully, you clearly understood and repeated it as it was told to you so that the only respond to you will be, "Yes, you got it!"

Some answers simply call for a closed ended response of "Yes" or "No." But a long winded person feels it necessary to expound when you simply want a one word answer. Suppose you are in a hurry and looking for a quick answer?

Here is another example of complaining versus explaining: **Complaining:** "Every time I asked you for a simple yes or no answer, you go on and on." **Explaining:** "I get confused when I ask a yes or no question and receive more detail than I need to know. I would appreciate it if you would tell me yes or no."

When you are trying to help a person concerning matters of behavior that the person is engaged in and the list is long, the person will consider you a complainer and rightly so. But to explain to the person why something is not working well and the person you are talking to is largely responsible, you will get a better response from him or her by explaining your point of view. The person would be more receptive and probably thank you for your time and interest. Complaining causes us to lose friends while explaining, for the most part, helps us to make and keep friends.

**We may all know what complaining is,
but may not be aware of our tone of voice and body
language.**

Not Getting Sidetracked

"Endure everything with patience."
Colossians 1:11 (NRSV*)*

Many people's aspirations, dreams, desires, ambition and goals are deferred because they allow themselves to be sidetracked.

What happens is we sometimes think that others know more about our abilities than we do and we rely on their judgment. Another reason is that we are not always confident of our own capabilities. We don't trust ourselves. We give up too easily. We lack stick-to-it-ness when the going gets tough. I like the saying "when the going gets tough, the tough gets going."

There are many other reasons why we allow ourselves to get sidetracked. If you have found yourself in this position, you might be interested in knowing what those reasons are so that you can begin to do what you need to do in order to stay focused and on course. In the event you do slip off course, you need to find out how to get back on track and keep going until you have achieved what you are aiming for.

Sometimes we give loved ones too much credit by thinking they know better than we what is good or not good for us. That is why it is so important to be selective with whom we share our thoughts and dreams. When planning a program or project it is best to consult with someone who has accomplished his or her dream in spite of great odds against him or her.

People who have never accomplished anything are the last persons to talk with because they see the impossibility rather than the possibility. So they discourage us in following our dream. It is because they don't feel that they are capable so they conjure many negative reasons why they and we can't possibly accomplish a certain thing or dream we may have. They have good intention. They think they are saving us from miserable failure. Failure actually results in not trying.

People who are successful and seem to accomplish much in life are persons who not only have a dream, but a desire to accomplish it. They visualize actually achieving it and they get very emotional about it. They feel good.

Even before we start working on our dream, our good feelings make up want to share it with the people closest to us, but because they cannot "see" and "feel" what we do, they discourage us.

For those of us who believe in a higher power, we know that whatever ideas come to mind or from dreams we might have, come from the Higher Power, And when the Higher Power gives us thoughts and ideas, we have the faith, confidence and trust to know that along with that comes the wherewithal to accomplish or succeed. Perseverance is one of our strongest traits.

Just as we are discouraged, we can be encouraged. To be in the care and company of people who believe that "all things are possible to those who believe" is the best company in the world. A large number of persons are believers because they have been positively influenced by other believers.

I think one of the best things a person can do is not to discourage someone who has a dream. Just telling him or her to "go for it!" is a motivating factor that we all need. Some people need more encouragement than others. It costs absolutely nothing to give words of encouragement at the time most needed.

Great people often tell us what someone has said that motivated them to be the very best they can be. It is usually mother, grandmother, father, grandfather or an aunt or uncle or a stranger.

It costs us nothing to let dreamers know that they should pursue their dreams, and if they truly applied themselves they can accomplish them.

Some people are content doing nothing and they don't take too kindly to us enthusiastically sharing our hopes and dreams with them. On the other hand, there are those who strive on your sharing and can't wait to hear of your progress so they can rejoice with you. These are the people who will help you not to get sidetracked. If you run into any difficulty, they will help you get back on track and keep going until the task is done.

It is so disheartening to be bursting with ideas, and while sharing it with someone you assume to be special, that person shows no interest in what you are saying. Good news, good feelings, grand ideas are to be shared with persons you feel close to and who are indeed close to you.

The reason friendship is so dear is because people who genuinely care about you love to hear good things about you from you, or from others who know and love you.

What we all need are friends who help us to stick to what we are engaged in that brings us joy, peace, happiness, and a sense of accomplishment. That is why our Creator included populating the universe. There is a feeling of wholeness when we have friends who truly believe in us and encourage us to be the best that we can be, whatever our endeavors.

So it is most benefiting when we are selective of the persons we call friends. The reason is because we are influenced by our friends more than we may choose to think. I like the saying that "family members are by chance and friendship is by chose".

If we plan to be successful and live an enjoyable and happy life, we would do well to select persons who have high aspirations for us as we do for ourselves.

It costs nothing to let dreamers know they should pursue their dreams.

NOT LETTING PROCRASTINATION
DETER OUR BLESSINGS

*"The harvest is past, the summer has ended,
and we are not saved."*
Jeremiah 8:20 (NIV)

When we put off doing anything just because "we do not feel like doing it now," we are procrastinating. When we procrastinate, we invariably short change and lose out on something valuable or important - perhaps the blessings of our answered prayers.

Experience has taught me when I do not do something because I don't feel like doing it now, I regret it. What about you? Has this been your experience?

Let us then begin to make some changes in our life so that we'll never again miss out on something God meant for us to have.

Blessings come in so many unexpected and strange ways. For a moment, let us take a look at sudden fleeting thoughts. We too often ignore them; push them away without giving a second thought of why we should follow through. Then again, sometimes these sudden thoughts seem to keep coming and we fail to do anything about them, and we say to ourselves, "I'll do it tomorrow." Day after day, tomorrow passes and we find ourselves missing out and regretting that we had not done what came to our mind, when it did.

Has this happened to you? If so, we are on the same page! Let us explore this so we can make a determination within ourselves to be more attentive to the potential blessings that are available to us if we would have been obedient to the "message."

There is something we can be sure of and that is something good is going to happen when we do what we are supposed to do, to let it happen. Another question – have you ever prayed for s specific blessing and subsequently received an urge to do something? You may not have known that the answer to your prayer was embodied in that urge, but you failed to trust it and did nothing. This resulted in your prayer not being answered because you did not follow through. In all probability you did not see the connection between the prayer and the urge

If that has happened in the past we can do nothing about that now. Right? But we can begin to give full attention to the sudden fleeting thoughts which come into mind today and our tomorrows. It has a name. It is called intuition. This doesn't happen just once in a life time, but it continues. When we begin to follow our intuitions, regardless how "foolish" we may think they are, we place ourselves in position to realize more blessings and what we pray for will come into fruition. The Bible says, "Faith without work is dead."

It is my guess that we do not follow through with all of our intuitions, but coming cognizant of them will enable us to give more attention to what's happening in our life. Life has so many inexplicable occurrences. When we try to explain them we really don't understand and it makes us appear foolish. (Heaven knows we don't want to appear stupid or foolish in front of our friends or foes). Do you think that is why we don't sometimes follow through with some of our fleeting thoughts? I that is the case, we should not be concerned with what others may think or say. We are doing the right thing in following our "gut" feelings. Do you agree?

When you listen to people who feel that have accomplished what they have set out to do, you will hear them say that they followed the lead of their intuition without concerning themselves what others may think or say. Actually, they have reached the point where they just don't care. I view this as solid and complete freedom.

Solid and complete freedom allows us to be ourselves, and in being ourselves we have a responsibility to make sure that we are not harming, hurting or debasing ourselves or anyone. The freer we are the more prompt we are to be obedient to our "inner voice" which attempts to encourage.

In bringing this message full circle, we all, of course, should know that the mystery of "gut" feelings, intuition, and inner voice sudden fleeting thoughts all come from our Creator.

If you happen to be a non-believer, I grieve because there are so many wonderful blessings coming from our Creator that you are missing and will continue to miss. But for those who believe and heed this essay, you will be amazed by the many, many blessings you are entitled to and will have if you followed through with all the suggestions given in this essay. You life will never be the same! And I am glad.

Solid and complete freedom allows us to be ourselves, and in being ourselves we have a responsibility to make sure that we are not harming, hurting or debasing ourselves or anyone.

NOTHING LASTS FOREVER!

"There is a time for everything, and a season for every activity under heaven."
Ecclesiastes 3:1(NIV)

Good times, bad times, happy times and sad times – all of these experiences do not last forever. During our grief, sorrow, discomfort, discontentment and disappointments we can ease the pain by saying, "This too shall pass." If we can manage some comfort while we are going through adversities, we can help ease the intensity of the situation.

We have many ways of easing the intensity of negative situations. Humor is one. Light touch can make even the worse situation seem not so bad and we are able to deal with the situation a little better.

Although some situations may seem that they are taking us to the end of the world, they aren't. Everyone experiences ups and downs. That's life!

Life is like a bed of roses and with their prettiness and fragrance, they have thorns. If you have been pricked by the thorns you will know the pain. But pain only lasts a short time. If you can laugh, the pain goes away and you can appreciate and enjoy the beauty and fragrance of the roses.

People are like roses. For the most part they look good and smell nice, but some have prickly thorns. They are the ones who seem to have unkind things to say about everybody and everything. Even a compliment from them has a little "dig." But to their loved ones they are much loved roses. Ultimately, their loved ones wish they weren't so thorny.

Even though we say nothing lasts forever, very thorny roses seem to last forever. Very thorny roses have pity parties and they like to have their loved ones join them in their "festivities." They get much pleasure in complaining and talking about all the things that are wrong with this or that person and who is doing what to whom. They delight in causing confusion and can be counted upon to be destructive.

Do you know of any such persons? You aren't one, are you? Most such persons are unhappy with themselves for whatever reason. Since misery tremendously enjoys company, the more "guests" there are in their pity parties, the "happier" they are. (See the essays *Happiness* and *Avoiding Bitterness)*. They talk about a better life for us as people.

People need to concentrate on happiness and avoid bitterness for themselves and others. As each of us should know, one can only give what one has. If you don't have it, you can't give it. It is unreasonable to expect persons to share joy when their hearts are heavy. The same is for peace when they are feeling nothing but turmoil. Those essays tell how to find happiness and peace coming from within the people themselves.

People are usually quite generous in sharing whatever they have. Happy people experience joy in sharing their happiness. They like to invite people to their homes and serve them sumptuous meals. Unhappy people like to share what they don't like. In both happy and unhappy persons, their "spread" is plenteous!

Most of the discontent in our lives is the result of our negative thinking. Our feelings are motivated by our thoughts, and, of course, our behavior follows our feelings. We can change our outlook on life by simply changing our thinking. It isn't easy so it is so important to be around positive people who find life wonderful, rewarding and expect something grand, or just good, everyday when they wake up. Positive people see themselves blessed and ready to take on whatever comes because nothing lasts forever. The difference is the optimist sees good replacing evil and the pessimist sees evil replacing anything that's good.

What a grand day we bring on ourselves when we wake up each day being receptive to the blessing of being alive and when we can see a vase of roses, looking and smelling good sitting on our night table. Since nothing lasts forever we enjoy then as long as they are still beautiful and their fragrance continues to tickle our nostril. Ah! What a life.

Life continues to give us many free choices. Which ones we make determine whether we have a festive life or a life of pity parties. Let's enjoy life to the fullest as long as we are here on earth. Remember, nothing lasts forever! It is up to us, you know. You can reasonably guess my choice, Can't you?

**People need to concentrate on happiness
and avoid bitterness for themselves and others.**

OUR COMMON BOND

"Dear friends, since God so loved us, we ought to love one
another. If we love one another, God abides in us, and
His love has been perfected in us."
1 John 4:11-12 (NIV)

There is a common bond (thread) that runs through the fiber of
our being as humans.

When our Creator made us in His image (Genesis 2:7) we were
given the breath of life and along with the breath, a commonality of
belonging to Him. And being belonged to Him we have a common
thread. The common thread is God Himself and His unconditional
love for us which we should have for one another.

Although we were fashioned by God, He made each of us unique.
We all have different talents, gifts and abilities (1 Corinthians 12:4).

Because of our diversities we are made able to come together as
a whole and all of us together are able to accomplish great things
individually and collectively.

What do we have in common? The Bible tells us (Galatians 5:22)
that we have the fruit of the Spirit which is love, joy, peace, longsuffering,
gentleness, goodness, faith, meekness and temperance.

Unfortunately, instead of concentrating and responding to our
common bond of love and the fruit of the spirit, we become more
attentive to our differences. Our differences in cultural, ethnicity,
talents, gifts and abilities are supposed to enable all of us to strive and
enjoy the blessings from God that each person has to offer.

Being more attentive to our differences:

It is most fitting that God's intent of diversity in His creation was
to enrich our lives so that each of us would give to others according to
our abilities so that all of us would profit as a whole and His people

would enjoy life in great abundance. Unfortunately, instead of sharing, we have the "have" and the "have not" amongst us.

There are the "have" who look down on the "have not" and instead of sharing with them so they, too, can enjoy life in abundance, they keep their abundance to themselves. Consequently, all over God's world we have people without food, persons who are homeless and people who feel powerless, helpless, and hopeless. This should not be.

The thread of love that is supposed to knit us together as one has been broken so that we have become selfish and disconnected. The attitude of "what's mine is mine" has cropped up and we see no connection to one another in terms of sharing our wealth.

Our wealth:

What we consider as "our individual wealth" isn't really ours. We do have the use of it while on the earth, but once we leave earth, our wealth is left behind. So in essence our wealth is borrowed until such time as we are no longer here to enjoy it or do whatever we wish with it.

Some people blessed with wealth see it as personal power without realizing that it is God who enables them to mass great fortunes and it is God who has given them the gifts, talents, and abilities to acquire or amass such wealth. And it is God who can take all away in a blink of His eyes if He so chooses.

It is apparently true that wealthy persons worked with great determination to succeed and become wealthy, but they should not fool themselves in thinking that there wealth is "self made." If God did not give them the talent and ability, they would not have been able to amass anything. And it is God who gives the strength and ability to gain their good fortune. Theirs is a blessing to be shared so that others are blessed as well.

The thread of love that was given to us in the beginning of humankind has been broken so that we not only have people of great wealth holding onto their wealth, but we have found ourselves wasting billions of dollar fighting one another because of our philosophical differences and greed.

There are countries where the rulers are wealthy beyond being able to count their wealth while there is hunger and poverty beyond the ability to count. Do you think that is what God intended in His creation of the universe and humankind in His image?

For some people, such as the very rich there is no common bond. For the very poor who are disenfranchised, there is no common bond. And the people between the richest and the poorest, there is no common bond.

It is sad to note that wealth to the wealthy means power, and the poorest of them have not seen themselves without power. So where is the power of love?

It is not too late to work toward what God intended and still intends, but in order to do that, all of us (especially the wealthy) have to be willing to follow the will of God and work according to His purpose. Then our common bond will have meaning for all of us, and in having meaning, we would be able to come together as one body of people under God. As one body of people under God we will be able to greatly appreciate our diversities and what each culture and ethnic group brings to each other in unity.

It is sad to note that wealth to the wealthy means power, and the poorest of them have not seen themselves without power. So where is the power of love?

Our Dependent
Adult-Child and Tough Love

"When I was a child, I talked as a child; I thought like
a child, I reasoned like a child. When I became a man, I
put childish ways behind me."
I Corinthians 13:11 (NIV)

While we can "manufacture" and have many excuses for letting our adult sons and daughters become dependent on us, we have to recognize that we made them that way. Oops! What am I saying? Hear me out. This is not going to be easy for us to hear. Denial saves us from hearing the truth and doing something about it, but recognition saves our life and gives us the strength to act in our own behalf, and ultimately on the behalf of our adult-children.

Although you may be tempted to skip pass this essay because you don't want to "hear" what you know is probably going to be said, I hope you will read it anyway.

Early in life, excessive dependence began with our blessing. The "cord" was being tied when we laughed at their first show of "cuteness." But they were actually testing their boundaries, discovering what they can get away with and what they can't. Children are often wiser than we give them credit for. How many times have I heard, "He/she is only a baby?" And the child looked into the face of the parent who made the statement and gave that parent the cutest smile that made the parent want to pick up the child and hug him or her. It may seem a bit of sexism expressed here, but girls are better at this than boys are. The wise little angel knows that she has just tightened the cord.

Sweet names as "My Little Angel" or "Pudding" regardless how old they are, remain with them. Even in adulthood they unconsciously think of themselves as that. For the most part they become self-absorbed and consumed with their own importance. The parents act if their special precious child needs special attention and that attention will be unconsciously demanded by the child and consciously responded to by the parents, regardless his or her age.

Some of our adult-children may remain home or leave home for a while and return with little concern about what their parents are going through or what their responsibilities are. They are happy to live rent free, having their meals prepared, their laundry done, and if they are not working, having spending change. If they are working, they enjoy their free time (after working hours) in their social pursuits. Strangely, they seem to have less energy than their parents and often forget to do something or too tired when they parents request them to do any tasks in the home.

In essence, the parents become servants catering to their children. And what do you think happens when the parents wake up or get tired of what is going on and decide to make changes benefiting to themselves?

The adult-children do not take too kindly to the proposed changes suggesting that they move on and acquire their own living quarters. The parents may be reminded of their temper tantrums when they were tots. They stopped only when their parents gave in to them, or until the next time when they wanted something else which the parents didn't want them to have. Guess what? The same temper tantrums appear and the now older parents give in for the sake of peace.

For the sake of the parents, the break has to come and it is going to take tough love in order to get their children to become independent and self-sufficient. Tough love isn't easy. Both parents have to stand together on this issue and speak with one voice. That is the only way the parents will be able to help their children move out and become independent.

It is going to take consistent prayers, steady persistence, unlimited patience and daily words of encouragement. Of course, no one (parents and adult-children) will feel good about forcing the situation. There will be lots of guilt on the part of the parents. And they can expect anger and lots of accusations on the part of the children. Why? The answer is because the parents created the situation consciously or unconsciously.

Sometimes, our adult-children find themselves needing help, but we as parents must be sure the help we give is temporary. We must do all we can to help them get back on their feet.

Here is a panacea that shows a combination of tough love and empathy for the problem that you may find benefiting to both parents and adults. Before moving back home, a written contract on their stay should specify all their responsibilities and they should be clearly defined and expressed. Included in the contract would be rent and other expenses agreed upon. The contract should plainly state a period of time (if possible) upon which they will have to find their own place to live.

If you want to help them to save money (and you can afford to), secretly, you, can put whatever monies you require of them in the bank. And when the date of departing from your premises arrives, you can surprise them by giving them a check. But you do not give them the check until the moment you are actually saying "goodbye."

Tough love isn't easy. Both parents have to stand together and speak with one voice.

"OUT OF THE BLUE"

"No one is like you O Lord, You are great, and your
name is mighty in power."
Jeremiah 10:6 (NIV)

This statement "Out of the blue" usually refers to incidents or happenings that seem to have no reason for being. Similar to the term co-incident, it is seen as just something just happening without rhyme or reason.

In reality nothing really happens for no reason. Every thing has a purpose. Since we don't understand the purpose, we pass it off as a "co-incident" or happening "out of the blue."

There are many things happening in the universe which we cannot explain. So we make up some kind of "explanation." But those of us who believe there is Power greater than ourselves know that we are greatly influenced in many ways by the Power.

People who do not believe in a Higher Power will quickly tell others who do that there is no such thing. Trying to convince them otherwise is often futile. But some of the disbelievers will get to know differently because of some experience that affects them personally. It can be a life or death situation which they explain as "strange" that really happened to them.

Those who are fortunate to have had an experience which caused them to suddenly believe that Power beyond themselves does truly exist will enthusiastically share their experience. They will also be willing to talk with anyone who shows an interest. Although they may not try to convince others of their phenomenal awakening, they are not able to stop talking about it. As much as I believe in the Power I still get goose bumps when I hear their story.

Some of the stories are about near death experiences when they were comatose and had an out of the body experience. It seemed that their spirit separated from their body, rising to the ceiling and they were able to see their physical body in deep sleep. The spirit traveled into space toward a great bright light. In some cases they have had conversations with a heavenly being, and they were told that they have to return because it was not their time to leave this life as we know it.

Each of the many stories I have read about is different. What really interested me is that the "patient" could repeat to the doctors the conversation they had heard while their spirit ascended toward the ceiling. I would imagine the doctors were amazed and admitted that they indeed had spoken the words repeated to them. Those who have experienced the phenomenon claimed they had never experienced such euphoria in their entire life. They felt such peace and contentment that they actually wanted to stay where they were.

For those who do not believe, it would be a good thing if they, too, had an out of the body experience. I would not call these experiences out of the blue because I believe they happen for the purpose of transforming the persons who experienced them. I understand that an immediate transformation takes place and they appreciate life as we know it even better. They also have expressed, although they wanted to stay, that they have placed greater value on life here on earth.

For persons who cannot accept the fact that nothing happens by chance, it would be nice if they had some kind of wonderful experience to show them that there is more to life than what we can actually see.

A very close friend had a different heavenly experience. While in a coma his experience was that he was in a place where there were many tall slender palm trees and a gentle warm breeze. He also had sweet chamber music as if played on violins. He was torn between staying and returning to earth. He said that he heard a voice pleading with him to come back. Sure enough his wife was talking into his ear as he lay in a coma. He didn't hear the words but he felt as if he were being pulled. When he came to she was right by his bed talking into his ear, telling him how much he was loved and missed.

He lived several years after gaining conscious-ness and was never tired of telling his story. In fact, his wife encouraged him to talk about it to anyone who would listen. I, of course, was never tired of hearing it. His return to us was a miracle. It was a special blessing to have him a few more years in our lives.

For persons who cannot accept the fact that nothing happens by chance, it would be nice if they had some kind of wonderful experience to show them that there is more to life than what we can actually see.

Overlooking the Obvious

"We all stumble in many ways…"
James 3:2(NIV)

Perhaps you can relate to this essay, or you can be the rare person and this has not happened to you. But most of us have a problem with overlooking the obvious.

Try these for size: Have you ever lost your house and/or car keys and you looked thoroughly for them? After a while you looked in the same places and there they were! Why? You simply overlooked them. Here is my explanation which you do not have to buy into. It is my theory, and I honestly believe this:

We do not stay focused on any one thing but for a short time. Our mind drifts off to the past or we are thinking about what we have to do at some future time. This happens the very moment we would ordinarily see what we are looking for. The saying is "it was right under our nose!" But we didn't see it.

Some of us spend a large part of your day looking for something we had before our eyes just a split second ago. Let's do some thinking back. How many times have you rushed to answer the telephone upon entering your home? Did you put your keys where you normally do? Where did you put them? Did you leave them in the door? Did you drop them on a table in passing? Did you put them in your pocket? Did you drop them on a chair?

Of course, these questions come up when you need your keys. After you answered the phone you went about your business doing some task. And now you need your keys and you cannot remember where you put them. So what do we do now? Probably we would try to retrace our steps. But the step we don't remember is where we dropped the keys. This is what I do. I try to relax and ask God to help me out again and then I do a task and before I realize it I am miraculously drawn to the area where the keys are. And I say, "Thank you, Lord."

You and I are working at our desks and we have three sheets of paper. At the blink of our eyes one is missing. Unknowingly, it has slipped between the desk and the wall and we are wondering what on earth could have happened to it.

Now, we can become frustrated while we are looking in all of the wrong places not thinking about the floor between the desk and the wall. We have a choice. We can either get terribly frustrated or we can talk to God asking Him to help us out again. Do something else, and we will find ourselves looking on the floor under the desk and there is the paper.

Now, this may blow your mind. The thought comes to you to do a certain thing and you, of course, put it off. It slips your mind. When the time comes that you need whatever it was and you don't have it or have the information. I have learned if it is at all possible to do whatever comes to mind the very moment it comes. You will not forget what you were in the process of doing. You just go back to it later.

Have you every thought of something so strongly that you "saw" yourself doing it, but you didn't? Later, you honestly believed you had actually done it and you can tell anyone the steps you took to do it when you hadn't done it at all. It was a figment of your imagination that led you to believe that you had done what you had to do. In this case the mind registered what you plan to do step by step as if you had actually done it.

Please remember you are perfectly normal. Nobody is playing games with you. There is no invisible people in your home playing hide and seek. That is another essay you will find in this book and it was written in jest just to add a little human to my serious writings.

There is another theory which I entertain as a defense mechanism, and that is proving to myself that I am not losing it in my first octogenarian year. The theory is that we are not breathing pure oxygen because of the pollutants in the air. The brains require pure, unadulterated oxygen to function at its best. Since we are not getting it, our mind is "cloudy" and we become forgetful.

Back to the keys, it is not that we forgot where we put them. It was that we were not paying attention in our rush to get to the phone. In the case of the paper, we were not aware that it had slipped off the back of the desk. These things happened in a split second. And they happen more frequently than we care to admit.

When we leave our home and travel in the street we must be aware of where we are and what we are doing. That is no time to think about the past or the future. We need to concentrate on the NOW, what we are doing at this very moment. Anything can happen at a blink of an eye. In an instance a pocket picker can bump into us and that quickly can lift something out of our back pocket or purse. They are extremely polite, but they are not sorry. They have what they want. So we have to be careful when walking in a crowd. We cannot afford to become distracted by any activity. That is no time to get nosy in a crowd trying to see what is going on. We become fair game for someone bent on stealing.

When traveling abroad and there are so many sights to see we can easily be distracted. In my travels we have been told to stay together as a group and do not venture out on your own individual sightseeing tour. Do not stop to talk while your group is moving on. There are persons who follow tour groups, either standing in back or the middle of a group looking for the opportunity to pick a pocket or purse because they know tourists have money. They know that the persons in the group are enthralled in whatever the guide is saying and pointing out.

We are human and we do not always take responsibility for being aware of what we are doing every minute of the day. It only takes a split second for something bad to happen. We do not want to become paranoid, just be more observant. As best as we can we have to make ourselves cognizant of what is going on around us and in close proximity to us. We cannot afford to overlook the obvious. Too often, people who are up to no good are just waiting for us to not be mindful of where we are, what we are doing, and how they can get that split second to "make a killing."

Sightseeing New Yorker don't have to travel overseas. 34th and 42nd Streets are prime places for pocket picking. In fact, any crowded street in any town or big city. People out to get anyone love tourists who are fascinated with our tall building and fast city life

This has not been written to frighten anyone. Wherever we go let us go with God, being surrounded by His angels and making sure that we are listening and being obedient to whatever they whisper to us in the crowd. We do not have to worry. We can feel comfortable and enjoy ourselves.

**When we lose anything we can become frustrated
or ask God to help us again.**

OYSTERS & PEARLS

"Do not give dogs what is sacred; do not throw pearls to
pigs. If you do, they may trample them under their feet,
and then turn and tear you to pieces."
Matthew 7:6 (NIV)

Some years ago I was a representative of a business called Empress Pearls. As a representative of the company it was my enjoyable responsibility to speak to interested groups. The participants would select and purchase one or more oysters kept in a container of water. I would then ceremoniously open the oyster and reveal the pearl.

When a foreign irritant (usually sand) gets into the oyster shell, secretion produced by the oyster surrounds the irritant to keep it from harming the oyster. More secretion is produced so the oyster is well protected. (Just between us, grains of sand were deliberately injected in the oyster shell by the company).

This procedure over time formed a pearl that was either pure white, brilliant black or pink. Can you imagine yourself in the company of others, sitting on the edge of your seat watching your very own oyster shell being opened and your pearl removed?

The most exciting group I had was with pre-school children. The experience was sheer magic to them. The pre-school children ("Tiny Tots.") could fairly contain themselves, and the teachers allowed them the pleasure of having their "magical moment."

The director gave each of the little students one oyster and that is when the excitement began. This was fun time and I enjoyed it as much as they did! After all of the oysters were opened and the "magical" pearls were given to each of the twenty children, they were instructed to vote on the best pearl. The director then selected the ring setting onto which the pearl would be mounted.

I am sharing this experience with you to illustrate a point. The point is - people can become pearls. And pearls come in all colors and sizes. But when love is withheld, little people become labeled as "bad apples."

Bad Apples and Pearls

When infants are born they are pearls because of their innocence. Babies are born with great innate propensity and capacity to love. But when the love is not given they become "bad apples." Children who are neglected and emotionally, physically, and sexually abused become emotionally disturbed and psychologically damaged. Until they receive the help they need and deserve, they remain difficult to manage. Pathetically, we (society) blame the victims and categorize them as "bad apples."

When children are not protected as the oyster is, the irritant of abuse does terrible damage to them. However, I strongly believe there is hope. Love conquers all.

If emotionally and psychologically damaged children are surrounded by pure unconditional love and given some counseling and therapy, they can be saved. We as parents, teachers, ministers, professionals, community leaders and politicians should rally around our children and young people and infuse them with all the power and wherewithal we have to teach them and simultaneously protect them from the irritants in society which lead them in becoming so called bad apples.

Bad apples need "psychological surgery." The damage of the evilness they have been exposed to has to be removed, and replaced with consistent unadulterated love. Children so damaged do not trust anyone not even themselves.

According to Erik Erikson's psychosocial development, when children are not shown love in their infant stage of development, they learn mistrust, and will grow up not even trusting themselves. Because of their mistrust, they are not very willing to accept the long over due expressions of caring and loving, but eventually they will.

By the time they reach adolescence they become hardened "bad apples." However, I truly believe that as long as there is life, the situation can change. People will always desire love. But it is difficult to trust love when it has only been given sporadically and by a few significant others. .

In the attempt to give strong dosages of love, the givers must realize that they will be tested. The testing process is intense, and the only way the givers will pass the test is to be consistent and **real,** Children can spot phonies the instant they present themselves. And phonies can and will cause further damage. It will take time, patience and understanding on the part of the givers in order to be successful in helping damaged persons to heal and to mend.

Being nonjudgmental is a necessary part of belated care giving. It is not easy. Persons working in the ministry of restoring bad apples into pearls have to realize that they could have been in the same predicament as those who are labeled as bad apples.

People have to be empathetic enough to really want to understand why people are hurting and for them the only recourse is striking back. That is learned behavior and the only way it can be changed and unlearned is by receiving love which is desired and needed in order to become whole persons as they were at the time of birth.

Every person reading this essay has a responsibility to do whatever he or she can to help hurting people (young or old) to heal their broken spirit. How do we help them?

"Please, Can You Spare a Hug?"

"By this shall all men know that you are my disciples, if you have love for one another."
John 13:35 (NIV)

To approach a complete stranger with such a question would not only surprise the person, it may cause him or her to wonder about your motive. Indeed, your sanity may be questioned.

While working as a houseparent in a sleep-in position in the Department of Social Services, Group Homes Division, I became known as "the hugger." You would often hear, "Here comes the hugger!"

Although for the most part they acted as if they didn't want to be hugged, they secretly wanted the indication of love and recognition. Many were unaccustomed to hugging because they were from families that did not display much affection, if any at all. But over time they began to ask me for hugs.

While attending a weekend child care seminar, I took advantage of the hugging workshop. It was quite interesting and much of which I learned and experienced with the young people entrusted in my charge I will share in this essay.

I learned that appropriately hugging is therapeutic and it helps to elevate the self-esteem of the ones being hugged. In fact the hugger and the hugged benefited from the exercise.

Hugging encourages conversation and effective conversation requires more listening than talking. Hugging makes possible a break through which affords introverts to open up and share (expose, if you will) a piece of themselves that they would never dare to otherwise.

Hugging workshop learning and experience:

First, the hugging must be real. This means it must come from the heart. People very quickly detect and feel when it isn't real, a hug that is not real makes a person feel uncomfortable. When it comes from the heart, it is felt as warm and comfortable.

What the workshop did was to allow participants to discuss their feelings after hugging. We discussed the feeling of recognition, acceptance, validation and level of comfort.

The weekend seminars we attended were found to be of such great interest that three of us decided to travel to Sweden, Russia and Denmark for further child care studies. From our studies we learned proper or appropriate application of discipline measures when working with abused children in the foster care system who found themselves separated from their families. Even abroad hugging was one of the topics discussed and role played.

I vividly recall visiting a day nursery and a two year old male child ran to me and gave me a very tight hug. Sadly, the visit was extremely brief and the young lad did not want to break the hug. I asked to remain there a few more minutes. A picture was taken for him to keep from an instant camera. That pleased him greatly.

In the group homes:

With hugging came a wonderful gamut of social interactions which helped all persons, (younger and older) feel good about themselves and they felt freer to express themselves in ways acceptable to themselves and society. For example: There was less name calling and when they got angry with the staff, they learned more appropriate ways to let their anger become known. And staff and residents learned how to respond rather than react which eliminated unnecessary hassles and reduced the escalation of negative behavior.

A note of caution dictated that child care workers of the opposite sex of the children in their care had to be careful how they hugged. Children who were not hugged at home often misinterpreted the physical contact. It was only when spontaneity clearly indicated a hug was needed, desired and respected and not interpreted as "hitting on" anyone and was not felt to be inappropriate. Under other circumstances where sexual identity was concerned, workers and young people of the same sex had to be cautious. The avoidance of giving the wrong message was paramount.

Basically, children learn to hug in infancy, but if it is not continued throughout their growth and development, it becomes somewhat foreign and uncomfortable. And in situations where the children were inappropriately hugged, as in a sexual way, hugs can be misinterpreted.

The three of us who had the occasion to travel abroad applied what we learned in our homes which became #1 in terms of overall effectiveness and the exemplary behavior of the residents.

Along with hugging, slapping fives, words of encouragement and recognition played major roles in the young people's behavior and pride in themselves and their home.

Young people will primarily give what is expected of them. Positive feedback and encouragement were paramount in their meeting the expectations of the caregivers.

Never feel bashful in asking for a hug if you need one. Because a hug is a sign of God's love. If you are perceptive to His "daily hugs," you are blessed indeed. And the way to share this blessing is to extend the hugs to someone who needs just that.

Basically, children learn to hug in infancy, but if it is not continued throughout their growth and development, it becomes foreign and uncomfortable.

PSEUDO-POWER
AND REAL POWER

*"For we do not dare classify or compare ourselves with
some who commend themselves. When they measure
themselves by themselves, they are not wise."*
2 Corinthians 10:12 (NIV)

There is a saying "it takes all kinds (of people) to make a world." This is true. And what a wonderful world this would be if we all welcomed and appreciated our differences.

The right blend of spices makes for a world rich in harmony and exquisite tastes.

Let us look at the real world as we experience daily. There are two kinds of people in our world that I would like to focus on in this essay. **The first** are those who feel helpless, hopeless, and powerless. With appropriate intervention they can be helped. One means of helping would be those persons involving themselves in a group with trained, qualified and professional persons facilitating the group. The so called helpless, hopeless, and powerless will find themselves able to help one another overcoming their feelings of being disenfranchised and alone to face the world.

Being involved within a group will afford them the opportunity to shake off their self-afflicted stigma that they find themselves stuck with. They, through their own self-help intervention will be able to become powerful; **that is with real power that God intends for us to have.**

The other group of people I refer to is those with "pseudo-power." Unlike those who feel powerless, this group has a false sense of power which is sometimes overbearing. This leads to many problems in their day to day interaction with loved ones, significant others, and associates if they are allowed by others to impose upon their peace, sense of security, joy and happiness.

This group is comprised of persons who either or within a thin line of emotional instability or have deeper manifestations of mental disorder. They are usually brilliant, highly intelligent individuals who are able to (unfortunately) convince others to their way of thinking. For the most part, those who are on the borderline are less detectable.

All persons we refer to as "normal" have idiosyncrasies which we tend to ignore by simply saying, "He or she is a little peculiar." However, when dealing with persons who have slipped over the mental border line we seem to tolerate them in their offbeat behavior because we do not want to make "waves."

I view the extent of emotional or mental disorders as "luke warm," "very warm," and "hot." Luke warm persons we tend to ignore their behavior. They fall in the category of somewhat peculiar which we pass off as "each of us has a right to be because variety is the spice of life."

Help is not always provided for the very warm (almost hot) persons who are troublesome because of their functioning from what appears to be normal to the really strange. Those persons do not cause any real harm. Nevertheless, they can be very influential because of the intellect and ability to express themselves using their very extensive vocabulary and manipulative acumen. Too often associates are so impressed by this that they follow along. The following along equips the problematic luke warm persons with pseudo-power.

The "hot" are receiving help according to the extent of their behavior and how safe they are to themselves and others. Along with this comes medication. The writer is not dwelling on this type of disorder because of having a better understanding, sympathy and empathy for those persons who actually cannot help themselves.

What happens in the luke warm and very warm cases is people who do not want to "rock the boat," in some instances, are persuaded to agree with the persons causing friction, and sometimes sabotaging something needed, beneficial or helpful. And, of course, others who are not as knowledgeable are swayed by smooth talking, well phrased comments and misquotes. Persons going along with them enable them to function in a manner which is not very healthy for others who may be affected by their behavior.

Some of the indicating signs of the very warm category are (1) disruptive behavior and validation of other persons' comments either negative or positive depending on how well the persons are liked or not liked at any given time, (2) speaking or not speaking to others according to the mood the luke warm person is in, (3) moodiness for no apparent reason, (4) having all the answers and can do anything better than anyone else, (5) will, if allowed, take over the leadership of the group in which they are a member, (6) very supportive to the leader if the leader succumbs to their power or gives them leadership leverage, (7) ridiculing the leader behind his/her back or will inappropriately chastise the leader and other members because of their judgment of the leader's inaptitude or inability to function effectively according to their standard of what functioning effectively is.

Even though the above are very obvious, no one seems to want to take on those persons regardless how nicely it is done, they resent being addressed and will make a major scene. Unfortunately, these persons attract others who are suffering with the same condition and they become codependent. We all know that is strength in numbers. Well, those persons certainly know how to gather and use their strength to the detriment of the character of others or the worthwhile of needed programs.

Although this may appear difficult in rectifying, it isn't. Pseudo-power is only possible by giving in to the persons. Their action is really a cry for help, but it reminds me of the tale of the snake when he asked to be put into the bosom of a woman for safety sake. When the woman complied, the snake bit her and reminded her that after all he was a snake. Cutting out the fang would have rendered the snake harmless. By the same token not giving in to them leaves them without the power to harm, hurt, and offend. In fact, it would leave them powerless.

It is through God that we are given real power and it is the power of God through the Holy Spirit that we are able to be whole persons enjoying the peace, joy, happiness, tranquility and prosperity we were created to enjoy.

**It is through God that we are given real power
which He intends for us to have.**

STUDENTS:
PASSING AND EXCELLING

"Whoever loves discipline loves knowledge, but he who
hates correction is stupid."
Proverbs 12:2 (NIV)

At the time this book was written I had enjoyed fifteen and one half years as an adjunct professor at Touro College in the Human Services Department, since retiring from the Department of Social Services.

There are no words to adequately describe my joy in seeing consumers being molded into students and students passing and excelling and moving on in their chosen professions. It is such a joy to see academic transformation unfolding from their very first semester to their final semester and seeing the students walk across the grand stage at graduation. It is an educator's delight!

This essay primarily speaks to persons of all ages who are either in college (or any school) or who are contemplating attending college and graduate school to earn their degrees. It is never too late. I was fifty-five years of age as a freshman, twenty-five years ago. The time was "ripe" for me. So when you find that the time is "ripe" for you, regardless to whatever age, I urge you to "go for it!"

My experiences as a student, a professional, and an educator have empowered me as I moved forward in each facet of my life. It is then my good pleasure to share with you what I have learned in terms of learning and teaching so that you will be able to pass and excel in your courses of study.

This essay continues on the assumption that you are now a student (younger or older). I am taking the liberty to give you some pointers on how to pass with high grades so that you may be able to obtain a scholarship for graduate school.

Here are five steps to class room learning:

Step 1 – Listen, stay focused, pay attention, do not allow yourself to be distracted by conversation with another student, question what you don't understand, use your dictionary to look up unfamiliar words. Take your dictionary to each class.

Step 2 – Take notes, but not word for word. Develop your own code or shorthand so you can keep up with the lecture or discussion. (Your professor/lecturer is not going to tell you how to spell anything).

Step 3 - Review your notes at home to be sure that you have grasped all that was given in class. If further clarity is needed, ask your professor. Another student may not have recorded the information correctly.

Step 4 - Read what your instructor has assigned for discussion in the next session. If the material you have been assigned to read is complication and/or complex, read it anyway. Warning: Do not stop reading because you are finding it difficult. When you get to class, and as the assignment is being discussed, it will become clear and you will find yourself getting excited and more interested in class discussions.

Step 5 - Participate in the discussion, but do not monopolize the discussion.

Rely upon your ability to learn. It is a matter of desiring to learn. Participate in role playing if you have them in your classes. It is a wonderful learning tool. Do not be afraid of making mistakes; they help you to learn.

The only person you should compete against is yourself. Do not compare yourself with other students. If you made a "B" on a test, and you desire to do better, fine but make sure it is because you want to better yourself, not because other students made higher grades.

Depending upon the course, internalize rather than memorize what is being taught or read. Why is this important? Internalizing enables you to visualize and "feel" what you are hearing or reading. Embodied in internalizing are some emotions (feelings) and that will help you to retain the information. Memorizing is learning word for word, and there is no guarantee that you know what you have memorized.

Of course, if you are taking courses in any of the physical sciences, you have to learn formula and that is done through the process of memorization. However, if there is any opportunity for internalization, by all means, include it.

Mentally remove any stumbling block that can keep you from learning. It is up to you. The brain is willing to work with you 100%. Don't tell yourself that you can't do anything. It will store whatever knowledge you want to retain.

The only person you have to prove anything to is yourself! You don't have to prove anything to your professors, fellow students, friends, parents or close associates. But you do need to show yourself that you are a winner as a student and whatever your desires are in life. Philippians 4:13 says, "I can do all things through Christ who strengthens me." If you ever experience moments of doubt, internalize that verse, and see yourself doing what you want to do.

Passing and even excelling are within your grasp, but you have to work at it and with it. I hope you get the opportunity to read another essay in this book, *The Brain: Your Innate Personal Computer."*

Now, for the person whom I assume is in college but isn't, and you are pondering whether you should go or not, by all means go! I was fifty-five when I stepped foot in my school as freshman. There were other students older than fifty. Each year you hear of someone graduating in their 70s, 80s, and 90s. We are never too old to learn. If you are sincere and determined, you will find younger students wanting to be your study partner or wanting you for a study partner. Because of your life experiences you will bring much to the class room, benefiting your fellow students and your young professors. Your longevity, professional, and worldly experiences will be a great asset to all listening to what you have to say in class. They will listen with rapt attention. And do not be surprised by seeing your fellow students taking notes.

Most college will give you life experience credits which means that you will graduate in less than four years. Inquire when you apply to any college of your choice.

As an educator I would love to hear from you. I would consider it indeed a blessing if we can correspond so that I can encourage you as you enjoy your academic experiences, passing and excelling.

The only person you have to prove anything to is yourself!

SWEET PEOPLE WITH FLAWS

"Blessed are they whose transgressions are forgiven,
whose sins are covered."
Romans 4:8 (NIV)

In order to be flawless we have to be perfect, pure, without sin of any kind. Humankind cannot be flawless because we tend to follow our own mind. In following our own mind we learn early as young children to rationalize. In rationalizing we find convenient excuses to "justify" whatever action or behavior we want to involve ourselves in.

There are some people who can be considered "sweet" but they are not flawless. Every living person makes mistakes during his or her life time. To be able to recognize our mistakes and correct them, if they are correctible, is a good thing and we will grow as well as learn to do whatever it takes to avoid repeating them.

Some people are able to move on and not be defeated by mistakes. Others seem to get caught in a web and keep on making the same mistakes. Those persons have a tendency to blame others. So as long as they blame others they do not see the error of their ways, and so they keep on making old and avoidable mistakes.

There are also persons who make mistakes but they are sweet people. What make them sweet are their disposition, attitude, and ability to laugh at themselves. Even though they make mistakes they are able to move on. They are also able to recognize that just a little carelessness or not being focused on what they are doing, allowed the mistake to happen,

For a brief moment this essay will dwell a little on those of us who find it very difficult to move on after making a mistake. In suggesting some reasons for this seemingly inability to pick up the pieces and move on and upward, I will attempt to show that things can change if we want them to

Here are some questions we can answer for ourselves. No one else needs to know our answers, but it is so important for us to be honest with ourselves and answer each question truthfully. This is so important because the only way we will be able to take ownership of our shortcomings is to recognize and become aware of the harm we cause ourselves. Some questions I am posing to you are: Are you more concerned about what others think of you than what you think of yourself? For the most part are you trying to please others when you are not pleased with yourself? Do you find yourself needing to be validated? Are you more concerned about what others think rather than what you think when it comes to making decisions concerning yourself? Are you easily discouraged? Are you afraid to try new things? Do you believe in trying to do the impossible? Do you know what the impossible is? The impossible is simply not being able to do a certain thing within our human ability, but relying on Spiritual ability, all things are possible to those who believe.

If you have honestly answered the questions and you truly desire to become more comfortable with yourself, you have to realize that making mistakes is just a part of life. Everyone makes them. Don't let yours cripple you. Forgive yourself!

I dare to say there are more people who love you than you may realize, but the real question is do you love yourself? If you do not want to hurt the people you love, why do you consistently do things to hurt yourself? When you allow other people to dictate what is good or not good for you, you are putting them in control of your life. There is no such thing as "co-controlling" They either control you or you control yourself. Now, when you attempt to break away from their control, they are not giving up the power that you have given them too easily. So this means that you have to be very determined to not let them over power you anymore. You owe this to yourself and you owe them nothing. You can expect them to lay guilt trips on you, but then you have to realize them for what they are and keep struggling to be your own boss.

This is not to say that you don't listen to the suggestions of others, but after listening and weighing what you hear, you are the one to make the decision. While making decisions, you may make some mistakes, so what? Some of the mistakes may turn out to be blessings. But the main thing is, good or bad; you are your own boss. And being your own boss should give you a good feeling and greater strength to stand up for what you want and who you are. Your own sweetness will not only be felt by you, but seen and felt by others, even those who tried to control you. In the long run, even they will admire you, respect you, and even consult you for advice or suggestions.

**There are also persons who make mistakes, but they are sweet people.
What make them sweet are their disposition, attitude, and ability to laugh at themselves.**

Stubbornness

"…they stumble because they disobeyed the messenger -
which is also what they were destined for."
I Peter 2:8 (NIV)

For the benefit of this essay, I looked up "stubborn." My Webster's New Universal Unabridged Dictionary (1983) listed many synonyms: a few them are harsh, rough, rugged, obstinate, tough, unyielding, hard, intractable, obdurate, stiff, inflexible, headstrong, pigheaded and contumacious. I like sound of the last word listed (contumacious), so I looked it up. The synonyms were insubordinate, rebellious, disobedient, and willfully resisting authority. Do you know of anyone who presents such traits? Before you get too happy about Mr. Webster agreeing with you in your dealing with someone in your charge, read this essay to the end.

Let us take some of the synonyms and place them in either a positive or negative category. While we are listing them, let's give some positive thought to using words as consistency, persistency, determination, toughness, unyielding, obstinate, rugged, and, perhaps, rough. The saying is,"when the going gets tough, the tough gets going." That, to my mind, means hanging in there to the completion of the task no matter what! It also means letting nothing defeat you. Another saying is,"nothing ventured, nothing gained." That is if you don't try you cannot accomplish anything.

Too often when we "decide" that something is too much for people in our charge so we try to discourage them from either trying or staying with it because it appears too difficult for us, and we are not able to accomplish the task. But, you see, it takes a person who is tough, rough, unyielding, obstinate, rugged in his or her ability to tackle a hard task and get it done.

We who are in charge of younger folk sometimes get agitated because they are stubborn and refuse to obey our demand to "give it up." Using the new word that I like so much, since the *contumacious* person ignores our demands and is willfully resistant to our authority; we call him or her rebellious.

Such a person visualizes the finished product while working to bring the task to completion. We see an impossible task. Many inventions took a long time to materialize, but the inventors could "see" the results of their dream. If they had allowed themselves to succumb to our demands to quit, many inventions would not have been made.

Sometimes in our persistence, there is an occurrence called serendipity. That is simply a thing happening either by accident or by doing something unintentional and it works well. I would imagine some new recipes have been recorded because a dash of this or too much of that was used unintentionally. It could also be possible that a machine that was to be used for one purpose did not work, but it was the ideal piece of equipment for something else and earned a fortune for the inventor who was "too stubborn" to give in to defeat.

The stubborn one in your household may be a budding genius. With his or her tenacity, disobedience and defying nature, he or she kept on doing what he or she had been instructed not to do. An example of this is a child who possesses strange powerful imagination comes up with stories that you see is that of a "psychopathic liar." That, of course, makes you fearful. That person may have the makings of a genius in creating and writing horror and gruesome stories. Remember Alfred Hitchcock?

How about one of your charges appearing as a clown when you want him or her to be more serious and act as he or she "had some sense?" Everyone finds him or her funny and enjoys what the person comes up with, while you are consumed by embarrassment.

Later in the person's life, he or she becomes famous as a comedian. You may find yourself secretly pleased that he or she did not listen to you and did his or her own thing. In such a case, would you still consider the person defying, disobedient, hardheaded, pigheaded, disrespectful or stubborn?

Indeed, those words can prove to be negative and cause harm to others in your charge or to himself or herself, if the person seems to have a propensity to be destructive. Rather than be led your own assumption, it pays to communicate with the one we so quickly unjustly label. While in the process of communicating, it pays to ask pertinent questions, listen and encourage the person to share his or her thoughts and feelings.

Your enthusiasm will greatly encourage your wards to share some of their deep feelings about what they are doing and why they are doing it. We must not be too quick to assume that something is negative simply because we do not understand what is going on. If we want or need to know, the only way to find out is to show interest in positive ways. Ridiculing because of unwarranted suspicion will cause problems and a "wall" to be built between you and the one you are responsible for.

Surely, any child spending too much time alone unsupervised can create harmful ways of expressing his or her frustration. Know what they are doing, what they think, how they feel about you, society and themselves

Every quiet child is not always "nice" or "up to something." But how would you know unless you have a good working relationship with him or her? All of us are due a certain amount of privacy. How much is determined by how much you really know about him or her and what he or she is really doing according to his or her expressed interest. It's foolhardy not knowing the interests of a child we are responsible for,

Now that we understand stubbornness a little better, perhaps we can be less fearful and more knowledgeable about persons we are responsible for. We are, and will always be, responsible for the behavior of under age young people, according to what society determines what "under age" is. The question is do we have a budding genius or a person bent on destruction?

We should know because we are placed with the awesome responsibility of being the one in charge, I shudder to think that we allow our under age persons to make major decisions without input and guidance from us who are, by law, responsible for their behavior and positive interaction in society.

"When the going gets tough, the tough gets going."

Talking and Communicating

If Alexander Graham Bell who invented the telephone were alive today, I wonder what he would have to say about cell phones. There seems to be an awful lot of talking on them. Every where one goes he or she sees and hears people talking on their cell phone.

However, talking is one thing and communicating is quite another. The difference is one can talk but there is no guarantee that the other party is listening. Communicating requires an exchange of words between the persons. And in order for the other party to respond, he or she has to listen.

Talking about communicating, can you imagine how peaceful, loving, and wonderful our world would be if we communicated with God and we were obedient to what He tells us?

We find it so easy talking (and hopefully communicating) with our friends, family and associates, yet when we mention communicating with God people seem to shy away.

We seem to have no problem communicating with people we know. And the reason for that is we feel comfortable with such persons.

Can you imagine how much better we would be if we got to know God? Many of us profess to know Him and others unfortunately claim they do not believe in Him.

Those of us who profess knowing Him need to tighten our relationship with Him so we can introduce Him as a Loved One to non-believers. Being able to do this depends on the way we privately and publicly conduct ourselves, as we go about our daily business and activities.

Whether we realize it or not, every person is observed by others. They observe the way we **talk and walk**. Our actions tell more about us than what we can say about ourselves.

We are always "communicating" even if we do not utter a word, but when we do speak, it should be in line with our behavior.

Dr. Melvin R. Hall

Although we talk a lot, we communicate much more by what we do. As you daily observe people, what do you see?

**We have no problem communicating with people
we know.**

TALKING TO OURSELVES

*"There is a time for everything, and a season for every
activity under heaven:
…a time to be silent and a time to speak."*
Ecclesiastes 3:1, 7 (NIV)

I would be the first to admit that I talk to myself, and I like what I am hearing, I answer. Am I crazy? Yes, I 'm crazy enough to not allow myself to become engaged in supercilious conversations, crazy enough not to get bent out of shape because someone's ridiculous opinion of me, crazy enough to listen to the voice in my head that tells me what I'm doing is not right and crazy enough to follow through with positive action rather than stay on the path of destruction.

You may laugh, but I'm willing to bet that you talk to yourself. Let's test this. Have you found yourself wondering out loud what you should do about something and the answer comes, and then you say,"Yes, that's what I can do!" Let's face it, you are crazy, too!

Never mind what anyone says, professional or layman; talking to yourself is healthy. So you have to be a little crazy to be healthy. And you definitely have to be a little crazy to survive in this crazy world. It is crazy because we made it so. Everything was okay and until the world was populated. Take a look at Genesis and read what Adam and Eve did that was absolutely crazy in allowing themselves to be beguiled by a serpent.

You know talking to ourselves is better than answering people who are trying to provoke us into an argument. As we talk to ourselves, they are thinking that we are talking to them and they are foolish enough to get angry. Talking about crazy, which of us are really crazy?

Have you ever been talking to yourself in a different room and someone asked you what you were saying? And when you told them you were talking to yourself they asked, "What about?" How crazy can that person be?

Now, I have come to the conclusion that there are two phases of craziness. One is positive and the other is negative. The core of this essay is on the positive. You may not see anything positive about being crazy, but I hope by the time you complete reading this you will meet me halfway in my thinking. So read slowly because it is going to take some serious pondering for you to get and accept my "drift."

You must have heard the expression, "It is better to be thought a fool, than to speak up and remove all doubt." Let us then say it is better that we are thought to be crazy than to act out and remove all doubt. Many times in life people will try to provoke us into being absolutely stupid. When they succeed we have proven to them that we are no better than they. Now, if we are prone to acting out by being easily provoked, we prove to our enemies or so called "friends" that we are crazy indeed.

The only reason why they attempt to provoke us is that they are jealous of us and they are trying to take us down to their level. When they succeed, they feel less bad about themselves because we are thought of and seen on a higher plane or level then they. While they are trying to pull us down, we need to talk to and remind ourselves that we are better than they, and we do not want to put ourselves where they have placed themselves. So what if they think we are crazy because we are talking to ourselves? Remember, we have to be a little crazy to live in this crazy world. But our craziness is positive while theirs is negative.

If we handle correctly what is happening in our cool heads, we may encourage them to emulate us. And by doing so, they will gain the respect we enjoy. I am willing to bet that we will have gained good and loving friends.

A little talking to ourselves will not hurt, but the warning is we must not talk too much above a whisper. Otherwise, we will draw attention to ourselves and the "authorities" may restrain us and take us to "professionals" who might just want to check us out for saneness. But if we do talk to ourselves in public, we should have our cell phone visible, but still do not talk too loud so as not to disturb others. We should be as creative as we can in public, but when home alone, talk as loud as we please as long as our neighbors are not disturbed. You know how thin the walls are in an apartment!

You know talking to ourselves is better than answering people who are trying to provoke us into an argument.

TEARS OF JOY

"These things I have spoken unto you, that My joy might
remain in you, and that your joy may be full."
John 15:11 (KJV)

Usually, when we see someone cry we think it is from something sad or bad or negative, but the best cry ever is one of sheer joy. Something good is happening and the only thing we can do at the moment is let the tears fall.

This is true of any person, but it seems to me that the tears of a happy child or man are most moving. First of all, a happy child is extremely contagious. We seem to identify with the child. We can almost feel the joy of the child. Now with a man, most of the time we as men try to stifle the tears, but when joy is felt, we cannot hold back. The more we try the harder it is to keep from crying. It may be a little embarrassing to some men who are not used to showing emotion, but at the same time it feels so good.

This brings to mind another thought and that is what other men feel when they see a brother tearing or crying. Some can't help but tear themselves. Others are embarrassed and feel that it is unmanly. However, there is no denying that it is therapeutic when a man cries.

If only all of us would not put so much effort in restraining our positive emotions, we would find others in our presence feeling more comfortable. For some strange reason we tend to think that showing our emotions in positive ways is a gender thing, that a man is supposed to be so tough that he should not show any softness. Well, Jesus as a man wept when he arrived at his friend's Lazarus tomb. As a Christian, He is our example. So if He wept so should we as men be able to, although his weeping was not from joy. Whatever the reason we weep it is right and proper that men show their strength in tearing or weeping.

The question that may arise in the reader's mind is if there is a difference between tearing, weeping and crying? Tearing seems to imply rather subtle weeping. For all practically purposes, crying and weeping seem to have the same degree of display of sadness. I love the biblical phrase, "Mourning endures for a night, but joy comes in the morning."

Although we (as men) think we are not being emotional, we express ourselves emotionally in negative ways. We sometimes avoid showing softness in matters of the heart, but are quick to show anger which is an emotion and we misguidedly think that is what men should do. Well, it may be what some men do, but that does not make it right. Our women-folk would much rather see a softer part of our nature that shows kindness and compassion.

Haven't you heard stories of grandfathers being kind and compassionate? Many a young man has opted to be just like his grandpa. Children learn more about being gentle from growing up and being in the company of men who are not only gentlemen, but gentle men.

Time has changed from the rugged days of the Wild West where men had to be rough and tough to survive. In those days the softness of a man made it difficult to live among men. In those days only the strong survived. For the most part, the men respected their women, but they showed a rough side to other men. In the changing of time, many other things gender-wise have changed. Can you imagine what an early pioneer would think of such a term as house-husband?

As the time has changed so must we. We don't live that kind of rugged life anymore. If a couple decides to change housekeeping and working roles, that is their business and no one should interfere with what works for them. People in their relationship have to do what brings them joy, peace, contentment and happiness.

As long as all of us work diligently toward keeping God's joy within our hearts, household, place of employment, and in our place of worship and wherever we go, we will experience the fullness of joy. Joy is contagious. And because it is, we can affect all of the people with whom we come in contact. So each man, woman and child should let his or her joy be known.

Children learn more about being gentle from growing up and being in the company of men who are not only gentlemen, but gentle men.

TELEPATHIC COMMUNICATION

"There are different kinds of gifts, but the same Spirit"
I Corinthian 12:4 (NIV)

Are you aware that every human (at times) communicates with others through mental telepathy? Do you know what mental telepathy is? Communicating by the spoken word is known to everyone as soon as we learned to talk. But before were able to able to talk we communicated non-verbally, and I might add, babies are most effective non-verbal communicators. We continue to communicate non-verbally the rest of our lives.

As strange as this may sound, the body language of an infant is usually clearer than some adults. To be sure of an adult's "messages," we sometimes have to ask questions. With a baby, as soon as we respond to his or her needs, the baby communicates his or her appreciation with a smile or coos and then drifts off to sleep.

All this was said to spring a surprise on some of you. The subject to expound on is prayer. For those of us who believe in God, we pray two ways – one with our thoughts and the other with spoken words. Even unbelievers may say, "Oh God!" Or "God help me!" when they are caught in an unhappy, dangerous, or disturbing situation.

Although the concentration of prayer will be for believers, I am respectfully asking that non-believers continue to read this essay. There may be a few surprises for you. At least you can whet your curiosity as to what this believer has to say about telepathic communication. I must add, however, that the utterances cried out in the above paragraph were not telepathic but spoken.

Telepathic Communication:

Telepathic communication is communicating mind to mind with others without any words spoken. Prayer is communicating from mind to mind with God, using or not using the spoken word. The beauty of this is that there is no specific time limit to our doing so. God's lines are open 24/7 all of our lives. He always answers with" Yes," Not now," or "I have something better for you." You will not hear those words, but your trust, faith and belief tells you He does answer.

Some very strong believers do not feel comfortable talking to God in the presence of others. That's okay. The reason why they may not feel comfortable is because they are overly concerned what others may think or say. This would not be a concern if they concentrated on God and not the people. Let me give you an example: If you are talking to a friend about something important but not confidential, you would not hesitate to speak to your friend regardless who may overhear. Once we learn how to give our thoughts and feelings to God, we will no longer concern ourselves with what others may think or say.

Telepathic communication allows us to share thoughts mind to mind even when in the company of others. In prayer there should be total concentration of our mind to God's mind and we should be able to "shut out" our surroundings in our work place, while using public transportation, or any place where there are people. In our home we can speak words or we can send messages telepathically. God receives our messages and loves the communication in whatever form we use.

Effective communication is achieved when there is an effective sender and an effective receiver. The joy of communicating with God is that one does not have to be perfectly clear as He knows what is in our hearts, and He knows that we are not always good at expressing our thoughts and feelings. When we are communicating with another human being, we must be clear or we will cause misunderstanding and create ill-will, to say the least of what can happen when we lack clarity.

How does mental telepathy work in communicating with others? Mental messages are transmitted by energy. What is energy? According to Webster's unabridged dictionary there are many definitions. But the one relevant to this topic is unseen "strength of expression." Simply put, it is a very powerful force that cannot be seen. However, since it is so powerful it can and will be felt by the receiver of the "message." I think an example is needed here. Have you ever felt something strange and you turned around or looked directly at a person staring at you? Well, the stare got your attention. Another example is your sudden desire to call a person. As soon as you dial, the same person says, "My goodness, I was just thinking of you and I was just about to dial you when the phone rang. What a surprise this is!"

What is important to be aware of is that only persons that you are very close to can you connect to in this manner. This is because love itself is energy and to concentrate on loved one is sending a message. They will feel your energy or "vibes" which some call energy. When a loved one is ill or in trouble, you will know something is wrong. Your thoughts remain on that person for a time and the feeling you have is an uneasy one.

There is so much going on because of the energy in our atmosphere and universe. We are affected in some ways by what is happening. Because you cannot see anything does not mean nothing is happening. You do not have to fear what is going on if you are communicating steadily with the One who created the universe and all its mysteries.

Sometimes God tries to reach us and warn us of something that is potentially dangerous or harmful to us. A good example of this is meeting a possible mate. This person from all appearances seems to be the special person you have always wanted to share your life with. The head is telling you of the person's good looks and charm. The heart is telling you to not move too fast and not get close to the person because something is wrong. The head sees what it wants and is often blindsided while the heart speaks the truth and tries to protect us. But if the head is bent on following its own sensations, there may be some trouble ahead.

Perhaps this essay will enable you to look into the possibility and probability of telepathic communication. Remember, much in this universe (all around us) is unseen. And to take the position "seeing is believing" can really cause some problems that we can avoid. *Judging a Book by its Cover* is a **must read** essay in this book that relates to believing in something that appears to be but isn't.

To those who believe and follow their intuition, there are many wonderful surprises. That is a form of communication closely related to telepathic communication. Let's enhance our lives by giving more attention to the art or skill of communication, especially telepathic communication.

Effective communication is achieved when there is an effective sender and an effective receiver.

"THANK YOU!"

"We ought to always thank God for you, brothers and
rightly so because your faith is growing more and more,
and the love everyone has for each other is increasing."
2 Thessalonians 1:3 (NIV)

This essay is about saying "Thank you" and the ramification of those two words. One would think such an essay would not be needed, but I think you will agree with me that there are people passed five years old who need to learn how to show their gratitude and express their thankfulness.

Before I continue this theme let me take the opportunity to thank you for purchasing this book of essays. I trust that you will receive as much joy in reading it as it was for me to write it. My essay "To God be the Glory" expresses my deep commitment to all of God's people to encourage them to be all they can be not only for themselves but for, and to, everyone they greet and meet.

Learning to acknowledge kindnesses and express my appreciation by sending thank you notes has been a part of me for as long as I can remember. Being a sentimentalist (encouraged by my mother who passed away when I was 13 years old) I love those two beautiful words, "Thank you!"

That is why I find it so hard to understand why our children beyond age five seldom, if at all, say those two little words. I cannot count the times that I expected to hear those words from people I have been blessed to help in some way. Not all children have been neglectful in saying thank you, but there are enough to be alarmed about.

Surely, all of us like to know that whatever we have done on behalf of others is appreciated. Sometimes I wonder if people of all ages truly appreciate what someone does for them when they didn't have to.

I have heard so many people complain because they didn't know if whatever was done was actually received. Packages have been sent and without asking, persons wouldn't have known they were received.

I would like to know what has happened that we no longer find this important or necessary. I know that little children are taught, but my experience has been children no longer are encouraged to express their gratitude.

Early in their growth and development I have heard parents (particularly mothers) say to their child who has been given something, "What do you say?" and the child says, "Thank you!" Later as they grow older I have not heard the words from the same children and their parents say nothing to them as a reminder of what they used to encourage.

Does this bother me? Yes, it does and it should bother you. I guess I am just old fashion and you know what? I am glad I am. Values should never grow old. Respect should never grow old. Decency should never grow old. They have always been with some families and should be with all families. Culture should have nothing to do with it. Ethnicity should have nothing to do with it. Words of thanks and appreciation are spoken in every language and they should be valued in every language.

While I am on the subject of teaching our children and giving them a frame of reference to live by until their dying day, I must state my pet peeve and that is parents having to tell their children over and over the same things to get them to be obedient. Children quickly learn how to be passively aggressive and get away with it. Instead of working with their children and letting them know certain behaviors will absolutely not be tolerated, they complain in their children's presence that they can do nothing with them. I have heard this and I have seen it. And although there was no humor in the statement I had to laugh (to myself) because they are telling the children that they have won. Can you believe I heard a mother say this in front of her three year old and can you imagine what the child learned in that instance? She learned that she at three is in control so whenever her mother gives her any instructions, they child sings her "no" song and begins her passive aggressive behavior and once that starts it is hard to break. But it can be broken! (See the essay, *Dealing with Passive-Aggressive Behavior.*)

In the parent-child relationship I am not saying that all of the old parent-child relationships I experienced have to be today, but there are basic ones having to do with good manners, respect, appreciation, and treating others as we wish to be treated. Is there anything wrong with that? We had poverty back then and struggled to make ends meet, but it was not used as an excuse for not being responsible as parents.

I understand from many of my friends who are teachers, that children bring their parents to beat up the teachers who are trying to discipline them as students. The "little angels" are given another lesson by their parents, and that is, they don't have to respect anyone in authority. Parents don't even know that beyond school age they will be summoned to court for the same angels who are no longer in school but older and on their way to prison for advance education.

The bad language parents use on their children only reinforces bad behavior. The screaming and the cursing teach the children a frame of reference which will be carried over to the next generation.

You may ask how did we get from saying "Thank you" to parenting children Embodied in parenting is all of that and it begins with showing gratitude and expressing thanks.

Persons who find that life itself is a blessing and are grateful for it, have no problem being thankful that every day is a new opportunity to be grateful for all of our blessings, big and small, known and unknown and we teach our children how these blessings came to be.

Is there hope? Of course there is! Parents who are finding it difficult raising the babies they chose to have can get help by asking. There are agencies and programs giving assistance in parenting. Why not make contact with your religious institutions in your community as a beginning? From there you will be assisted and directed to professional help. Meantime, we have to begin to show our appreciation by simply uttering two words each time someone blesses us in any way. Whenever some asks you how you are and you respond with, "Fine, thank you!" That could be the first step.

**Saying "Thank you" expresses a person's
appreciation and gratitude.**

The Blame Game

"We are hard pressed on every side, but not crushed;
perplexed, but not in despair..."
2 Corinthian 4:8 (NIV)

I seriously believe that each of us (at one time or another) has played the blame game. What is the blame game? It is when we blame others for our action or behavior. Borrowing Sigmund Freud's ego defense mechanisms - denial and rationalization - we show a lack of "guts" in not taking ownership of our particular negative behavior, character and/or personality.

We come up with a variety of excuses. Our denials and excuses in not claiming our wrong doing are simply our "covering up" our weaknesses; and that creates more problems. Until we are able to take ownership and not blame someone else, we are unable to make necessary (needed) corrections in our lives.

As has been mentioned in several other essays you will find in this book, none of us is perfect and will never be. However, there are things in our behavior, character and personality that we can change. But it requires serious recognition and taking ownership.

Is it easy? No, because we always like to appear as being right even when we are wrong. We have to learn to do the right thing at the right time. Ever heard of the expression, "You can run but you cannot hide?" Whether we know it or not, the very persons we are running from are ourselves. Regardless how we try to avoid ourselves during the day, when night falls, and before we drift off to sleep, we have to face ourselves and recognize our negative behavior. Do you know what I'm talking about?

So before we drift to "slumber land," it would be in our best interest to make some decisions about a change in our lives so that we will be able to be happier with ourselves, and we do not have to blame anyone about anything. When we are happy with ourselves, we are happy with others. When we are happy with others, we can relate to them in a manner that adds even more to our own happiness. It is a wonderful cycle we find ourselves in. I love it!

The happiness and the experience will boost our ego. Did you know that everyone has an ego? What is an ego? It is how and what we feel about ourselves. So naturally when we feel good about ourselves we are able to accomplish seemingly impossible tasks. A good, strong, healthy ego makes us feel capable of doing whatever we need or want to accomplish. It also puts a smile on our face; it encourages us to feel and know that "all things are possible to those who believe." In case you happen not to know where that comes from, it comes from the Bible where we find instructions, guidelines, directions and a way of living our lives exceeding our fondest dreams.

A good healthy ego allows us to know that there is a greatness in us that can change not only us, but our world. What is our world? It is all that is around us, in us, about us, the people and the activities that influence our life and help us to be whom we are. What a wonderful feeling it is when our world embraces us with love. Just think of the times you felt loved. Why don't we feel it all the time? There is no reason why we shouldn't.

Although we are not perfect people, there is a perfect time to make whatever changes we need to make and that time is NOW! The decision is ours to make. No one can make it for us. Any procrastination just puts off or delays our personal happiness.

Did you know that you were born for greatness? We were created and equipped with all the "tools" necessary for greatness. Something happened between our births and now that has caused us to lose sight of the fact that we were indeed born for greatness. Only we know what has come into our lives that has somewhat destroyed our motivation to strive for greatness. Whatever factors there were and may still be, we can shake them off if we are determined to "go for the gold." (Look for the *Go for the Gold* essay in this book.)

Going for the gold requires using all that we have been gifted (blessed) with and to do our best in all situations, regardless how large or small they are. What may be insignificant to us may mean a great deal to others. Let me give you an example: A small thing as a smile from us may well brighten the spirit of someone. Another example is that just listening to someone sharing some pain or hurt may keep that person from taking his or her own life. We may never know what our very presence and loving interest means to another.

Even though playing the blame game may seem to help us to get over for the moment, there is a consequence. And that consequence may serve to hurt us in the long run. We do know that it does not enhance our sense of well-being, and it does not make us feel comfortable about ourselves. Why then don't we take full ownership of our negativity and decide to take a leap of faith into doing what is positive and right by us and others?

When we take the right course of action, traveling down the right road, we find that we have greater companionship in those traveling with us. In essence, whenever and wherever we are traveling, there is plenty of company with us. Now, which would we rather have – the company of people who will enhance our lives or the company of people who take great pride in helping us destroy our lives? I know what my choice is because I want to reduce my playing the blame game. More importantly, what is your choice?

Although we are not perfect people, there is a perfect time to make whatever changes we need to make, and that time is NOW!

The Brain: Our Innate Personal Computer

"Whoever gives heed to instruction prospers,
and blessed is he who trusts in the Lord."
Proverb 16:20 (NIV)

The greatest aid and power given to humankind is the brain. It is as powerful as we allow it to be. It has power extending well beyond the most extensive imagination! All you have to do is to give it the freedom it was created to have. Yes, I am talking about our personal innate "computer."

There is a process in the use of our computer. The process begins with the mind. Every second our mind is busy with thoughts coming and going. These thoughts are processed before being programmed or not programmed into our computer. Decisions have to be made as to the acceptance, rejection or the need to give further thought and final deliberation to what visits our mind.

How does the mind do that? Imagine three "baskets" – file, hold and waste. Accepted material/information goes into the file basket and is programmed by the mind and enters directly into the computer as facts for future use and a frame of reference. The hold basket collects information that is to be reviewed as soon as possible to determine where it should go. It eventually will be sent to the file (computer) or to the waste basket. The waste basket is for information that is disbelieved or not accepted.

Caution: All information stored in your computer automatically plays out at sometime in our life. It appropriately fits in when and where needed. Some simple examples are talking, walking, dressing, and all other skills including emotional and physical behaviors we have learned throughout life. Recalling an incident which occurred earlier in life, even many years ago, will evoke the same emotions experienced then.

Sometimes our recall may cause some physical reaction such as rapid heartbeat, elevated blood pressure, fears, nervousness, anger, joy, peace, happiness, contentment, and a surge of confidence – all depending upon what we programmed into our computer. Unless the computer is reprogrammed, all will remain with us our entire life.

Why do some people give the impression of absolute serenity? Why do others express anger and discontentment? Why are some very confident? Why some people are so negative and complain about everything? Why does nothing seem to bother some folk? Why do some people get bent out of shape by the most trivial incident and everything is problematic? The answer to these questions is that many times young children growing up have experienced situations which have caused them to be either positive or negative. And they will remain that way until they reprogram their computer.

Getting back to the baskets, when the hold basket overflows because persons have not taken the time to sort out the content, they begin to feel overwhelmed. This feeling causes them to become agitated and annoyed; it is not unlikely that they will blow up over even small matters because their hold basket is overflowing with decisions which have to be made. There is a strong possibility that the persons will eventually have emotional and/or mental problems if they don't properly empty their hold basket. Often, what they are holding belongs in the waste basket. Because of that they will suffer emotional and mental anguish.

Based on what you have read so far, you can probably imagine what happens when the waste basket is not properly used. When important factual information is discarded in the waste basket, what do you think may happen? Well, when the time comes to use the vital information that has been placed in the waste basket, the computer does not have the information to enable the person to function successfully in a given task.

On the on the other hand, can you imagine what happens when waste material has been programmed into the computer? What a mess we make of our lives! That is why it is so vitally important that we consciously file in the appropriate baskets the things that affect our lives. (There is another essay on thinking and how it affects us negatively or positively. If you read it you will see how it ties in with this essay).

In addition to being able to file appropriately, we can also see the harm we can cause ourselves and others by not knowing how our personal computer works and that we have options as what to do with information (stuff) that is momentarily and daily fed to us.

Very quickly, some of the stuff such as gossip and negative opinions that hurt others and ourselves, false beliefs, and negative thoughts that we feed into our computer will cause devastating damages which we will have no small amount of difficulty correcting. This will lead to many wrongs having to be righted through recognition, apologies, and asking and receiving forgiveness. So we may find ourselves having to put some of our computer stored information in the waste basket. Yes, negative information stored in the computer can be deleted and replaced with positive, factual, helpful and healthy thoughts and deeds.

We can always improve our quality of life. It's up to us. Any change can be made if we recognize the need and have the willingness to put forth the required effort. Our own determination is powerful enough to enable us to do what we have to do as expediently as we can.

One of the things that of what we need to learn to do is to be less hard on ourselves for our errors and faux pas that each of us are guilty; in reality none of us is in position to point fingers. At the same time be kind to ourselves. The way we unconsciously treat ourselves is the way we treat others.

Each of us is unique and special in some ways. So we cannot "measure" ourselves by other people's standards. The only standard that is perfect is God's and He made us as we should be. The question is - are we following His standards or our own? If we can answer the question honestly, we will find that we will be better able to use our three baskets appropriately. Consequently, we will be better able to live with others and ourselves.

You see, human beings change from day to day and it is difficult (and impossible) trying to keep up and please others. Let us make it easier on ourselves. Just remember we only have to please God. Let us strive to do just that!

The brain (computer) is a powerful 'tool' that God has endowed us with. Centering His love into it and into our hearts enables us to be successful in all of our faithful endeavors.

THE CHOICES WE MAKE

"...choose you this day whom you will serve...
But as for me and my house, we will serve the Lord.
Joshua 24:15 (KJV)

From infancy we make choices. As time passes, hopefully, we are able to make better and more sophisticated choices. Not making a choice is actually making a choice. If you happened to have read my essay *"Decisions, Decisions, Decisions"* in **Our Times**, you will in all probability connect that essay to this one. If you have not read it, you will still be enlightened. And if you take heed to what I'm saying, you will be the better for it.

How does an infant learn how to make choices? As soon as a child comes out of the womb, that child learns how to get attention. Instinctively, the child learns certain actions on his or her part - to take in order to get desired responses.

As the child grows he or she learns how to "push the caregiver's buttons." Subsequently, the child learns how to have his or her way or not have his or her way. Be not mistaken, children are smarter than we give them credit for. Any caregiver who says in the hearing of a child, "I cannot do anything with this child," is actually teaching the child how to be in control. The child immediately learns how to have his or her way. The choice for the child is immediate gratification which the caregiver makes possible.

From then on, depending upon who is controlling whom, the child becomes more difficult and selfish, thinking only about what he or she wants. If this keeps on, the child does not learn how to appreciate anything and will become self-centered. It is all about him or her... It is very difficult trying to change children when they have been taught all of their young life that they are the center of the caregiver's life. Attempting to change this behavior causes a lot of disturbance in families, and regretfully the older adults will find themselves at odds with their children unless they give in to their every whim.

At some point when the adult "in charge" refuses to bend to the child's (now adult) will, he or she will accuse the senior adult of not loving him or her. Does this sound familiar? During the time of maturation the caregiver made the choice of giving in too much to the whim, desires, and demands of the child or children. And the children, although now adults, expect the same treatment and relationship until death.

After living as the receiver for most of their lives, they have not learned that it is "better to give than to receive." For them it's "better to receive than to give." They don't concern themselves with bad choices. They act from their own wants and desires knowing if they get into any trouble (financially or otherwise), their caregiver, continuing from infancy, will bail them out by taking care of any problems they create.

These persons will forever call upon their caregivers to right their bad choices, and the caregivers, for whatever reason, will continue to find ways to "save" them incident after incident.

Even though the caregivers have their own set of problems (financial, health or emotional), the dependent "spoiled" persons are more concerned about their own personal problems than those of their caregiver.

Initially, who do you think made bad choices? Not only did the caregiver make wrong choices, the caregiver taught those naturally dependent on him or her as very young children to continue to depend on them.

Moving on to others making bad choices, the desire to be loved can play a role in the choices we make. The fear of having no one loving us sometimes leads to our acceptance of poor behavior of those we love. The key words here are *fear* and *desiring love*.

Every human being desires and needs love, but we do not have to pay a price for it; however the fear of not having it causes us to make bad choices. So actually, fear is the evil that causes many problems. And that fear usually stems from something happening early in our own lives.

The greatest fear in the world is rejection. People will do a lot of things and make bad choices from the fear of being rejected. Unrequited love is painful. To love someone (regardless who it is) with all of one's soul, heart and mind and then to discover that the person cares nothing about you seems to be the worst thing that can happen to a person.

As hard as it may be, we still have a choice. We can remove ourselves from the person and allow ourselves the freedom of finding someone to replace him or her. Or we can try to hold on with all the pain, hurt and heartache we have to endure in our attempt to make that person love us. That, of course, is a bad choice.

The fear that in this big wide world we can find no one to love us is real for some folks. It is real only because that is what they believe. What really is real is that there is someone, somewhere looking for you. It may be in close proximity or may be a few miles away or hundreds or thousands miles away. Once you stop grieving and hurting, your heart, soul and mind will be free to let the new person in.

Life was not meant to include much of the discomforts we bring upon ourselves by making choices we should not make. The sooner we learn that our destiny is in our own hands, the better our lives will be. We sometimes depend on others when we are very capable of handling and dealing with many matters ourselves. And when we find that some matters are beyond our control, we have Power beyond us to treat the matter. The Power I am referring to is the power of the One Who created you and me.

The right choice, then, is to let go and let God take over. I encourage you to test His power.

And caregivers encourage those depending upon you too much to begin to depend on God. His shoulders are broader. He is tougher. He wants you to take a break and live for yourselves. His love is sufficient!

The right choice is to let go and let God take over.
I encourage you to test His power.

THE CORE OF YOUR BEING

"Do everything without complaining or arguing."
Philippians 2:14 (NIV)

It is most unfortunate that all persons do not know who they are deep down to the core of their being.

Because of myriad life experiences, they have internalized a definition of themselves that is not true or complimentary. As little children they had no control over the adult authority who was supposed to love them, protect them, help them and provide a quality of life that would ensure a healthy, happy and a peaceful and loving existence so that they would grow up to be strong and confident adults.

I am talking about the inner-self - so race, ethnicity and culture have nothing to do with what I am saying because God made all of us according to His image. Even though we are different, He has placed the seed of greatness into all of us. But without the proper loving, nurturing and encouragement, the seed stays dormant.

This essay is a wake up call. You may not ever have been told that you have the seed of greatness inherent at your conception. Some have been told, but somewhere in their growth and development, they have wandered off and no longer realize who they are. So deep in the core of their being they have experienced hopelessness, helplessness and powerlessness. In that state they think "What's the use? I will never become anything of worth, and I don't deserve any better than the situation in which I find myself."

It is not their fault they that believe that lie. God did not make any junk! So let us look at their predicament from two perspectives. The first perspective is the internalization from birth that they are nothing and will never be anything. The second perspective is that they grew up in a healthy, peaceful, and loving home but found themselves in the steady company of people who feel worthless, and they allowed themselves to be defined by them. Sometimes association brings on assimilation. This reminds me of the cliché that says,"You lay down with dogs you get up with fleas."

The first perspective: A child quickly learns whether he or she is wanted, loved and respected. If that love is not given by words and action, the child begins to feel he or she is not wanted. But the child will attempt to elicit love because it is a powerful force we all need to survive; the child will do anything to get it. Unfortunately, there are adults just as needy and will use the child for their own purpose, whatever that may be. So the expression, "Misery likes company" is at play in that instance.

Some children, not finding the love they crave, turn bitter. In their bitterness they seek to harm and hurt others as they hurt. Unless someone comes to them offering the love that only God can provide through them, they are doomed to a life of hell, and they will give to others a portion of what they have to give, and that is hell.

The second perspective: Sometimes persons as children have received good treatment, but decided as young or older adults to wander off into a different life style and are influenced by others who have come from the first perspective, never knowing what love is. Yet, there is a strong possibility that they will eventually turn back to the love they knew. That is, if they find someone who will help them to change back into what they once enjoyed.

The beauty of even the worse scenario is that as long as there is hope, there is a great possibility and probability to be transformed into the person they were created to be. Contrary to the thinking of unloved persons, the core of our being should be love not hate and bitterness. The absence of love leaves a big void in the heart of too many people. That void is filled with hate and bitterness. And they get back by destroying what is good. It is the same as pigs not respecting the value of pearls.

My heart aches when I meet persons who are bitter. And even though I don't know the full circumstances which caused the situation, I know that they were not born that way and that something happened that should not have happened. However, most people are afraid of such persons and tend to shy away and do not want them in their company. They then perpetuate the same feelings instead of helping them to overcome their bitterness. Even though the average person is not trained to deal with them psychologically, the one ingredient we all can give is love. Believe it or not, love neutralizes the situation to a degree. Along with that we can minister a heavy dose of patience, endless compassion, unconditional love, fairness and being void of judgment; this will help the needy persons to perhaps seek professional help. We who seem to be "well" are quick to judge and say what should not be, but we don't know what the individuals' circumstances are, and it is only by God's grace that we are not in their condition.

We have to "walk in their shoes" to truly understand what they are going through on a daily basis with seemingly no help or relief. Yes, we are quick to judge and react and that compounds the feelings they are already harboring.

Here are some things we who are blessed by not being in that situation need to know: Unloved persons do not trust anyone because they have been let down so many times while seeking the love they (and all of us) need. So your reaching out may not even be accepted by them immediately. Overtime, if you have the patience to keep trying, you may make a little "dent" into their hearts, and you may be able to convince them to get counseling from a professional. Understand that your patience will be tried because they need to know that you are true, sincere and really concerned and not trying to run a game on them as others have done, including their parents.

If you feel it is your "Christian duty" to help them with their "demons," watch out because you will be addressing issues you know nothing about. It is easy to simplify something you know nothing about but think that you do because of your religious beliefs.

If you truly practice the love of God that you have in your heart, your empathy will allow you to meet as much of the needs the person has that you as a non-professional and not trained in emotional and psychological disorders, are able to do. The best you can do, after winning the person's trust, is to find some means of financially supporting the person's counseling service.

Now, the question is how can you truly help such a person? You need to know that you cannot do it on your own. I would not recommend that you venture into this vital ministry without fortification of the Holy Sprit. If you truly know God for yourself and you have a personal relationship with Him, you are safe and armed with all that you need for the ministry of helping the person to change. And the person will only be able to change when he or she sees that you are different from all the other people he or she has been dealing with. Your God-like behavior with him or her will cause the person to want to change, and of course, that is going to take all the unconditional love that you can give. God will supply all you need and will direct you how to handle him or her. Don't count on religion. It will give you incorrect information that the persons are caught up in their "sin" when they actually have been destroyed by not being given what we are all born to receive and that is LOVE, unconditional love, the same love God gives to you and me.

Much more can be written on this piece, but my point in writing about the core of our being is two-fold. One is to let people know who are out there hurting that there is help. Even though they did not receive unconditional love in their earlier years, it is still available through the power of God and His people. The second part of this is for people to understand that they who are more fortunate should do all they can to help those persons find peace, joy, and happiness through the power of love. I am hoping those of us who have been blessed with love will not be so quick to judge and to label others. We don't know their psychosocial and psychological history or anything about them actually. When the core of your being is made clear to you, you will know who you are and the same applies to me. It will be made plain to me who I am, as well.

If you feel it is your "Christian duty" to help them with their "demons," watch out because you will be addressing issues you know nothing about.

THE DAMAGING EFFECT OF TOXIC THINKING

*"Those who live according to the sinful nature have their
minds set on what that nature desires; but those who live
in accordance with the Spirit have their minds set on
what the Spirit desires."*
Romans 8:5 (NIV)

Everyone should know that anything that is toxic is bad for our physical, emotional and spiritual health. So what is toxic thinking? Toxic thinking is entertaining thoughts that will cause damage to us as whole persons. If we want to live happy and productive lives, we need to weigh our thoughts by being very selective.

Every moment of the day we are thinking about something. Wrong or harmful thoughts will creep in. In order to keep toxic thoughts from playing a major part in our thinking, we have to consciously weed them out and "kick them to the curb."

Unhealthy thoughts are like weeds. Weeds impede the growth of healthy plants and will take over if not pulled out by their roots. So if we think of unhealthy and damaging thoughts as "weeds," we will be more prone to get rid of them as soon as they crop up in our heads.

A good way of getting rid of toxic thoughts is to say to ourselves, "That's not true." Follow that with asking our Creator to help us think good and healthy thoughts and be less judgmental. Philippians 4:8 tells us *"...whatever things are true, whatever things are just, whatever things are pure, whatever things are lovely, whatever things are of good report, if there is any virtue and if there is anything praiseworthy - meditate on these things."* And I Timothy 4:15 says, *"Meditate on these things; give yourself entirely to them, that your progress may be evident in all."*

What is the difference between thinking and meditating? Thinking is really thoughts coming to mind or to our heads. When we examine or give more or deeper attention to them, we are meditating.

Meditating usually refers to pondering good and honorable thoughts over and over. We consider quiet, calm thoughts, when we communicate with God. Meditation is peaceful, relaxing and motivating. It helps us to view ideas from a clear and positive understanding. Some persons refer to meditation just before dawn, others mid-day and others around midnight. Whatever time is best for you. It is such a pleasure to enjoy the peacefulness of your soul. It is when your soul, your mind and your heart come together in unison, concentrating on our Creator. Wow, what an experience that is!

Meditating is wholesome, healthy and beneficial to our spiritual, emotional, and physical well-being. That is why it is important to make it a daily exercise. Collecting one's thoughts keeps one calm and positive.

The opposite of meditating is worrying. Worrying seems to draw negative forces. Worrying is not looking for a solution, but just reviewing the "problem" over and over without seeking a solution. Worrying is holding on to problems without seeking help. Worrying is definitely toxic. I will say that holding on to worrying issues will result in a great deal of problems that will adversely affect us.

Since worrying is toxic let us concentrate on finding a solution to our problems. Let's focus our mind on everything that is good, healthy, productive, and that will help us to increase our ability to enjoy life more abundantly.

Since we know all good things come from God, we should keep in daily communication with Him through meditation or worship or both. Praising Him brings wonderful results. God is simply amazing! The amazement of God may be an essay you may want to read. Following His instructions, there will be no coincidence that you will come upon if that is on your "wish" list.

You cannot actually see toxicity with the naked eye, but you better believe it is prevalent, and like the oxygen we breathe, it's all around us. Thoughts cannot be seen, but they manifest themselves in more ways than you can possibly count; and they affect everything you say or do. That is why it is so important not to hold onto negative thoughts too long. One thought brings on another, and we find ourselves inundated with them. And you can bet that they will negatively or positively affect the outcomes of our lives according to the thought (bad or good) that we are entertaining.

Toxicity we do not need. So why spend even a second thinking toxic thoughts? Just ask God to clear your mind and let you think positive. While asking Him, concentrate on Him and you will find good things happening to you spiritually, emotionally and physically.

It is really strange how we draw upon the wrong things looking for good results and then we wonder why we get into more hot water than a tea bag.

In order to keep toxic thoughts from playing a major part in our thinking, we have to consciously weed them out and "kick them to the curb."

THE EPITOME OF INTELLIGENCE

*"Boast not of thyself of tomorrow; for thou knowest not
what a day may bring forth."*
Proverbs 27:1 (KJV)

To me the epitome of intelligence is how well a person simplifies the complicated rather than complicating the simple.

There are reasons why people find importance in making simple matters complicated. I am going to cite several incidents or situations and perhaps you can relate to them. Your relating to them may not have anything to do with you, but is just a part of your daily observations.

I hope you enjoy the humor as well as the seriousness of what I am about to share, coming from my own observations in and out the class room. I have to tell you that I take great interest in observing people because of my training and interest in studying body language, known by social scientists as non-verbal communication.

Here we go! Some people have a need to impress others. This reminds me of children performing when they are given recognition. All of us have a need to be seen, recognized and validated. There is nothing wrong with that, but when the need is obsessive, there is a problem. When we apply for a job (particularly a high powered position), we have to be impressive because a potential employer is looking for certain qualifications. However, the best way to impress a potential employer is by being real. Whether we either have the qualifications they are looking for or we don't. We can't fake it.

Some people need to be impressive in order to feel good about themselves. For the most part that is their struggle because of their childhood experiences. Some may have been put down by their parents, peers, teachers, acquaintances, or significant others. They try to compensate for the feelings they have internalized because of the action, behavior and poor relationship with people who meant the most to them. They have unconsciously "bought" into the nonsense that they are less than anyone else as a person. They need a big "dose" of confidence from loving, empathetic and understanding new persons who have become a part of their life.

Others have difficulty admitting they don't know when asked a question. So they cover up their lack of knowledge by responding in a language they don't even understand, hoping they will be able to impress the person inquiring by using misplaced words. They are not cognizant of how ridiculous they sound. What would be more becoming and command respect would be to simply acknowledge not knowing.

The extreme cases are those persons who have to make sure they are seen by everyone they consider important. They make such a fuss over "important" people while ignoring persons they consider less unimportant. Their movement throughout the crowd gives the impression of genuineness, but their aim is simply to be seen. That hunger is more prevalent than we may realize. But, as I said, they are extreme cases.

I have great admiration for a speaker who has a message from the heart rather than from the head. It doesn't matter how complex the subject is, if the person is free to let his or her feelings flow, the audience will be captivated. The complex subject would be done in a manner that the listeners will be able to understand and enjoy. When some listeners have difficulty understanding the speaker and a joke from him or her drew laughter, the listeners may laugh with the crowd as a face saving technique.

A question was asked in my Values and Ethics class. It was "What makes a person important?" As you may have expected, most of the answers had to do with money associated with power. After asking all of the students, the last answer was how well one treats others and how one shows empathy, understanding and kindness. This led to an interesting discussion from an altruistic point of view. Finally, we came up with, if we help others to feel good about themselves, they will acknowledge us as also important.

I have always had an affinity for "sweet people" and considered them important because of their kindness, understanding nature, patience, being good listeners and having motivational skills.

295

If you do not consider yourself a "sweet person," you can become one. It is up to you, Let no one tell you anything to the contrary. Becoming that kind of person puts you in the category of having the epitome of intelligence along with your other fine attributes; this makes you desired as a good person to hang out with because of your importance.

The extreme cases are those persons who have to make sure they are seen by everyone they consider "important."

The Freudian Mystique

*"For God speaks once, yes twice, yet man perceives it not.
In a dream, in a vision of the night, when deep sleep
Falls upon me, in slumbering upon the bed, then he
opens the ears of men, and speaks their instruction."*
Job 33:15-16 (NIV)

Sigmund Freud (1856-1939) the father of Psychoanalysis (Psychoanalytic therapy) believed that when we say something quickly without thinking (and then regret having said), that thought comes from the unconscious mind and we are unconsciously letting it out. We, even then, wonder how such words could come from us. Personally, I have found this quite embarrassing; I have said to myself, "I don't feel this way, so why on earth would I blurt that out?"

A common way of explaining this is called "a slip of the tongue." Some people call it a "Freudian slip." Do you recall ever having such an experience? According to Freud, that is something buried in our subconscious mind that needs to be released.

Another of Freud's theory was dream analysis. In conversing with people, I have been told that they do not dream. I don't believe this is so. I believe that people dream but they don't remember dreaming because the dreams occurred early after falling asleep and by the time they wake up the dreams are forgotten, or the fact that they did dream. I am definitely a dreamer, but I do not always recall the dreams in their entirety. Then there are times I remember a dream very well even to the smallest detail.

I always play an active role in my dreams. I am not just a spectator. Sometimes I wake up quite tired as it seems I had been extremely busy. I am usually the facilitator or director. It seems I am usually the one responsible for getting the tasks done. I even wake myself up talking loudly, giving instructions. If Freud were alive he would have a "field day" with me.

Freud as a psychoanalyst interpreted the dream for the client/patient, rather than ask the client/patient what he or she thinks the dream means. During a session he would ask the persons to share as much details of their dreams as fully as they can recall. You see, a psychoanalyst probes the subconscious mind, dealing with what happened in the past, while other therapists are dealing with the present and would like to know what is happening presently in the conscious mind of their clients.

Other therapists after having the client share their dream as fully as possible, find that questioning their clients as to the meaning of the dream is more helpful in helping the clients to understand how they think the way they do. This is a faster method of getting to the core of what problems the clients may have. Those therapists are known as short term therapists while Dr. Freud was known as a long term therapist. You can easily see why it would take quite a bit of time getting to the root of a problem by probing into the subconscious.

Some of my dreams are very specific. There are many of my close friends who are deceased, but in my dream they are still alive. The dreams for the most part are pleasant and enjoyable. But then I have had dreams that are actually nightmares. You will find reference to this later in the essay.

Do you dream often? Do you dream nightly? Are your dreams pleasant? Do you dream of the dead as if they were alive? Are you disturbed by any of your dreams? These are some of the questions a therapist may ask you.

I am seldom disturbed by my dreams, but I wonder why I dream so much. Freud believed that much is hidden in our subconscious that comes to our consciousness while we sleep. As strange as this may sound, I dream while taking naps sitting in my favorite recliner (supposedly watching television) with the same intensity as in the bed.

Freud also believed that through dreams we deal with unfinished business in our life. We may or may not resolve them while sleep. That may be so since I am the facilitator of whatever is happening or taking place in the dream. I do recall seeking advice and help in how to go about accomplishing certain tasks in my dream.

Have you ever been in a fight in your dreams and found your arms too heavy to defend yourself? Have you tried to escape from someone and found with all of your best effort you were moving but not getting any place? Have you ever seen yourself with wings and flew short distances with your feet a few feet off the floor? Have you had a dream of a sexual nature?

The only one I can recall (although I am sure I have had many) was interrupted by an urgent call to the bathroom. I could hardly wait to finish my bathroom relief because I was eager to get back to the dream. Fortunately and strangely, I was able to resume where I had left off.

Nightmares

I have had two kinds. One was when I was trying not to fall asleep because I felt as if I were drifting into something unknown and frightening. I was extremely uncomfortable, scary, and fearful. I was wrestling with a strong desire to keep my eyes from closing, and they felt so heavy. I just knew that the minute I closed my eyes I would drift into an unwanted (inexplicable) experience. Have you had that experience?

The second nightmarish experience was when I was actually asleep, and it seemed I was trying with all of my might to wake up. The dream of monsters was terribly frightening. I could not move my body, and I felt as if I could I would be able to wake up. When I was finally able to wake up, I was in a cold sweat. Have you ever experienced that?

For several nights after those experiences I was reluctant to go to bed, even though I was tired and sleepy. I am thankful for being able to overcome my reluctance because I do indeed enjoy a good night's sleep and rest. Do you?

Engaging the services of a counselor/therapist does not mean that there is anything wrong with you. Some people hesitate to get the help they need because of a stigma they feel is placed on them by their friends, associates, and relatives.

We all need help. We all need to express our feelings. We have various degrees of need. But when we find ourselves not happy, longing for peace, not having a sense of worth, and lacking in trust in ourselves and others, we need to talk to someone. That is why friendship (genuine friendship) is so important.

A genuine friend who is quite secure with him or herself and is a good listener, but does not have the training or skill in counseling, will suggest that you consult with someone who is trained.

It is not everybody's business that you are seeing a counselor, but you do not have to be ashamed. Actually, you are wiser than most. It takes a big person to admit to needing help. Many persons who would mock you for seeking help need help very badly themselves, but they are not wise enough to know that. You cannot let an unwise (or foolish) person validate your action.

Wise people seek professional counselors. Foolish people seek fools. A truly wise person does not desire the validation of a fool.

THE GIFT OF LAUGHTER

"To everything there is a season,
A time for every purpose under heaven:
A time to weep and a time to laugh."
Ecclesiastes 3:1, 4 (NIV)

Being able to laugh is not only a gift, it is a blessing. It is therapeutic. It reduces tension. It stimulates the various cells in our body and causes them to produce new cells bringing about healing. A good hearty belly laugh a day is something we all can use.

My heart goes out to people who seem to not have any sense of humor. People who cannot find anything to laugh about place themselves under terrible strain and tension.

When I speak of laughter, I am talking about people being able to laugh at themselves either alone or with others. I don't see anything right about laughing at or poking fun at people. Quite frankly, I find such behavior lacking in sensitivity and hurtful. But to laugh heartily at oneself indicates to me that a person is confident and quite comfortable with who he or she is as a person.

If you are the kind of person who sees the good in most situations, you must also see the humor, and that is good. Sometimes we take things too seriously. And other times we may not be as serious as we ought to be.

I don't think everything is laughable. And I don't think we need to overly exert our tear ducts either. Have you ever seen a person laughing and crying at the same time? I think in that case they laughed so hard they caused their tear ducts to join in the merriment.

I like being around people who love to laugh. They are good company and they make me feel good about them and my world. I must state again that I don't care to be around people whose laughter is brought about because they are laughing at someone.

When our best laughter is because we are laughing at others, there is something wrong with us. People who are confident in who they are and are quite pleased with being themselves do not get any joy from laughing at others. They don't need that to make them feel good about themselves. People who need to poke fun, whether they admit it or not, are somewhat insecure. They are much like bullies, and probably were bullied as children.

I have to admit that when I was a child I did laugh with other children when they were poking fun at someone I didn't particularly like. But the only reason why I didn't like them is because they poked fun at me, and I got a little satisfaction seeing them as the butt of a joke or being made fun of. I thought they deserved it. But having matured into older adulthood, I then see the error of my ways.

As a teenager I learned how to deal with being laughed at. Poking fun at me was short lived because I avoided being defensive. I learned that if I laughed along with them, their fun poking was short-lived. A lot of times the object of the persons making fun of me was to make me feel bad. But since laughing right along with them did not enable them to achieve their objective, it stopped. However, sometimes another tactic was to call me "stupid" because I was laughing at myself. Learning to have more confidence in myself, allowed me not to let name calling bother me. But I must say that I was never one to engage in name calling because I was always sensitive to other people's feelings.

In fact, as a child, I would quickly come to the defense of anyone small in stature who was being picked on. Most of the fights I had were because of defending someone who seemed unable to defend himself.

Laughter serves many functions. For me, it was a defense against unfair attacks. Later, it became a bridge to friendship. You see, laughter is contagious. If you are around people who are enjoying good hearty laughter, you will find yourself laughing, too. On many occasions I have laughed with a group of people, and we ended up laughing and crying at the same time.

Some people are naturally humorous and we can expect them to say something that is going to crack us up. When those persons approach us, we begin laughing in expectation of hearing something funny. Has this been your experience?

To me, being able to laugh easily is not only a gift, but a blessing. Being in the company of persons who are able to tell clean jokes and funny stories of interest makes for a good day together.

You may realize from time to time that, for whatever reason, there are people who cannot laugh. Their life is so sad or they are in such poor physical condition that having a sense of humor plays no part in their life. Just think how sad this is.

How about you? Do you like to laugh? If you do, you are blessed.

**I don't think everything is laughable,
and I don't think we should overly exert our tear
ducts either.**

The Giving of Love

"The good man brings good things out of the good
stored up in his heart."
Luke 6:45 (NIV)

The most important thing that determines not only our survival but also our quality of life is not for sale. It is absolutely free and more precious than any precious stone. The more we give of what we have, the more we have. It never runs out!

If you are wondering what "**it**" is, take another glance at the title of this essay. You can't buy it. You can't steal it. You don't have to ask for it, just give it. We are born with the propensity to love and receive love. The world was created by Love. God is love. Now, what we do with our inherent love determines how our lives will be.

Tough unconditional Love:

Tough but unconditional love is a powerful and positive force that practically guarantees our sense of well-being, self-esteem, self-improvement and respect for self and others. In essence, it has a lot to do with our appreciation for all living things and our quality of life, as well.

Genuine love has a kind of "sweetness" that softens the most hardened heart, deeply penetrating and changing the heart of the person who seems unlovable. Genuine love is tough because the persons dispensing it are more concerned about another person than being loved. The persons who dispense tough love are all about love and feel comfortable about themselves, and the love they have for another is greater than their concern about being loved. Why? The reason is because the persons who give tough unconditional love feel comfortable in their love simply because the source of their love is God. Tough lovers love people but they will not tolerate negative behavior.

People who have not had the benefit of being genuinely and unconditionally loved develop a "hardness" in their heart to protect their ego from further damage. Everyone has an ego. An ego determines how and what we think about ourselves. If we feel good our actions (behavior) will reflect that. The reverse of that is if we feel badly about ourselves, we will act badly.

We should not fool ourselves. We might think that everyone feels loved, but that is not so. To take this further, parents allowing their children to have their own way is not loving. That is why good parenting calls for tough love. Discipline (not punishing) is a major part of tough love. Disciplining is lovingly correcting bad behavior so the young persons learn life has boundaries, rules and regulations and everything is not okay. This has to be learned in the home where one is nurtured. What has to be learned is that the larger society is not going to tolerate negative behavior. So it should not be tolerated in the smaller society (the home).

Discipline and Punishment:
The difference between discipline and punishment is: (1) discipline is administered with loving concern with a desire to correct negative behavior, (2) punishment has an attitude attached to it, and the person meting the punishment usually shows some anger and the punishment does not always fit the behavior of the person being punished. Discipline usually includes an explanation why the person is being corrected. Punishment gives little explanation (if any) and teaches the recipient to strike back in some manner. This is a very controversial topic, and the reader may not agree, but the essence of this discussion is to show how to administer tough love while not condoning bad behavior and letting the recipients know that they are loved.

The Need for Love:
Each person needs and desires love. Too often, we find ourselves doing wrong things to gain the approval of someone who does not care about us and will use us. People are very quick with their "you ought to know better!" Sometimes knowing better has nothing to do with our situation.

Someone should be able to recognize or realize that our behavior stems from a strong desire to be accepted (loved) and if someone would lovingly direct us to positive thinking and acting by tough love, we will be accepted by doing what is right.

This writer strongly believes that love changes things. If we care about people as we claim we do, rather than being critical, we should demonstrate tough love and help our loved ones do what is required in order to have a better quality of life. There is nothing wrong with telling our loved ones who are on the wrong path, "I love you, but I do not like what you are doing to yourself and others. In fact, it hurts me the way you are hurting yourself." Of course, what you say must be genuine not dramatic.

Unfortunately, some of our brothers (and smaller number of sisters I have seen) think exposing their colorful boxer shorts is fashionable. They do not realize that such a display tells an uncomplimentary story about them. Whether right or wrong it gives a bad impression about them. When I saw a teenage son of two teachers who are friends of mine parading with his fancy drawers showing, I was appalled. But his parents simply said, "It's just a phase he is going through," Exercising tough love would make a parent say, "Boy, pull your pants up and keep it up!"

Tough love is usually not immediately appreciated. If fact, our children may find it not to their liking, but that is not a reason not to administer it. Later in life they will even mention to their children how "strict" their parents were. I am certainly glad my mother was strict with me, although I think she operated somewhere between disciplining and punishing. Along with that I could swear that she could x-ray me with her staring eyes and could read my thoughts. So I didn't dare to even fleetingly think any thoughts, but understand what she was saying and be obedient. Along with discipline, she demonstrated love, but she never hugged after disciplining me. I really don't remember being kissed by her, but then that would have been a little embarrassing for me as a self-conscious child.

The worse thing a person can say to any loved one is, "If you do …I will love you." And the best thing a person can say to a loved one is, "I love you regardless, but I just can't stand your attitude and behavior because they do not show who you really are." Ultimately, who we are and whom we are will be discovered. All of us are children of God, created and unconditionally loved by Him. That is good to know. Knowing this helps to realize that we have a support system that is infallible and we should rely on it in every thing we do. To ensure success in anything we do, we should first ask our Creator for direction; follow it with no doubt and we will be crowned with success. We have to remember to give Him thanks and praise for our successes. God is all about love, and as He gives we give back to Him by giving love to His people.

Genuine love is tough because the persons dispensing it are more concerned about the persons they love than being loved.

The Highs and the Lows in Life: These Too Shall Pass

"... For when I am weak, then I am I strong."
II Corinthians 12:10 (NIV)

Each and every adult in life experiences highs and lows. We often refer to our situations as mountains and valleys.

Mountain Experience:
These are highs of joy, happiness, contentment, peace and comfort. The world is full of good and wonderful things!

Valley Experiences:
These are the lows with feelings of sadness, disappointments, impatience, lack of confidence and anger. The world (everybody) is "dumping" on us!

Can we control the extent of our valley experiences? Yes, we can. We can overcome the temporary and short term ones ourselves. For others, we need help. No man is an island. No man stands alone. All of us need each other. We were created to help each other. Someone experiencing the mountain can help someone in the valley.

There is Help. Where? Who?
Everyone needs someone he or she can trust. It is important not only to trust the helper but know that the helper can be relied upon to keep confidential matters that a person does not want known to others. The helper must be a good listener and nonjudgmental.

Most of the times we want people to listen to what we have to say without giving any advice and without the person having all the answers. As we talk, the answer sometimes comes and we are able to clearly see our contribution to our problems. When we ask for help, God sends the right person.

A Good True Friend Who Believes in God:

Usually, a good true friend is the one who is most helpful when he or she does not try to impose his or her values and will on others and accepts others for whom and what they are. Now, a good friend who believes in God can be very helpful. Do not be misled. Do not mistake a very religious person as always a God loving person. Most religious persons are judgmental. Their judgment is about others and not judgmental enough about themselves. However, a person who truly believes in God and has a personal relationship with Him is open and understanding and nonjudgmental. Very religious people too often are caught up in ceremonies, rituals and appearances. So if you have a bad experience with ultra-religious folks, do not let it stop you from communicating with God loving folks.

How do we know the difference between truly God loving folks who have a personal relationship with God and those who claim to love God and are very religious? God loving folks are understanding, kind, patience, loving and willing to admit they too have faults and are not perfect, but are working on improving themselves. A good and true God loving friend will invite God into the conversation. The three of you: God, you and your friend can work together on whatever problems that are causing you to be in the valley.

From the Valley to the Mountain:

What a magnificent experience that is! When the mountain experience replaces the valley, the feeling is unexplainable and wondrous. The experience will make one want to help others who are in the valley.

A person who has a daily relationship with God is usually spiritually connected to our Creator. Just think; God created heaven, earth, moon, sun, stars, and animals of all kinds, from the smallest to the largest. If God created all that (and much more) than we can imagine, taking us from the valley to the mountain is small stuff, don't you think?

One of the joys of the mountain experience is the realization of not having to bother with the valley experiences anymore and enjoying your divine blessings of safety, peace, harmony and freedom. All of the things that happened in the valley may be remembered for a short time but the time will come when all the valley memories will slip away.

As you enjoy your mountain experience do not forget the folks still in the valley. They need you to help them to get where you are, through the grace of God.

Peace and love to you!

The three of you: God, you and your friend can work together on whatever problems that are causing you to be in the valley.

THE HOLY GHOST PARTY

"I rejoiced with those who said to me, 'Let us go to the
house of the Lord.'"
Psalm 122:1 (NIV)

There is a song that says, "Ain't no party like the Holy Ghost party 'cause the Holy Ghost party don't stop." That song has great meaning for me. I know that the grammar is incorrect but the message is more important than the grammar. For some strange reason I feel that which was originally stated has more meaning than the grammatically correct saying, "There's no party like the Holy Ghost party because the Holy Ghost party doesn't stop."

The first version is repeated over and over until someone decides to change to another song. Repeating the incorrect grammar seems to add much to it, as it is coming from the depth of our soul, expressing our love and personal and direct connection to our God.

What's my point? The point is that for us who truly believe in our Lord and Savior, the song helps us to continually look forward to that day when we spend eternity"partying with the Holy Ghost."

Even before we get to eternity, we can enjoy the Holy Ghost party on earth, that is, if we truly believe in God as we proclaim we do. Proclaiming belief, of course, is not just our words but our deeds.

Our deeds, behavior, or action, purely demonstrate if we are or are not a true member of the party that seeks the Holy Ghost. All we have to do is be receptive to the Holy Spirit or Holy Ghost. When He takes over, the feelings and the experiences are indescribable!

Some act as if they think being " active" and "serving" in the many important committees, boards and agencies gives them "status and position." What they are doing may be wonderful and helpful, but real status comes from accepting and being obedient to the Trinity (God the Father, God the Son, and God the Holy Spirit). Persons in ministry under the influence of Holy Ghost power are happy serving God by doing what the Trinity want them to do in carrying out their assigned ministries.

Some of us are seeking self-importance; we complain about how busy and involved we are while at the same time wanting the world to know how "religious" we are. Sometimes it gets to the point where we think we are almost indispensable and no one can take our place or do as well as we can. We claim the "position" as ours. The truth is when we move on or out, God replaces us with empowered persons with fresh ideas.

A "job" becomes a ministry when we place ourselves in ministry to do God's work. A job is a function we are hired to do. A ministry is what God appoints us to do and it enables us to experience the joy of servanthood.

In fact, servanthood extends outside of the church. It has no barriers or boundaries. A job is simply a function in the church. And it will not alone get us where we say we want to go.

Where we want to go has been prepared for us (John 14:1-4) by the blood shed by our Lord and Savior. In order to get to that place, we have to be active in the Holy Ghost party which encourages us to praise the Lord without reservation or fear of what others think or will say about us. Moreover, it will enable us to join in with those who are praising the Lord and telling of their marvelous experiences.

More often than I care to hear from well meaning Christians fellow worshipers are complaints about the Holy Ghost party being "too noisy," "too much like the Baptists," "Sunday services too long," and other complaints. The complaining is bothersome especially while worship is in progress. It is also distracting. My purpose in being in church is to worship and to learn what adjustments I need to make in my spiritual journey to our heavenly home prepared for us.

Attending church is not a formality, something we have to do each Sunday or Saturday, for some. It is not a time for just going through the motions of praising God, but truly praising Him. True, some of us are more audible when we become so moved by the Holy Spirit (in our Holy Ghost party) that we shout out such expressions as "Hallelujah," "Amen," "Praise the Lord," "Holy," or whatever the Spirit gives utterance.

The Holy Ghost party members, in their worship, go to church to have a good time in the Lord. If all of the members were there for the same purpose we would find ourselves not caught up in cliques (except the clique in Jesus Christ), and not getting upset by something said in God's message to His people.

How sad it is when people go to their place of worship to hear the Word of God and leave angry because the message offended them. They missed the point. God gives us opportunities to hear about ourselves and to make amends. So when we are angered by the message, we miss an important blessing. Being angry invites the negative part of our nature to attract and absorb more negative words and deeds to consume us. What's even sadder is that so many good, and otherwise wonderful, "loving" people get caught up in this turmoil of thoughts and feelings that eventually lead to unchristian and unbecoming behavior from persons who claim to be "Children of God."

Being Children of God means studying the Word regularly so that we know the Word and are therefore obedient to the Word. When this happens, the Holy Ghost or Holy Spirit freely enters our lives (thoughts and feeling, and action) and all that we do and say confirms that we are indeed Children of God.

Again, referring to the point of this essay, I would much rather be ridiculed for being "like the Baptists" or "Pentecostals" than to risk my chance of not going into the second phase of life, of living with God in the place He has prepared for us. Since the Holy Ghost party provides all that I need to get me there, I proclaim that I am an active member of the party and derive great joy, blessings, and benefit from partying with those more concerned about the Holy Ghost than what others think of them. The Holy Ghost party feels strongly about serving God in spirit and in truth.

In fact, every time we come together and worship is "party time." Each of us has his or her own definition and feelings about worship. One of the many definitions listed in my very old, well used dictionary says that "a party is people drawn together for a specific purpose." What could be more specific than worshiping in church and inviting the Holy Spirit to dwell within each soul individually and collectively?

When the Holy Spirit is invited and freely given the opportunity to express Himself, then we have a party which we believers call the Holy

Ghost Party. There is no party like it and there are many gifts called blessings associated with the party.

Again, "Ain't no party like the Holy Ghost party 'cause the Holy Ghost party don't stop!" If you are skeptical, just place yourself in the midst of persons in the "heat" of the party.

**Even before we get to eternity, we can enjoy the
Holy Ghost party on earth, that is, if we truly
believe in God as we proclaim we do. Proclaiming
belief, of course, is just words but our deeds show
the depth of our belief.**

THE HUMAN TOUCH

*"...the Lord God is a sun and shield: the Lord will give
grace and glory: no good thing will He withhold from
them that walk uprightly."*
Psalms 84:11 (KJV)

One cannot over estimate the "magic" of the combination of a firm and sincere handshake while smiling into the eyes of another person. Both parties will enjoy the meeting of the heart, mind and soul of the other. The human touch is so important to each of us even though we deny this when we are hurting. It is when we are hurting that we want it so badly. Sometimes, when we say "I'm alright," we are actually saying, "I'm in pain and wish someone would care about me. I am afraid of being rejected again."

The human touch encompasses shaking hands, eye contact, a smile and hugs.

Unfortunately, some people have not learned how to shake another's hand. Often they are too shy even to look into the other person's eyes. Some do not feel comfortable smiling at strangers. And there are persons who have a very weak handshake which means that the person who gives a good firm strong handshake will hurt the hand of the weaker shake. If both handshakes are firm and strong, no one's hand will hurt. Then there is the person who shakes another's hand with a pen or pencil or keys in his or her hand. That is callous and most disrespectful.

A Firm Handshake:

A firm handshake usually denotes character, confidence, sincerity and integrity. This is especially true when the firm shaker smilingly looks into the eyes of the other person. This simple act is a language unto itself. It brings a sense of acceptance to the recipient. However, shy people usually feel uncomfortable and a little embarrassed. Enough handshaking will (hopefully) enable a shy person to relax a little more when meeting strangers who are inclined to properly shake their hands.

Eye Contact:

Depending upon the person's culture, there are some "dos" and "don'ts" to be considered, and we always try to be culturally correct. Staring and gazing is out of place unless we are "appropriately flirting," and we are at a time and place where this would not only be acceptable, but encouraged. That should be a sign that a person is "looking" for that special someone in his or her life (being single). Otherwise, gazing and staring will seem rude, distasteful and downright uncouth!

A Smile:

A smile melts a cold heart and raises the temperature of the cold or lukewarm heart. It speaks a universal language of its own. A shy person of any culture will melt and if that person happens to be in a place or country where his or her native tongue is hardly heard, can you imagine how that person will respond hearing his or her language being spoken by someone who is smiling? Wow!

Speaking of a smile having a language of its own, try instantly responding to a person with a smile sitting across from you who happens to be looking at you. The person will respond in kind. But if you do not respond instantly, the person will avoid looking in your direction or at you. Your smiling immediately acknowledges the person. Being hesitant implies a "put down." All this is unconscious, mind you, but the person is affected by your action or lack of action. Try this yourself and see what reaction you get. Who knows, just that alone may make a person want to get to know you, especially if you are looking good and smelling good early in the morning!

I wonder how many persons met, became friendly, courted (dated), and became engaged and married just because of this acknowledgment early in the morning. The person may hope to see you the same time another morning and so on.

To the shy persons who are hoping to find Ms. Right or Mr. Right, why not let a smile be your umbrella? Many people find shy smiles very attractive, especially the protective male who is looking for that special person who can possibly share his life.

If that male (attracted by her shy smile) is really interested, all he has to do is think of that person in positive ways, going over what attributes he recalls (good looks, posture, dignity and quietness) and in his thoughts compliment her on those qualities. Thoughts carry a great deal of energy and send messages. No doubt he will run into her again. When he does he can smile and say "Hello!" The energy exhumed known as vibes will be picked up by her and she will, even shy, give some response (if she is single and looking).

Perhaps you have read my essay, *"Please, Can You Spare a Hug?"* It tells of the importance of hugging (appropriately hugging this is). If you have not read it, please do and let that piece be a part of this essay, *"The Human Touch."*

A form of communication that is not talked about much is vibes. We are all affected by this strange experience. Positive vibes can be so invigorating and exciting, while negative vibes make us ill at ease. Keeping on a positive note, regarding human touch, I prefer to put more emphasis in the positive rather than the negative, even though it would be wise to understand the affect of each one,

Males seem to pick up negative vibes quicker than positive vibes. Women seem to more readily understand and pick up positive vibes. There may be an exception to this theory. But it is my observation in having many conversations with women. There are no hard and fast rules. There are many factors involved in attracting a person and they are too numerous to name.

It is real that a smile, firm handshake and eye contact and hugs will make a difference in your life in terms of meeting people, feeling comfortable about yourself and your world. Be happy; do not be afraid to let the world know that you are a happy person. It will pay big dividends wherever you are because it is "part and parcel" of the human touch.

A smile melts a cold heart and raises the temperature of a lukewarm heart.

THE PERSON IN YOUR MIRROR

"Do not conform any longer to the pattern of this world..."
Romans 12:2 (NIV)

You can travel a trillion miles, but you can never get away from the person in your mirror. Every mirror reflects you. So how well do you know the person?

God knows the inside of that person. Do you? You can play all the games you wish, but you cannot get away. You can be in denial, but when that person looks into your eyes, you know that person knows all about you.

So how do you make a real connection with the person in the mirror? How do you get to know that person better? Will you ever get to know him or her completely?

These and other questions you can ask the person, and if you sincerely ask the questions, you will get answers. If and when you follow through, you will see and experience favorable results.

Take a break from this reading for a minute and take a good look at that person, deep into the eyes, smile and frown. Pay attention to the person as you do these things.

Do you like what you see? Are you happy with that person? Without any game playing with that person, how honest are you in answering the following questions? Is the person perfect as far as you are concerned? Is the person attractive? Is the person happy? Is that person depressed? Is that person pretty much contented about life? Is the person willing to grow in ways needed to make life better, happier, pleasing and satisfying? Can you make changes in the person you see in your mirror? Yes, you can!

There is one certainty, if you are not able to give positive affirmative answers to those questions posed to you, you will not find happiness with that person or any other person. Happiness begins with the person you see in the mirror and is extremely contagious. You will find not

318

only happiness, but other feelings (good or bad) that you harbor about that person.

If you don't like what you see you can always make changes. Yes, you can! It only takes a desire and a positive thought which can start instantly. Do not wait. In fact, the longer you wait the more likely you are to lose the desire to change.

It costs you absolutely nothing to change. Some people think that they need professional help to change, but the thing is that even a trained and experienced professional cannot help you if **you are not willing** to change.

You are no different than I am (was). We look, act and think differently, but there is a common thread of love from God who fashioned us in His own image as human-beings that is binding us together. We have the same desires and propensities in lesser or greater degrees, but we express them differently. We are all embodied with the desire to love and be loved.

It makes no difference how many degrees we do or do not have. It makes no difference whether we are tall or short. It makes no difference whether we are considered rich or poor. Our outward appearance, of course, is different, but it makes no difference. The person in the mirror is more interested in what is in the heart. Is there love in your heart for the one in the mirror? If it is, that is all you need. Use that love to get you where you want to go. What you need is absolutely free. You can be the richest person in the world, but not be able to buy happiness, even if you spent every penny. Love is the secret. Use it beginning with the person you see in the mirror. Dare to extend it beyond that person and see what will happen to you.

If you see or feel no love for the person in the mirror, ask for it for him or her. Ask that the love of God comes into the person's heart. Keep asking every day as you look into the mirror until you see a smile on that person's face reflecting the deep love in the person's heart, soul and mind. Recognize and acknowledge what and how you feel about the **new person** in your mirror. Your mirror will not lie to you. What you see is what you are and who you are.

Warning: After you have made whatever changes needed, your mirror will reflect a smile so bright and beautiful coming from the depth of your heart, soul and mind. You will be so surprised that you

Dr. Melvin R. Hall

might think the person in the mirror has been replaced by someone else. Make that correction NOW. I did!

**Can you make changes in the person you see in
your mirror? Yes, you can!**

THE SEEDS WE SOW

"Be not deceived; for God is not mocked, for whatsoever a
man sows, that shall he also reap."
Galatians 6:7 (KJV)

Never in my wildest imagination can I think that I will grow collard greens when I plant tomato seeds in my garden.

Life is like a garden. We reap just what we sow, so then, why is life so complicated? Wouldn't it be simpler if we just planted what we want to harvest? And from each seed or plant comes abundance. Think about that for a moment.

As simple as it may seem, it isn't easy. And the reason it isn't easy is because we do not seem to think about the little formula of life that warns us **what goes out comes back in greater abundance.**

Too often we blame others for our situation. All of our emphasis is on trying to get others to change when we are the ones who need to change; we talk about our mistreatment all the while we are doing the same or worse. How then do we expect to be treated differently? The simple truth is what goes around comes around.

Perhaps we need a wakeup call. In one of my previous essays in <u>Our Times</u>, *the Person in Your Mirror,* gives a thought along the line of sowing seeds. According to the essay, we need to take a good look at ourselves internally. By doing so we can give some thought to the seeds we plant. Any changes that have to be made in our lives must begin with us. I am reminded of finger pointing. While one finger is pointing to a person, three are pointing back. What do you think that is telling him or her?

Let's look at some seeds we can sow so that we can reap a glorious harvest in our garden of life. A smile would cause others to smile back. Charity would be a blessing to someone needing help. A kind word would lift the spirit of a person who is sad. A word of encouragement would help someone, who is struggling to accomplish a difficult task.

A surprise gift would bring joy to someone, and a wonderful sense of humor will enlighten someone's spirit. If we stretched our imagination a little, we can come up with many more seeds.

I am very pleased when persons give me something they want me to have. And I am pleased when I can give others something I want them to have. The giver receives a blessing of having lifted someone's spirit. The receiver has the blessing of being thought of and loved. Do you know of persons who love to give but have a hard time receiving? The first thing out of their mouth is, "You shouldn't have." How do you think that makes the giver feel? A simple response to receiving a gift is "Thank you so much!" That is being gracious and it makes the giver feel good.

How many times have we asked God for something and when it comes through a person, we are not gracious in accepting it? It seems as if we expect God to deliver it Himself. Each of us at some point and time becomes the conduit through which God works to deliver a blessing. The more God uses us the more we are rewarded, even though whatever we do is not for the reward. But it can't be helped, because it is the law of divine nature.

We are not always careful of what we say to another. Sometimes we are so focused on getting a certain job done that we forget to speak kindly to the person doing the job. And too often we are bent out of shape over small matters.

When we allow ourselves to become more aware of what we do to others, we will find others thinking of us more kindly and will treat us better. A good rule is known as the golden rule, and it is, "Do unto others what we would want done unto us." If we could just do that, what a difference this world would be! Just imagine how flourishing our gardens of love would be.

Sowing seeds of selflessness instead of selfishness would help to make our world a better place in which to thrive and live. You know selfishness harvests weeds that choke the desired growth of love, devotion, caring, understanding, complimenting and consideration of others' feelings. But if we are not careful, the weeds of disrespect, lack of interest, ridicule, agitation and other undesired habits will take over the garden and we will find all of the good flowers of love choked to death.

Actually, no one wants a garden over run with weeds. So what we have to do is start nipping the weeds in the bud so that they will not thrive and ruin our gardens. Actually, a better thing to do is to pull up the weeds by their tender roots before they increase in size and thickness. It's easier that way. Once a weed is allowed to gain strength, damage is done and feelings are hurt. The job of removing weeds becomes harder and very irritating.

Why don't we then check to see what weeds we are sowing intentionally and unintentionally? Without the weeds choking our plants we will be able to supply everyone the fruit of the spirit which is **love, joy, peace, patience, kindness, goodness, faithfulness, gentleness and self-control** (Galatians 5:22) from our gardens.

**Sowing seeds of selflessness instead of selfishness
would help to make our world a better place in
which to thrive and live.**

THE STRENGTH OF OUR ENDURANCE

*"And He said unto me, 'my grace is sufficient for thee: for
my strength is made perfect in weakness.'"*
II Corinthians 12:9 (KJV)

We will never know the strength of our endurance until we are tested. And life has many tests. Too often before we attempt anything we say that we are not capable of doing it. The thought of not feeling capable comes to our thinking and we buy into it.

It is most unfortunate when that happens because we are capable of doing many things we have not even thought of. That is why it is so important to expose children to many positive things even before they learn to read.

Children's early exposure to learning is by the process of internalization. They internalize what they see much more than what they hear. And yet, they have good memories and will often repeat something their parents or others have said to the chagrin of the persons who wished they hadn't said it. If you have been in the company of children you know exactly what I am talking about. This can prove quite embarrassing.

So the strength of our endurance begins to build early in our growth and development from the cradle to the grave. Can you imagine being nurtured in a household of adults who have a strong sense of accomplishment? Such a household does not believe and do not use the word "can't." That household evidently believes we can do all things through Christ who strengthens us.

My heart goes out to people who have so little self-confidence that they don't even try. They feel they are incapable. We are not going to talk too much about them, but what is truly delightful is watching children who seem to have so much confidence in themselves that they seem to want to know how to do anything and everything. Regardless of what you are doing, they say they know how to do it. Well, often they are not really up to the task of doing it, but we don't want to discourage them and we don't want them to make a mess or destroy or break anything. So we have to find a way of letting them express themselves while we are teaching them the proper way of handling whatever it is. This requires some creativeness and imagination on our part. Children who are confident are full of imagination and creativity. This brings another thought to mind. We do not want to stifle their imagination and yet we do not want them to create major problems. At the same time we do not want to instill a great deal of fear into their little minds.

We want to keep building their strength of endurance. If you want to enjoy moments of humor many years after you have raised your children and they have become quite successful in their professions, we can think back to the time when it took every ounce of our strength of endurance to raise them.

Gifted children are very talented. Children seem to be born with the ability to learn how computers work while we older folk have some difficulty trying to master it. For most of us as adults we need to take a course in computer literacy or some kind of training. Children can sit at a computer and amaze you with their learning on their own. Do you dispute this?

I know a family in Manassas, Virginia where all of the children in this family seemed born with athletic and other skills. The youngest one in the family complex has known "everything" since the day he started talking. This child (now 9) has had a grand sense of confidence since age 1.

Now, such a child can drive you bananas at times, and it takes a great deal of patience because not only does he profess to know everything, he practically does accomplish tasks that will surprise you. His parents have to give him some "brake fluid" at times, but for the most part, he's okay. The problem is he sometimes wants to take over what you are doing without your invitation. That along with doing something that can prove dangerous calls for the application of "brake fluid."

Now, he, like all of the other persons before him who are now professional adults with excellent professions, has the strength of endurance that successful persons admire and respect.

Let me share with you about this family from which this little 9 year old hails from. His grandmother at her present age of 84 is the winner of many senior Olympics gold and silver medals from the age of 70 plus.

Fortunately for me, I have known this family over forty years and I have seen the dynamics of each generation of accomplishing members. It is understood that not going to college is not an option. I don't think the possibility of going to college is as much talked about as acted upon. The fact is mother went to college and daddy went to college and there is no question that the children will go to college. Many of them have received athletic scholarships. One of the mothers is an athletic director at her school.

Now, the patriarch at 87(father, grandfather, great grandfather) of this esteemed gifted family is the married partner of the lady who has won and is still winning gold and silver medals in the senior Olympics. Although he has been retired from his profession for a large numbers of years, he is still active in another and is the most beloved sexton (pro bono) of his church.

To each and every member of this family (children and grandchildren) their strength of endurance is amazing. Their self-esteem, motivation, inspiration and encouragement of one another easily draw the admiration of everyone in the City of Manassas. Talking about role models, they are that indeed!

I am surprised they have not been interviewed on national television. The matriarch as an Olympian has been written about, but I believe the family is too modest and humble to even accept an offer to be televised. Of course, the 9 year old is an exception. I believe he would welcome the occasion and would hold his own because he is just that confident and articulate.

When I speak about having the strength of endurance, the family I have spoken of naturally comes to my mind. You may know of many other families, but the point is - all of us are created by God to draw from the limitless supply that He continues to provide for us; so that we will be able to become our best and to do the best we can for the betterment of ourselves and others.

Yes, we all have the ability to have strength of endurance. I would strongly suggest that we continue to read about many persons who have made tremendous progress coming from a life of poverty, discrimination and great despair and negativities stacked against them.

How did they make it? When we desire to be achievers we can do what they did. They called on God (their) and our Divine Source. They asked, listened, and were obedient and faithful. When we do the same, we will be amazed how strong we will become in our strength of endurance

**People who have never accomplished anything are
the last persons to talk with because they see the
impossible rather than the possible.**

The Sweetness of Forgiving

"The troubles of my heart are enlarged: O bring me out
of my distresses, Look upon mine affliction and my pain,
and forgive all my sins.
Psalms 25:17-18 (KJV)

For whatever reason or reasons some people have a problem with forgiving some wrong or hurt they have experienced. If you happen to be one of those persons, this essay is for you. I would like to invite you to the sweetness of forgiving.

The person or persons who directly or indirectly caused you hurt or pain may or may not have long forgotten the incident or incidents, But the reality is, you, yourself can rectify your individual situation by forgiving the person or persons who inflicted the pain. You can be pain free. It is all up to you now.

Let us say whatever happened occurred early in your very young life and you have been holding onto it ever since. Being realistic, the only person who knows your pain is you and when people say, "For heaven sakes, you are an adult now! Get real. Why are you dragging the past into your life now? Why don't you move on?" They are partly right, but they don't really understand what you have been through in your young life and how your experiences have become so ingrained in your soul.

They are partly right because you do not have to continue to suffer. On the other hand it is not so easy to forget about what happened and the impact it made on your life. Actually, you do not have to continue to suffer. It may appear to others that it is just that simple, but it isn't.

Sometimes our pain makes us bitter and we may resent and reject anyone prying into our lives, but the truth is we need help. We need to find someone among our **real friends** whom we trust to talk with when we have a genuine desire to release the bitterness.

The only way the bitterness is going to be released is by forgiving the person or persons who hurt us so badly. I want you to know that I am not speaking strictly from my training in matters of this sort, but from experience as well. I have found there is real sweetness in forgiving and I want to share that with you because you deserve to live a life that is going to enhance your joy and sense of worth not impede all that you were created (born) to receive.

What happens all too often is that persons influencing us to feel the way we do about ourselves may no longer remember, or are dead, but we are keeping the pain alive simply because we feel we cannot forgive. In actuality, we may never forget, but when we forgive, the pain is no longer prevalent and the relief is so sweet!

It would be of little good for me to disclose what caused the pain I carried for years, but I do think it would be helpful for you to know how I was able to release it and move on.

I went to a professional, recommended by my minister, who dealt with such matters At first I had serious reservations because the professional was a psychiatrist. My minister was eventually able to assure me that I did not have to have mental problems to consult with a psychiatrist, but I did have problems that affected me emotionally.

Well, after talking with the good doctor I learned that I had to release the hurt feelings; part of that process was talking with him (a professional stranger) who assured me that our talk was strictly confidential. The words that I distinctly remember him saying were, "You must fully forgive them." I did, and from that very moment I felt as if weight had been lifted off my shoulders and my soul felt free!

Subsequently, my training in human relations taught me that I must not internalize the negative sayings and actions I am daily surrounded and confronted with; I do my own judging about me because I know my circumstances better than anyone.

My dear friend in pain, you can begin to free yourself. No one can do it for you. Only you can decide that you want to be free and the only way you are going to be is to forgive those persons whom you have let influence your life much too long.

If you feel you need to talk to a professional, you should. However, if you have a close trusted friend who will keep in confidence every word you share, then you do not have to engage the services of a professional.

You and I are not the only ones who now have (or had) this experience. There are many persons just like us who are wasting so much time being caught up in pain and bitterness. But since you are fortunate and blessed to have come across this essay, what are you going to do for you? Why not discover for yourself the joy and sweetness of forgiving?

The only way the bitterness is going to be released is by forgiving the person or persons who hurt us so badly.

THERE IS NO BETTER TIME THAN THE PRESENT

"To every thing there is a season, and a time for every purpose under the heaven."
Ecclesiastes 3:1 (NIV)

The past is dead. Tomorrow is not promised; all we have is the present which is now! Think about this for a moment, and please continue to think about it as you read this essay.

You may not find the first paragraph acceptable, but keep reading with an open mind. An open mind along with belief makes it possible for us to achieve anything we desire.

For those who feel hopeless, powerless and enslaved to the past, this essay will release you from feeling stuck to becoming free and finding the happiness that you truly want and deserve.

The Past:

There is absolutely nothing that you can do about the past. It is true that we are influenced by it to some extent, but it does not have to define us nor does it have to dictate or control the present. Much of the past we had no control over. Some we had, but we now have the opportunity and the responsibility to leave the past in the past and do all we can now to change our negative situations to positive. Therein lays the happiness we seek.

About tomorrow:

There is no guarantee that we will see tomorrow. We have no control over our own departure from this life as we know it. Every day that is added to our longevity is a blessing and we ought to treat it as such. Every day that we wake up in our "right" mind, and we have the use of all our limbs and faculties, that is a blessing so we ought to be grateful and treat all that we have with the greatest respect.

Today:

Today is all we have. It is that special gift given to us to do what is right not only to ourselves but to everyone that we come in contact with. Today we can find whatever we need to make our life complete: the wholeness we seek, the peace we desire, the ability to find and give love. Today enables us to make whatever changes need to be made.

The joy of that is we do not have to do it alone. There is help. Our Creator, the Magnificent Designer, is ever willing and ready to come to our aid. He has the wherewithal to change anything at any time. His unconditional love is always present and He wants to shower us with love in meeting our individual and unique needs.

Do you know who the Creator is? Do you recognize the power He has? Well, today is the time to seek His help. We can never ask too much of Him. We often ask too little. We often think we are self-sufficient and that is a fallacy. As independent as we think we are, each of us depends on someone for something. We were created to help each other and God supplies the means. All we have to do to get help is simply to ask Him sincerely and earnestly, and He will supply everything.

Most unfortunately, there are some people who do not believe that God exists. Those persons act under the delusion that they control their own life. What a pity because God wants the best for us and He provides for those who ask. As long as we have breath, we can ask and His help is ever present. He works through each of us to help others. As we receive, we give. We do not give to receive, but it is inevitable that what goes around comes around. The Scripture says it is more blessed to give than to receive. Think about that. But one cannot give without receiving.

For those who do not know our Creator, it would greatly benefit them to make themselves aware of His greatness and love. He freely gives without a moment's hesitation. Those of us who know Him a little need to know Him more so that we can make ourselves available for all that He has to give. We just have to ask, listen, follow through and be obedient. The Bible spells it out perfectly. It is the book instructing what to do, how to do it, and it gives God's promises to us if we simply obey His instructions. His communication is like no other. We ask, He answers, and we obey. He supplies. He gives us power to do what we call the "impossible."

Spend some time reading the Book (Bible). I suggest you read from the translation that you best understand, and at the same time, ask Him for greater understanding.

You will find yourself enjoying life more with blessings overflowing. God is so awesome! You will wonder why you didn't seek Him in the past, but the joy of it all is that you are seeking him now (today). And the results are going to be amazing. Trust yourself in placing your life in His hands. You have placed your life in the hands of others and what did that bring you…heartaches, frustration, unhappiness, a sense of powerlessness, and hopelessness? Remember, all you have to do is ask the One who created the universe and us. You see what an awesome job He did in His creation. He will do an awesome job in you starting today. You see, there is no time as the present!

There is no guarantee that we will see tomorrow.

TIME MANAGEMENT AND ORGANIZATION

"… Deal courageously, and the Lord shall be with the good."
II Chronicles 19:11 (KJV)

Some people seem to have the ability to accomplish a great deal from day to day. Others don't seem to manage to get done what they hoped or expected to. They do not seem to have enough time. Why is there a difference? There is a difference because of time management and organization.

Just what is time management and organization? It is simply being focused on what one has to do or what one has decided what he or she wants to accomplish. So the person goes about the task of starting and working at a pace that will ensure that the work is done in a timely fashion.

The "enemy" of time management and organization is procrastination. The "friend" of time management and organization is a strong desire for accomplishment and pride in the completion of various tasks. A person desirous of this has to be positive in thought and action. Additionally, the person has to have confidence in himself or herself. This person knows without a doubt that he or she can accomplish anything through the power of the Holy Spirit. "It is God who girdeth me with strength and maketh my way perfect." (Psalm 18:32).

Faith and trust in God will release any doubt a person has about him or herself to accomplish any task. Consequently, one does not have to concern him or herself how the job is going to be done. He or she knows that having God's approval empowers, enables, and motivates him or her to accomplish all things through God who gives them strength and fortitude to stick with the tasks to its completion.

Procrastination clearly shows doubt, lack of interest and confidence in one's own skills and abilities. This results in one losing focus and direction often at the point of his or her feeble (procrastinated) beginning.

Proactive people who enthusiastically tackle their tasks do so with the thought of nothing short of getting the job done and done well. Those persons are also known as achievers.

Achievers are believers who enjoy being successful in whatever they commit themselves to. The problem with some achievers is that they do not allow themselves the luxury of resting and relaxing. They are always busy working on some project or program. The negative side is not being able to say "no" when their plate is full. So administrators, supervisors or people otherwise in charge call upon them, the busiest ones, because they are the ones who will get the job done efficiently and in a timely fashion.

Strangely enough, because the busy person gets the job done, the one in charge will pass over another worker who is supposed to be equally qualified to do the task. And, which is most unfortunate and unfair, the achiever is the last to receive promotion and salary increases. You may hear that the person is too valuable to be promoted out of the department. Well, if that is the case, why not give the person an appreciative increase in salary? Otherwise, the person may move on to another employment that truly appreciates his or her work ethics.

Let us not kid ourselves. We all know that everyone desires recognition and appreciation for his or her special efforts in employment or service. So why don't we regularly reward the worker whose work is done accurately, efficiently and expediently?

Mr. or Ms. Skilled Worker: If you are topnotch workers why stay on a job that does not recognize your skills, efficiency and dedication? You must speak up for yourself if the one who is supposed to recommend you for an increase in salary or a promotion does not.

Mr. & Ms. Manager: Good workers are hard to find these days. Most people do not want to give an honest day's work. When you find persons with excellent work ethics you should reward them showing your recognition and appreciation. By so doing you will be acting with courage.

Good workers like to work under the supervision of supervisors who have the courage to demand more for his or her workers. You will find other workers wanting to be transferred to his or her department. That supervisor's own reward may be a promotion matching his or her skills. That may be the beginning of his or her upward mobility to the position of manager and then to administrator. From there he or she might find him or herself in position of training of persons on supervisory levels on the treatment of employees who are skilled in time management and organization.

We all know that everyone desires recognition and appreciation.

Transformation

"Do not conform any longer to the pattern of this world,
but be transformed by the renewing of your mind."
Romans 12:2 (NIV)

When I started writing for *Our Times* one of my essays was about the physical transformation of the caterpillar into a butterfly through the metaphoric process.

The transformation that I am writing about in this essay is about the spiritual transformation of humankind. With all transformations, whether physical or spiritual, the change leaves no resemblance to the old self. Notice the difference between the caterpillar and the butterfly. (That essay is also in this book.) Now in the spiritual transformation, the physical difference may be only the countenance of the person showing a change. That physical difference will be a smiling face replacing frowns.

The spiritual transformation produces a real and complete change of heart and will find persons thinking more positively about themselves. Consequently, their behavior changes and good thinking, good feelings and good behavior dominate their entire being.

In the physical transformation the caterpillar has no control. It cannot make the decision to change. It was created to automatically change when the time is right according to the plan of our Creator.

We as human beings have a choice. We were born innocent. By association and exposure we adapt to the environment in which we live. If the environment happens to be negative, we become negative. However, we do not have to remain that way. We can change, but not on our own. We did not become negative on our own. We had help to become negative so we need help to change.

When we decide that we are tired of the unhappy way we live and cannot seem to find a way to reap more joy, peace, contentment, love, happiness and a wonderful sense of being, we can call upon our Creator to change us into what we were originally meant to be.

God, our Creator, is the way, the truth and the light. There is the best selling book called the Bible. It tells us how to become the better person that we desire to be. When we have searched for love, acceptance and understanding in all the wrong places, the Bible will guide us to the right Source. What better Source is there than our Creator who made us in His image? A humorous way of stating this is "going back to the drawing board." Another way of saying this comes from a hymn "God is the Potter and we are the clay."

When a lump of clay is not being fashioned into the shape that we want, it can be remolded. In a sense we go back to the Creator (the Potter) so we can be reshaped. Our hearts become filled with love. Our thoughts are no longer the same and our actions are consistent with our hearts and thoughts. Wow!

None of this is easily understood. That is why faith (believing what we cannot explain, see or truly understand) is the key to being able to change.

When we are tired of being on the losing end of everything while others seem happy and smiling most of the time, questions should run through our heads such as: "Why can't I be like them? How can I find peace in my soul?" Again, there is a book that continues to sell more copies than any other book ever written and that book gives us instructions and powerful messages of promises that God makes to us if we follow His direction.

It isn't enough to have the book in our possession. It isn't enough to put it under our pillow thinking it is going to ward off evil. The science of osmosis doesn't work from under our pillow into our heads and hearts. It has to be read. I suggest daily readings when you find yourself in a state of turmoil and you don't know what to do or to whom to turn. This book will direct you to God and God will direct you to (or send) the right person or persons to you.

Don't be fooled in thinking that everyone who goes to church is the right person. As you read your Bible, you will learn to discern who in the church you should seek solace from and who you should not. A measure of discernment is knowing that action speaks louder than words. One of the many things that have brought you to the state that you are in is words from the wrong people (some in church and some are not).

One of the wonderful results of transformation is that we become empowered with and by love. We discover discernment, and then we are able to connect ourselves to the invisible and powerful positive forces in the universe. There are good (godly) and bad (evil) forces that affect every living soul. We become able to attract the good elements and become affected by them through our thoughts.

Some people wonder why everything they touch turns "sour." I often hear, "It does not pay for me to do anything because it is not going to come out right." It doesn't. And the reason nothing comes out right is that the persons are attracting the wrong invisible elements. Ever heard of self-fulfilling prophecy? What's wrong here? The persons need to change their hearts and their thinking and likewise their behavior. The difference is love dwells in the heart. A loving heart produces loving thoughts about others and self, even of seemingly unlovable people.

A loving heart carries more power than you can imagine. Why? The reason that is God dwells in the heart. So there is nothing you need to do when you run into unloving folk but to let God's power in you fight your battle and deal with the unloving person. Initially, they are going to provoke you to stoop to their level. When they see that you are not fighting back, the persons will hastily depart from your presence. Don't be surprised if they express their frustration by departing with a curse word or two. I have experienced that more times than I can count, and each time I smiled and said, "Thank you, Lord!" There are too many persons getting caught up in negative elements without any effort on their part. All it takes is to think negative. The elements will embellish their thinking with more negativity. In such cases they find themselves helpless, and, of course, their self-confidence goes down to zero. With zero self-confidence, a multitude of problems beset them and they find themselves in all kinds of trouble. At that point they are out of control. They do things they really do not want to do, but feel they cannot help themselves. What happens then that is they keep going down until they find themselves in a bottomless pit (also "known as rock bottom").

The good news is at that point and in any condition in our life we can change. If you have any doubt about this there are many books written about persons who have been transformed. They have become new creatures. Their happiness knows no bounds. The smile on their faces will melt your heart. They are people you need to talk to. They will tell you that they have "been there – done that" – now they are happier than they have ever been. I can hear them saying, "If I can do it, so can you!" When your transformation is complete, you will do the same. This is a truly wonderful cycle. Can you imagine being transformed and sought after to tell your story? Also some televised stories have also shown persons who have been transformed and you can actually see and feel their radiance.

So if you are looking for unconditional love, happiness, peace, joy, contentment, self-confidence and prosperity, I trust that reading this essay will lead you to the Source and to the Book (His words) where you will find these words, "Seek me, come to me, and I will give you the Kingdom," He says. Reach and take His outstretched hands and "see" yourself enfolded in His arms saying, "Take me Lord, just as I am!" With just those words sincerely and desperately spoken, you will find yourself being transformed into the person you were born to be. You must have heard the declaration"**being born again!**" That is what you will experience and you will not be able to keep it to yourself. Not only will the world see it in your face, the world will hear it in your talk and it will be confirmed by your walk.

The good news is at any point and any condition of our life we can change.

Two Bosom Buddies:
Envy & Jealousy

"A heart at peace gives life to the body, but envy rots the bones."
Proverb 14:30 (NIV)

Two evil and destructive buddies (actually, very close pals) are envy and jealousy. When you see one you usually see the other. However, envy travels solo at times. But you can bet jealousy is not too far behind. When envy does travel alone, it checks in to the hearts of normally good people. It really cannot make a home in the heart of good people because they are basically trying to do the right thing and attempt to treat people fairly.

But, in that weak moment that good persons experience at times, envy stops to rest itself without jealousy catching up with him.

Now, really weak persons gladly invite envy and jealousy, welcoming them to take residence in their hearts. You see, really weak people carry evil thoughts in their minds. So to have more company of like nature is no problem for them. Envy and jealousy are always looking for homes for themselves. There are more weak persons for them to live with than you might be able to imagine.

Envy and jealousy are out to destroy happy and successful people in any way they can. They will do whatever they can to bring them down. A primary difference between the two bosom pals is envy carries heavier resentment and has a tendency to be destructive. And if it doesn't restrain itself, it will definitely seek to hurt the object of its disdain. Jealousy seems to have more control, but is unhappy about the accomplishment of someone it is secretly competing against.

They convince weak and downtrodden cooperative persons that they have enemies in unsuspecting, innocent persons who are going about their daily lives minding their own business - being productive and prosperous. They convince weak persons that prosperous folk are taking from them and that is why they aren't successful, too.

Understand that envy and jealousy do not like to see people prospering. They conjure all kinds of evilness against people and often the object of their attempted destruction is not aware of what is happening.

This may sound preposterous and farfetched, but it is more prevalent than we may want to think or believe. However, we don't have to fall prey to their nefarious behavior because the truth wins out in the final analysis, and envy and jealousy will be exposed for the evil they are.

Good and honest people do not have to prove themselves. When so called friends have doubts about your goodness, they were never friends anyhow. And, be mindful of so called friends who lend themselves to the antics of those two bosom buddies. They never were your friends. And because of their envy and jealousy, they were always taking advantage of your generosity.

Naturally, when you try to do your best by others and those two culprits play their game, it hurts. Please know that they will be found out as the phonies that they are, and they will have their own price to pay. What goes around comes around, and it is usually in greater abundance when it comes around.

True believers know that there is evil all around us. But we don't have to fight our own battles as long as we remain faithful to our Creator and read His word and act accordingly.

All persons have some ordeal through which they must suffer through, and while we are experiencing it, what is helpful is to know that and to say, "This too shall pass." In the final analysis, after it passes, the world will know the truth!

Understand that envy and jealousy do not like to see people prospering.

Unconditional Love, Compassion, Grace & Mercy

"Grace, mercy and peace will be with you from God the Father, and from The Lord Jesus Christ, the Son of the Father in truth and love.
II John 3 (NIV)

There are some people who wake up each morning dreading the arrival of another day. They don't see the awakening as something good, something special and a new opportunity to make whatever changes they need to make in order to feel good about themselves and their world.

To them each day is just another day of the same old thing that has happened to them day after day, and year after year. It is most unfortunate that they do not see the bright side and the good that is afforded them just by being alive. They don't see the brand new day as an opportunity to squarely face their problems and resolve them or ask for help.

Do you fit in this category? Are you one of those persons? Does life seem hopeless to you? Do you feel as if no one cares about you? Do you feel that you are lost in the crowd? Do you feel there is nothing in life to laugh about?

If you are one of those people, know that you are not alone. It does not have to be your fault that you find yourself in your condition or situation. I strongly, but lovingly suggest that you read this essay very slowly and carefully. As you read you may find your eyes tearing and that's okay.

What you may not know is that there is someone who can in an instant wash these feelings away and can give you a different outlook on life. This Person loves you unconditionally. This means regardless of what you have done in your life, you are still loved. The love that you can claim immediately is yours for the asking. Why? It is because this Person has compassion. He knows that you are not perfect (as none of us is) and He doesn't really expect you to be because to expect you to be perfect is to expect you to be super human. No one can fill this bill. It is impossible; however, we must strive to be our best.

If you are wondering who this Person is, read the quoted Scripture just under the title of this essay. Yes, God's grace is a blessing which means that it is given unearned. Added to this is His mercy and mercy is forgiveness.

Forgiveness is not always because of what you have done to someone else, but what you have done to yourself that places you in the condition that you are in.

Some people have placed themselves in unhappy positions because they do not believe there is anyone who loves them unconditionally and has compassion, grace and mercy. But this writer wants you to know that the One who created the universe is the One who loves you unconditionally.

If you have any doubt believing, how do you think the world came into being? Do you think humankind keeps it working in good and perfect order? What about the seasons: spring, summer, fall and winter? Do you think humankind is that smart and has such control? Do you really think that humankind has unconditional love, true deep compassion, grace and mercy? What about the stars and planets, sun and moon. Are they controlled by humankind?

Let us address your feelings about yourself upon arising in the morning. Wouldn't you like to wake up with a feeling of excitement of what blessings the day will bring through God's grace and mercy? Wouldn't you like to feel God's love? If your answers are yes, all you have to do is simply ask God for what you want believing that you will receive whatever you ask for. Matthew 7:7 says, "Ask, and it shall be given to you. Seek and you shall find. Knock and it shall be opened to you."

This may be new to you. If it is not new, maybe you have forgotten what it feels like to be happy and looking forward to good things happening to you. In any case, when you are alone and in a quiet place, imagine that you are talking to a warm, understanding and kind friend; just pour out your heart, asking for His peace, compassion, grace and mercy. Let Him know how you feel and what you want in your life. Feel the warmth that will engulf your body as your heart fills with His love. If you feel the tears in your eyes, don't hold them back. Let them flow. That is part of the love entering your heart and soul.

Suddenly you will feel as light as a feather. That will be the Holy Spirit filling your soul. The key is to believing that all things are possible to those who believe. "And all things whatever you ask in prayer, believing you will receive" (Matthew 21:22).

Tomorrow morning when you awake you will experience a difference. You will jump out of bed ready for the day and the blessings the day will bring through the power of your Lord and Savior Jesus Christ.

When you are alone and in a quiet place, imagine that you are talking to a warm, understanding and kind friend; just pour out your heart.

UNSOLICITED ADVICE

*"I said, I will heed to my ways, that I sin not with my
tongue. I will keep my mouth with a bridle..."*
Psalm 39:1(KJV)

Have you ever had a strong desire to talk to someone, but you
didn't want any advice? Did the person listen without saying anything
but showed signs of listening by a nod or just a word or two? How did
you feel?

Have you ever tried to talk to someone about a burning issue
and the person started talking and advising you what to do at every
sentence? How did you feel?

Did you ever had a burning desire to release some bent up feelings,
and as soon as you began to talk, the persons took the conversation
away from you and began expressing their own feelings? How did you
feel?

I have had two of the three experiences and I have been sorry that
I approached the persons to talk. Can you guess which two? I have
learned that when I was not seeking advice and just wanted to talk,
my first sentence should be "I just need you to listen. I am not seeking
advice or your opinion. Okay?"

First of all, when there is something on your mind and you feel
the need to talk to someone, you first have to carefully select the right
person. It should be a friend because you don't know how a stranger
is going to accept what you have to say without being judgmental.
Secondly, you need to know that the friend will treat what you are
sharing as confidential. Some friends are quite talkative and for whatever
reason, they just have to "share" your business with one or two of their
other friends who may or may not be a friend of yours. However, even
if the person is a friend of yours, it is not the business of the persons to
whom you are speaking to say anything to anyone, friend or foe.

I know from first hand experience the anguish one can suffer from opening one's heart to the wrong person. I seriously thought a person was my friend, but I found out too late the person was "my friend" for selfish reasons. Loyalty was not included in the friendship. The anguish resulted from his betrayal and the blame I placed on myself for not being wise in my selection of the person as a friend. That was a terrible experience in terms of my own judgment because genuine friendship had always been profoundly important to me.

Sometimes we encounter a person who poses as a friend because of our generosity. Persons reading this essay should be aware of such people. Usually they are willing takers and give just enough to have you think they, too, are giving persons. Do you have friends who are "your friends" for what they can get from you? Maybe you need to become more aware of who is a friend and who isn't. What do you think?

All persons at sometime in their lives need someone to talk to. That is why listening is not only a skill, but a responsibility. To be able to listen with your ears and your heart is a learned skill.

There are some people who are extremely good listeners and who, by nature, don't talk much. Have you ever heard of the expression "still water runs deep?" Such persons are usually good judge of character, but they only respond if asked a specific or direct question. And even then there is no guarantee that they will give you an answer. Now, that is a good person to have on your list of genuine friends. If you have at least one, feel blessed.

While we are talking about unsolicited advice, where do you find yourself? Yes, I'm asking you, the person reading this essay. Are you quick with answers even though you don't know the facts? Are you quick to give advice when you have not been told the **whole** story?

We should all know that when persons come to us, they are only telling us their side, and if we give any response (advice) we are wrong. Do you fashion yourself the "community/ neighborhood counselor" who is free with giving advice? Every community or neighborhood has at least one.

It would be wise to still your tongue of which you have only one, and use your ears of which you have two. If you are giving unsolicited advice it is probably to each person only once. You may notice that persons no longer come to you and you wonder why. The reason may well be they wanted your ears but you gave them your tongue. There is a saying "do not put your tongue in action until you put your brain in gear." So giving any kind of advice without thinking it through is wrong and potentially dangerous.

Unfortunately, we function more by our emotions - influenced by what we think and not know. Good listeners are always desired and needed. Persons will highly praise us as wonderful conversationalist when we hold our tongue, and use our ears twice as much as our tongue.

**We should all know that when persons come to us,
they are only telling us their side of the story.**

VENEER

*"We...will not boast beyond proper limits, but will
confine our boasting to the field God has assigned to us."*
2 Corinthians 10:12 (NIV)

According to Mr. Webster, my consultant whom I visit quite often, the word *veneer* refers to a thin layer glued over a cheaper substance. He calls it superficial display.

A thin layer glued over a cheaper substance serves well to define veneer when we are talking about physical things.

Many years ago when I left North Carolina and returned two years later, I was surprised to see a cousin's framed one story house brick veneered. When I compared it to the two stories all brick home of my aunt, I couldn't see any difference. In terms of beauty, both looked great!

This essay is not about veneered tangible things, but actually people who appear quite differently than they really are. This brings my thoughts to the word *façade* which Webster defines as "front part of anything; often used figuratively, with implications of an imposing appearance concealing something inferior."

My mother could spot a person's façade immediately. She and I enjoyed having private conversations about people as human-beings. Although I enjoyed those private times together, at my young age of ten, I think it was more entertaining to me than educational. Her intent was to educate me on learning people for who they were, rather than what they pretended to be. Of course, as an adult, I now appreciate the value of her lessons.

It is my belief, even with her ability to "spot" people; she was disappointed and hurt by persons she thought were her friends. As a friend she thought she should help them by raising their self-esteem and self-worth. My mother classified herself, even though a maid, as a professional person. She wanted her friends to see themselves as professionals as well. The story I am about to share demonstrated this.

Mother was a natural organizer and she believed in justice and fair treatment of people. She worked in an exclusive area in North Carolina as a sleep-in –maid. The entire area had sleep-in-maids.

After reading a book on "collective bargaining," she decided to "educate" the other maids. She hoped to start with one whom she supposed to be a friend. Mother suggested that the friend during her time off read a book and she and the friend would discuss the contents.

Together they would encourage the other maids to do the same once a week during their few hours off during the day. Unfortunately, the "friend" shared the information with her employer and the employer called my mother's female employer.

Mother's employers were fair-minded people and I am sure they did not agree with the racism that took place in the southern town of North Carolina. Mr. & Mrs. A appreciated my mother's thirst for learning and knew that my mother liked to read.

Mrs. A approached my mother after supper one evening saying, "Martha, I know and understand your desire to help the other maids and I think your plan is an honorable one, and I personally approve of it. But you see your friend went to her madam and complained that you were causing them to rebel against their employers.

I know that was not your intention. You wanted them to enjoy reading as you do and to share the knowledge they would gain by reading books. That would give them something constructive to think and talk about instead of gossiping when you all are together on your breaks."

Mother's employers had a great deal of admiration and respect for her as she was valued as a highly intelligent employee and she understood my mother's intent to "educate" her peers. My mother felt being a maid was an honorable profession and she took great pride in her work. Mother's intent was purely to raise the level of intellect among the maids so they would take greater pride in their profession and in themselves. I think her secret wish was for them to change their speech pattern as she had done, living in New York for many years before migrating back to the south. And I think she would have loved the opportunity to "teach" them to accept and present themselves as professionals and not mere maids.

My mother was crushed and greatly disappointed, but she learned to keep her thoughts to herself, and until her death I was her only audience. I was quite willing to be it because I learned much from her. I've been blessed by our experience together. She taught me more about human nature than all the sociology and psychology courses I was required to take in both undergraduate and graduate schools. In fact, because of her, I excelled in those courses and decided to spend my life working directly with people. What a blessing that has been and still is!

The basic lesson I learned from my mother was observing people who found the need to "cover up" what they lack by wearing a veneer of "knowledge" they don't really have. The veneer looks good, but, unlike something tangible that you can see and feel, the real self comes through loud and clear to those who take the time to learn people's behavior and why they behave the way they do.

People who feel they have to" front" are unhappy. And the reason they are unhappy is because they are afraid they will be found out who they really are. This fear causes them to do many unnecessary things, and by doing so, they draw attention to themselves.

How do they draw attention to themselves? One attention getter is their propensity to "know everything." They attempt to take over when they don't have a clue as to how the task is to be done. They will dare to tell a trained and experienced person how to do the task based on their opinion. Rather than fight, the experienced person steps aside and lets them "run the show," in order to avoid arguments and a negative situation.

Another way of drawing attention to themselves is their false sense of leadership. They take their "position" of being facilitators who have all the answers and those working with them to work "under" them when all should work together democratically, having the same opportunity in the discussions and decision making. In most cases, the "leaders" are so caught up in being "leaders" they forget that leadership means helping people to be a part of a team. It is team effort that gets the tasks done.

Such "leaders" are carried away with their "power." This often results in strife, disgruntling, flared tempers and arguments. Some persons in the corporate world are so self-possessed that they are difficult to work with. So workers would rather be transferred to a position with less status with someone they can enjoy working with. Adversely, there are some wonderful administrators and supervisors with whom others would love to work with because they know who they are and are confident of their abilities and know-how.

Apart from the corporate world, there are "unpaid" positions in clubs and organizations where power is seen and felt. There is a great deal of competitiveness and fronting. The desire to be seen as the "ones in charge" or the "ones in authority" runs heavy. That is where you find the greatest display of personal veneer. Among such persons you will find competitiveness for attention, recognition and validation very strong and that seems to carry an undercurrent that is felt throughout the organization. It is not always something you can readily point out or identify, but the tension is thick and heavy.

Persons operating as administrators who possess the same veneer buy into this so called power over the employees directly under them. They protect each other, but eventually someone wakes up and begins to look closely at the different operations and the final results. That is when appropriate changes are made. The status quo operation seems to have been operative for quite some time before someone at the top takes a good look down the line and weeds out persons who are ineffective or less effective. This usually happens when the person at the very to top is replaced.

"Fronters" know who they are. They know how they feel. We all desire to be in situations that promote peace, contentment, joy, happiness, and etc. We have to be honest and truly face ourselves and to find the way to change. Once we stop playing the game of denial, we are in position to make a change. As quickly as we make our decision to change, we can find help all around us, starting with a very close friend whom we admire and trust. And who respects confidentiality, at the same time, be nonjudgmental.

The process can begin by approaching (in confidence) our highly esteemed friend, letting him or her know of our respect and admiration.

Simply admit that we are unhappy with ourselves. Let him or her know that we see him or her as a role model. Spend quality time with the person communicating and praying together. Then we will be able to like and love the person we are without the needless veneer. Even our mirror will reflect us as we genuinely are.

Some persons in the corporate world are so self-possessed that they are difficult to work with and nobody wants to work with them.

What is A Worry Wart?

"Cast all your anxiety on Him because He cares for you."
I Peter 5:7 NIV

When we define "worry wart" we are describing a person who worries excessively, and that is about everything. As human beings all of us worry from time to time because that is the way we are. Can we change? Yes, of course we can. Do we want to change? Some of us do and others say "Don't worry about me being a worry wart."

Whether we worry excessively or occasionally we find more negative things happening in our lives than we really want. All worrying is a sheer waste of time. If we accomplished anything its aggravation, agitation, and many other negative feelings adding to our discomfort. Not only are we physically affected, we are emotionally unstable. Strangely enough, we do it to ourselves.

When we worry even occasionally, we hurt ourselves more than we hurt others. However, we do hurt our loved ones and those we interact with because they are affected simple because they are not happy with how we treat ourselves. People who worry a lot pull and send negative vibes. A vibe is a feeling and a negative vibe is a strong overpowering feeling that seems to work on the nervous system. It is an uncomfortable feeling. There is nothing to see but the feeling is strong. And, of course, the worry wart feels it all the time which leaves the person feeling anxious, nervous, uncomfortable, agitated and aggravated. You name it. All of the negative feelings seem to want to out do the others.

You may have heard people say,"I worry all the time; I can't help it!" The correct response is,"Yes, you can if you really want to rid yourself of the disturbing habit." The feeling of helplessness and powerlessness can be overcome, but it takes determination supported by a strong desire.

People who profess a strong belief in God and continue to be a worry wart either are not letting God do His work, or their faith and trust are not as strong as they profess them to be. We who worry occasionally have to remind ourselves of what the Scripture says (Matthew 13:22, Luke 8:22-25) and Philippians 4:6-7 has an antidote to worry. Reading the Gospel books (Matthew, Mark, Luke and John) also helps to change the habit.

Some people actually feel they are not able to change, and, of course they can't on their own. But if we seek help we will find it. And what better source can we find than consulting the Bible?

Worrying was not meant to be a part of our daily existence. Some people confuse concern with worry. If you happen to be one of those persons you might be interested in knowing what the difference is. It is this: concern shows interest in something and helps one to make an effort to do something about the problem or a challenge. Concerned people see challenges which they can work on to reach a solution or to accomplish a task. Concern is a positive response to a problem or situation. Concern enables a person to seek to find the answer needed in order to eliminate or correct a problem.

Worry, on the other hand, is allowing a problem or situation to fester in ones mind without attempting to find a solution. It is a do-nothing but think about how it is affecting oneself. Along with that negativism is hopelessness, helplessness, powerlessness and other negative thoughts which cripple. The "woe is me" attitude takes over, adding to the browbeating that one puts on oneself as a worrier.

As long as there is life, there is hope. Regardless to what negativism we experience in life, we must believe that this too shall pass. We can help it to pass if we want to. Our loved ones want us to enjoy life to the fullest. They laugh with us. They cry with us. They rejoice with us and they grieve with us. Not only do we see it, we are a part of this wonderful cycle of caring, loving, being there and wanting the best for those we love. Right?

If the term "worry wart" is one you can claim, claim it no more. You know what to do to rid yourself of this destructive habit. Doing what you need to do will make those who love you happier, and you will be happy as well.

People who profess a strong belief in God and continue to be a worry wart either are not letting God do His work, or their faith and trust are not as strong as they profess it to be.

WHEN GOD SPEAKS!

"And He said, 'O man greatly beloved, fear not; peace be unto thee, be strong, yea be strong'. And when he had spoken unto me, I was strengthened, and said, 'Let my Lord speak; for thou hast strengthened me.'"
Daniel 10:19 (KJV)

A friend who I have known for about forty years asked me this question, "When do you know when God speaks to you?" I gave a quick one sentence answer which did not answer the question. We were in a setting where it was not conducive to give a long discourse. Subsequently, the opportunity came one morning and that is the reason for this essay you are reading. I have emailed my friend the message contained in this essay.

I hope you, the reader, will experience the same pleasurably feeling that I did when I recalled one of my many experiences of God speak to me when writing this essay.

It was during one of my morning mediations that I pondered over some of the many times God has spoken to me. Let me share a situation with you and then we will talk more on the subject. I am trusting that this essay will bring to your memory some of the times God has spoken to you.

Here is my story regarding a very serious situation: It was December 31, 1976 and I was the only person on duty as a male in a girls' group home in a brownstone in Manhattan. The girls had invited their boyfriends to celebrate the arrival of the New Year, 1977. They were in the dinning room located on the ground level of the brownstone. I was in my room on the first floor exactly over the dinning room.

I was hired December 13, 1976 as a sleep-in-work known as a "houseparent." I heard my girls and their dates laughing and seemingly having a merry time, but what bothered me was the sudden unfamiliar pungent odor coming from the dinning room. Upon investigating,

I discovered the girls and their guests were smoking marijuana and drinking alcoholic beverages. With great authority I admonished the girls, stating agency policies and state regulations against such behavior.

The unofficial leader of the girls responded with her extensive knowledge of expletives and invited me to take my "so and so" back upstairs and to mind my own business. I was in a state of semi-shock because at the age of forty-eight I had never been spoken to in that manner by a teenager, even though I had worked with young people for about twenty years. So I did just as she instructed.

When I arrived in my room I sat in my rocker and prayed, asking God to guide me and to give me the courage to deal with the situation. After a few moments of prayer and calming sitting in my rocker, God "spoke" to me. I found myself in a trance-like state causing me to feel as light as a feather. I suddenly felt myself standing on my feet and literally "floating" downstairs.

When I arrived, I asked to speak with the same young lady's boyfriend whom I had gotten to know the same weekend I started to work in the group home. I called him to come to me at the foot of the stairs. I asked him why he had disrespected me and he responded that he hadn't said anything. I told him that was disrespect because he said nothing to his girlfriend about her behavior and language to me. I reminded him that I had made sure that he had his bread pudding, which he had made known to me he liked, each time he visited his girlfriend.

He then apologized and turned to the girls and the guys and told them to either pour what was in their cups into the liquor bottles or pour it in the kitchen sink. He instructed the girls to go to their rooms and the guys to open the windows and door to air out the room and they vacuumed and cleaned up taking their used cups, bottles and roaches (marijuana butts) with them. After each apologized and wished me a Happy New Year they quietly departed. Returning to my room I thank God for doing what He does best, and that is answering a believer's prayers.

I did not hear one sound from the girls the rest of the night. The next morning when they finally got up, the girls wished me a Happy

New Year and acted if nothing had happened. Neither they nor I mentioned the aborted celebration.

I could cite many other experiences of God speaking to me in myriad ways. Just as He speaks to me, He speaks to you. Being able to discern his speaking is a blessing in itself! There are many more blessings to be had if only we would trust and obey Him.

To answer the question how do we know when God speaks to us, I will have to say that God speaks to each of us differently. It depends upon our individual relationship we have with Him. Sometimes He speaks in a dream. Other times he speaks through the thoughts in our heads. Sometimes He speaks through other persons (known or unknown). God is so creative. Though our own personal relationship with God we can learn how we individually communicate with Him. As in all effective communications, He listens as we talk, but we must listen when He talks. And if we want good results, not only do we listen, we obey.

Can you imagine the problems I would have had attempting to demand respect and obedience to agency policies and state regulations on my own? I do not want to even think about that. But to avoid conflicts we can depend on God to see that we victoriously succeed in whatever comes before us. God tells us any battle that we might have to face is His, not ours.

Surely, God has spoken to you many times in myriad ways. Now, do you know when God speaks to you?

**Being able to discern His speaking is a blessing
in itself!**

WHEN LITTLE THINGS MEAN SO MUCH

"The tongue has the power of life and death, and those
who love it will eat its fruit."
Proverbs 17:21

We are all moved by small acts of kindness, but we do not always think about performing or expressing ourselves in this manner.

Most men need to learn what most women already know; and that is that little things can mean so much to another's enjoyment.

Men do concern themselves with little things, but they are usually negative. Men enjoy arguing about minor things. Many arguments ending in fights have occurred over very small insignificant matters such as discussions over a professional baseball player's batting average. If you have any doubt about this, just sit in a barbershop waiting your turn. That is also the place to "learn" about politics. In fact, any subject is good for a thorough discussion.

What I find annoying, at times, is that the barber gets so caught up in the argument that he stops what he is supposed be doing to make his point in the argument. That means I am sitting there waiting for him to finish the work on his customers before me so I can get my little work done and go on about my business.

The comments made concerning negative little things are merely for entertainment and humor. But the little things that mean so much have nothing to do with negativity. Rather. it has to do with the positive things we can do to make others feel good about themselves, other people, and their interaction with others.

What this essay is really about is to make all persons aware of the small positive things that we can easily do without costing anything in terms of money. The only cost is a little time and interest.

History records much of this. Many, many years ago before the invention of the telephone, the main medium of communication was letter writing. Personal letters and romantic letters with a "hint" of perfume delighted the hearts of men and women who were the object of the writer's affection.

This does not have to be a lost art. People still enjoy personal letters, even those of us who are emailing. We may have to leave off the "hint" of perfume due to today's "scare" of envelopes containing a harmful substance.

An occasional personal or romantic letter delivered by a mail carrier can still be a special joy to the recipient, even if the letter is mailed to someone in the same household. However, if you want to save the price of a postage stamp, just slip the letter under the pillow of the person it is intended for.

If you don't feel like writing a letter, why not write a note saying something "sweet" and pleasing? Another suggestion is a quick phone call to a loved one. Tell the person that he or she is very much loved and you can't wait until the person gets home. If he or she lives somewhere else, let the person know you can't wait until when you will be able to see him or her.

Another suggestion is to occasionally hide a gift. It does not have to be expensive, just something the person really likes, and have the person search the house for it.

Come on now, use your own imagination. You know what the object of your affection likes; why not just provide it?

Life would be much sweeter if we would think more about pleasing others than pleasing ourselves. It would be wise for men to know that one of the best "investments" they can make is to concentrate on little things to please the object of his affection. Women like to out-do men positively or negatively.

Any man who is foolish enough to think he can out-do the object of his affection needs to stop the arguments on small matters with his buddies and discuss and learn how women "tick." In some unisex barber and beauty shops, the female beauticians can add "spice" to the arguments or discussions.

It is not only the object of our affection that can benefit by small deeds of kindness, but everyone we encounter should reap some benefit of having associated with us in some manner. Everyone enjoys small expressions of joy, peace, love, interest, and appreciation.

Try this yourself and see how it enhances your quality of life. It may start with just a simple but sincere compliment. Do not be surprised if you find yourself more cheerful, smiling, and feeling better about yourself, your friends, and your world. Try it. You have more to gain than to lose.

What this essay is about is to make all persons aware of the small positive things we can easily do without costing anything in terms of money. The only cost is a little time and interest.

WHEN YOUR FRIEND BECOMES YOUR FOE

"When the wicked, even my enemies and my foes, came
upon me... they stumbled and fell."
Psalm 27:2

Viewing the court shows has caused me to think about this topic. Persons who claimed to have enjoyed wonderful friendship for so many years become bitter enemies over what appears to be a simple matter.

Although this essay is primarily about what happens when love turns sour or when a beautiful friendship (for whatever reason) no longer exists, personal loans or co-signing for loans seem to be the biggest reason for breakup between family members and friends according to the cases I have seen coming before the courts on television.

One of the most enjoyable experiences during the time of friendship is sharing secrets. Some secrets may be about the involvement of just the two friends or they may be about one friend telling another something about his or her interaction with a third party. That once shared is no longer a secret. When anyone tell anything which is supposed to be between just two other people, what we call a "secret" no longer exists as such.

People who genuinely consider themselves friends with persons they consider "special" persons have no reservation of sharing any and everything, even though one may get a feeling that something ought not to be shared even to a close friend. The feeling is ignored. After all, sharing is what friendships is all about, isn't it?

At the time it never crosses our mind that our friend is not going to be our friend forever. We could swear that we will be "tight" until death parts us, but one never knows what the future holds. That is why we should listen and obey that "still small voice" that whispers to us to not say certain things at times.

Whereas you may feel very close to your friend, regardless what happens, he or she may not feel the same about you. At the time of "great friendship, "no one has the slightest idea that the friendship will not always be. When it does not last, two persons are hurt.

People do change. Other than the loan mentioned earlier, what other circumstances are involved in some break-ups? Do genuine deep loving friendships ever break up? I don't have an answer to these questions. Do you? Has this happened to you?

How can love turn so sour? Was there ever love between the two friends? It may have been some kind of love, but it was not unconditional which is what real love is. Unconditional love allows us to accept people the way we find them. We may not always like certain things about them, but it is unconditional love that enables us to continue to enjoy time and space even though there are some things we may not like.

There is a strong possibility that some of the things we don't like are because we may be guilty of ourselves and that is why we were unconsciously drawn to that person in the first place. We may see ourselves in that person. So it would benefit us to honestly and earnestly look in the mirror of our own soul to see if we possibly have the same trait or traits.

Now, if we find out this is the case, then being real friends we should be able to talk about it in a loving manner. This will allow both of us to make appropriate changes of what is coming between us. Unconditional love is usually not only strong, but genuine and it should allow us to discuss any matter affecting the relationship.

Getting back to what is seen while watching case after case being brought before the court on television; it is hard to believe that unconditional love was a component of their relationship. Whatever love they felt must have been conditional. This means as long as someone is giving and the other is taking, there seems to be a "good match." But when one friend lets the other friend have a loan and the friend reneges on paying it (claiming it was a gift), it is obvious that something is wrong with the friendship.

Then, there is the friend who co-signs, but the borrower does not do what he or she is obligated to do and the friend takes him or her to Judge Brown or one of the other judges on TV. That is where you see the ugliness between two friends. All secrets are exposed and there is so much anger. The borrower broadcasts all their "dirt" without realizing that he or she is implicating himself or herself. Strangely, the borrower usually appears angrier than the lender.

Is it reasonable to say that money can break up relationships when conditional love along with selfishness and greed becomes a part of the friendship? It seems to me that conditional love is clearly displayed when a friend becomes a foe by the borrower refusing to pay the loan and gets down right nasty in court. Rather than to deal with the issue of the loan, secrets are told by the borrower.

It is said," If you want to make a mountain out of a molehill, just add some dirt." Well, when your friend becomes your enemy; he or she seems to have an unlimited supply of dirt to share with whoever listens. So it truly pays to listen and obey the still small voice that tells you to refrain from saying certain things even to a friend. And the voice surely must warn you about giving a loan to a friend or co-signing for that friend.

At the time of the "great friendship," no one has the slightest idea that the friendship is not an everlasting one, and when it does not last, two persons are hurt.